MAO ZEDONG
on
DIALECTICAL
MATERIALISM

CHINESE STUDIES ■ ON ■ CHINA

THE CHINESE COMMUNIST PARTY'S NOMENKLATURA SYSTEM
Edited by John P. Burns

THE ASIATIC MODE OF PRODUCTION IN CHINA
Edited by Timothy Brook

BASIC PRINCIPLES OF CIVIL LAW IN CHINA
Edited by William C. Jones

MAO ZEDONG ON DIALECTICAL MATERIALISM
Edited by Nick Knight

MAO ZEDONG
on
DIALECTICAL MATERIALISM

Writings on Philosophy, 1937

Edited by **NICK KNIGHT**

M.E. Sharpe, Inc.
Armonk, New York   London, England

Library of Congress Cataloging-in-Publication Data

Mao, Tse-tung, 1893–1976.
   [Selections. English. 1990]
   Mao Zedong on dialectical materialism : writings on philosophy, 1937 / edited by Nick Knight.
      p. cm. — (Chinese studies on China)
   Translations from Chinese.
   Includes bibliographical references.
   ISBN 0-87332-682-2
   1. Dialectical materialism. I. Knight, Nick. II. Title. III. Series.
B5234.M35M3413   1990
181'.11—dc20   89-49016
                                                                                CIP

Printed in the United States of America

MV   10   9   8   7   6   5   4   3   2   1

CONTENTS

MAO ZEDONG
on
DIALECTICAL
MATERIALISM

IT

tion: Soviet Marxism
Development of
long's Philosophical

Dialectical Materialism

During the early Yan'an Period, Mao Zedong wrote in draft form a number of philosophical essays which have had in their post-Liberation versions an enormous impact on Chinese Marxism. These essays, *On Practice* and *On Contradiction*, are rightly regarded, alongside a number of other documents by Mao, as the cornerstone of the variant of Marxism which has developed in China.[1] For those interested in the development of the thought of Mao, and the emergence and development of Chinese Marxism, these essays represent a crucial starting point.

However, another lengthy text on philosophy written at exactly the time (July, August 1937)[2] that Mao penned *On Contradiction* and *On Practice* has only ever been published in post-Liberation China in *neibu* form (that is, as a confidential, internal Party document and not for general circulation). This is a document entitled *Dialectical Materialism (Lecture Notes)*.[3] While it is not true that this text has been left "to the gnawing criticism of the mice" by the Chinese as was once suspected in the West, and indeed has been published on several occasions as study material for cadres and academics,[4] it is certainly the case that the Chinese hold *Dialectical Materialism* in much lower regard than the "celebrated philosophical essays"[5] *On Contradiction* and *On Practice*. Indeed, when questioned on his authorship of *Dialectical Materialism* by Edgar Snow in 1965, Mao feigned ignorance of it, although his denial of authorship was not categorical.[6] The Chinese view of *Dialectical Materialism*, its origins and contribution to Chinese Marxism, has thus been an ambiguous one, and I will return subsequently to a more detailed analysis of the contemporary Chinese evaluation of this document.

While the Chinese perspective on *Dialectical Materialism* has been ambiguous, a very negative judgement has been rendered by Western scholars as fragments of the text have become available in the West from the early 1960s. Doolin and Golas, for example, declared *Dialectical Materialism* to be "a rambling, vague attempt at philosophical discourse".[7] Similarly, Wittfogel argues that this essay indicates Mao's "inability to expound comprehensively the concepts inherent in Hegelian-Marxist dialectics", and that it can be regarded as a manifestation of Mao's "peculiar conceptual limitations".[8] A further example is Cohen's view that *Dialectical Materialism* is "primitive and philosophically erroneous" and "sheds revealing light on his incompetence as a philosopher".[9] Some years later and following Mao's interview with Edgar Snow referred to above, John E. Rue rehearsed the known evidence (both conceptual and historical) relating to *Dialectical Materialism* and came to the conclusion that Mao "probably did not write it at all", that it may have been a forgery "planted by Mao's old enemies in the CCP" to discredit him.[10]

A lone dissenting voice is that of Stuart Schram who found it hard to take seriously the view "that Mao's text was a mass of crude blunders". Schram's judgement was based on the fact that *Dialectical Materialism* was heavily dependent on Soviet philosophical texts of the 1930s (an issue we will return to), and that the philosophical level of the essay was therefore at least the equal of that to be found in these sources.[11] Schram also argues that it is a mistake to regard the three philosophical essays - *On Practice, On Contradiction*, and *Dialectical Materialism* - as written separately and for different purposes; they belong, rather, "to a single intellectual enterprise, namely Mao's attempt to come to terms with the philosophical basis of Marxism from the time he was first exposed to it in July 1936 until the Japanese attack of September 1937 turned his attention to more practical things".[12] The implication of this judgement is that *Dialectical Materialism* must be given due consideration in the attempt to understand the origins and development of Mao's philosophical thought; not only was this text contemporaneous with *On Contradiction* and *On Practice*, many of the concepts contained in it emerge and are evident in these other better known essays and in his subsequent writings. I will argue below the validity of Schram's judgement that these three essays represent a "single intellectual enterprise", and will suggest that a more constructive and less dismissive analysis of the philosophy contained in *Dialectical Materialism* is consequently called for than it has hitherto received.

The opportunity to attempt this more detailed and constructive analysis has been made possible by the publication in Chinese of a number of versions of the complete text of *Dialectical Materialism.* Prior to the early 1970s, Mao scholars were constrained to make their judgements on the basis of fragments of the larger work. The judgements rendered by Wittfogel, and Doolin and Golas, for example, were based on analysis of Chapter 1 only;[13] and Schram's position was founded on an examination of Chapter 1 and sections 1-6 of Chapter 2.[14] Since the early 1970s, however, two seemingly complete versions of *Dialectical Materialism* have been published.[15] The first appeared in *Mao Zedong ji* (Collected Writings of Mao Zedong), an edited collection published in Japan under the auspices of the Japanese Mao scholar Takeuchi Minoru; the second appeared in 1984 in the supplementary volumes of the *Mao Zedong ji.* The discovery and publication of this latter version is significant in a number of important respects. First, it is very clear from a comparison of this document with that published in the early 1970s in the *Mao Zedong ji* that there are a number of differences between the two texts. Indeed, the annotations appended to the translation which appears below indicate over ninety variations between the texts. Many of these are minor variations, for example, the alteration of a word or phrase; others are more significant and include redrafting of several sentences. Such variations indicate that *Dialectical Materialism* was revised in the early to mid-1940s prior to its republication in the two sources drawn on in the supplements to the *Mao Zedong ji.* Whether Mao himself was responsible for this revising and editing remains a matter of conjecture, but it is certainly probable that at the very least he gave his blessing to editorial changes made to the text by others. Consequently, it is now clear that the text of *Dialectical Materialism* has its own history in which a number of versions have appeared. This history includes: the creation of the text in 1937 involving heavy reliance on Soviet philosophical sources and writings of the influential Chinese Marxist philosophers Li Da and Ai Siqi,[16] its complete publication in 1938,[17] publication of fragments in 1938 and 1940,[18] its revision during the early 1940s,[19] its republication in a number of sources in 1944 and 1946,[20] and its publication as a *neibu* document in post-Liberation China in 1958 (complete text),[21] in 1960 (text divided into extracts),[22] in 1972 (Chapter 3 only),[23] and in 1982 (complete text).[24] *Dialectical Materialism* also circulated during the Cultural Revolution in a compilation entitled *Mao zhuxi wenxuan* [Collected Essays of Chairman Mao].[25] The links in the history of *Dialectical Materialism* are thus much less shrouded in mystery than was hitherto the case, and reveal that the text which was originally written in July and August of 1937 (and republished in 1958 and 1982 in that form) has appeared in other versions. The comparison and analysis of textual variations in Mao's writings constitutes an important component in the development of Mao studies; for, as John Bryan Starr has suggested, until Mao scholars are able to work from a definitive set of Mao texts, interpretations and judgements rendered by them will unavoidably be based on an uncertain empirical foundation.[26] The textual comparison of the different versions of *Dialectical Materialism* and the other texts on philosophy which appear in translation in this volume represents a modest contribution to the larger project of compiling a definitive corpus of the Mao texts.

The version of *Dialectical Materialism* which appears in the supplementary volumes of the *Mao Zedong ji* is also significant because the two sources from which it was drawn also contain versions of *On Practice* and *On Contradiction*.[27] *On Practice* appears in both sources, while *On Contradiction* appears only in the volume entitled *Dialectical Materialism* published by Dazhong Shudian. The publication of all three philosophical essays in one volume under the title *Dialectical Materialism* reinforces Schram's view that they represent "a single intellectual enterprise".[28] It moreover suggests that the attempt to understand the development of Mao's philosophical thought needs to confront the philosophy contained in all three essays, rather than concentrating on the two officially sanctioned essays which appear in *Selected Works of Mao Tse-tung* as has been the case in many Western interpretations, or *On Practice* alone, as has been the tendency of contemporary Chinese Marxism. The evaluation of these texts in concert can, it is argued below, allow significant insights which may be concealed if analysis is limited to one or both of the two better known texts.

It might be queried whether *Dialectical Materialism* deserves serious consideration as a philosophical essay reflecting Mao's own philosophical views. After all, as Wittfogel and Schram have pointed out, *Dialectical Materialism* is in many parts a direct plagiarism of a number of Soviet essays on philosophy.[29] Wittfogel estimated that some 40 per cent of Chapter 1 "consists of passages that are either literally or with some editing taken from Chinese translations of Soviet presentations of dialectical materialism". Moreover, he argues that the rest of Chapter 1 is merely a paraphrase of ideas which can be found in these Soviet sources.[30] We will return subsequently to a more detailed consideration of this plagiarism and also of the influence on Mao's philosophical thought of Ai Siqi and Li Da, the Chinese philosophers who translated into Chinese and edited the Soviet sources on which Mao relied, and who themselves wrote extensively on the philosophy of dialectical materialism.

However, to dismiss *Dialectical Materialism* as unworthy of serious analysis and consideration on the basis of Mao's heavy reliance on Soviet philosophical sources of the 1930s is to miss a number of significant points.

First, it is important to note that when pressed to provide an explanation of Marxist philosophy it was to Soviet sources, replete with categories and themes of contemporary Stalinist Marxism, that Mao turned. Obviously, Mao's choice of reference materials was severely limited due to the nature of the historical context, as several commentators have pointed out.[31] Nevertheless, it is significant that Mao regarded the philosophy contained in these reference materials as reflecting the orthodox response to problems of philosophy within the Marxist tradition.

This indicates that Mao was undoubtedly influenced by categories and concepts of Soviet philosophy, and although his adherence to some of these wavered over time, they contributed significantly to the construction of the theoretical framework from within which Mao observed and interpreted the world.

Second, if Mao was not to derive his understanding of Marxist philosophy from Soviet sources, from where was he to obtain it? The answer to this question is never directly broached by Mao scholars concerned with this issue, but the implicit suggestion is that Mao should either have come out with something startlingly original, or at the very least avoided reliance on the Soviet theoretical writings of the period with their "extraordinarily low level".[32] While the former expectation might well be warranted given the often exaggerated claims for Mao's prowess as a philosopher, the latter suggestion appears to ignore not only the contextual limitations on the development of Mao's philosophical thought, but also the genealogy of many of the categories incorporated within Soviet Marxism. Such categories did not emerge from a theoretical vacuum, but can be traced back, as Lucio Colletti and other scholars have demonstrated, via the writings of Lenin and Plekhanov to Engels.[33] Engels' various forays into the realm of philosophy (*Anti-Dühring, Dialectics of Nature, Ludwig Feuerbach and the End of Classical German Philosophy*) were assumed by many Marxists to reflect faithfully the philosophical views of Marx himself, indeed they are still so regarded by many commentators on Marxist philosophy.[34] Yet, and as Colletti argues, there is a significant difference in approach to questions of philosophy contained in the writings of Marx and Engels. Engels' philosophical writing elaborates a materialistic position which is rather mechanistic in its approach to problems of ontology and epistemology, attempting as it does to create a philosophical system in which all phenomena are invariably constituted of matter which observes a number of fundamental natural laws. For the most part, it was to these writings of Engels that Marxists turned in the attempt to elaborate a Marxist philosophical position. Mao's own *Dialectical Materialism* and the Soviet sources on which he relied are thus not surprisingly replete with references to Engels, and to Lenin who built on the materialist foundation provided by Engels. And the reasons for this reliance on a philosophy whose pedigree begins primarily with Engels are not far to seek. In the first place, Marx himself wrote comparatively little on purely philosophical questions, consciously abandoning philosophy for political economy from the mid-1840s;[35] and in the second place, those philosophical writings of Marx from the early 1840s were to become available only in the late 1920s and early 1930s,[36] by which time the formalisation of Soviet Marxist philosophy based on Engels was well developed. The philosophical writings of the so-called "early" Marx (*Economic and Philosophical Manuscripts, Critique of Hegel's Doctrine of the State*, etc.) could not easily be incorporated into Soviet Marxist philosophy, based as they were on concepts such as alienation and estrangement, "themes absent from the work of Engels, Plekhanov and Lenin alike".[37] These philosophical writings of the young Marx were thus largely ignored, emerging from hibernation only in the post-Stalin period to contribute to the renewed interest in Marxist philosophy which has developed within European intellectual circles. To judge harshly Mao's reliance on contemporaneous Soviet philosophical sources is thus to be wise with the benefit of hindsight, for neither the Marxian texts on philosophy nor a willingness seriously to entertain their content were present when Mao commenced his theoretical apprenticeship in Marxist philosophy.

Mao's heavy reliance on Chinese translations of Soviet philosophical sources is thus not accepted here as sufficient grounds for the dismissal of *Dialectical Materialism* as unimportant to the project of understanding the development of Mao's philosophical thought. At the very least, Mao's use of Soviet Marxist categories in the 1930s and their subsequent reemergence in later writings throws doubt on the widely held view that Mao broke entirely with the orthodox Marxist tradition in a number of important respects. Let us take a few examples.

Ontology and epistemology

It is often suggested that Mao deviated from or broke with orthodox Marxism by distancing himself from the materialist premises on which it is founded.[38] From very early in his revolutionary career, these accounts suggest, Mao inverted the ontological assumptions of Marxism by delineating a distinction between thought (consciousness, ideas) and matter, a distinction in which thought had causal priority. Consequently, the material preconditions for the emergence of a particular form of consciousness need not necessarily exist, for consciousness was not dependent on, and indeed could create, a particular material environment. In this respect, Mao is accused of "idealism", "voluntarism", and the like.

However, an opposite interpretation can be taken from the position articulated in *Dialectical Materialism* and his other two better known philosophical essays. The ontology contained there is unmistakably a materialist one. From the outset, Mao refuses to entertain the possibility of a dualism between mind and matter predicated on an ontological distinction. In rejecting such a dualism, Mao argues that everything in the universe (thought included) is comprised of matter, and that the unitary character of the universe derives from its uniform materiality. "Materialism", he notes, "considers the unity of the universe to derive from its materiality, and that spirit (consciousness) is one of the natural characteristics of matter which emerges only when matter has developed to a certain stage".[39]

Indeed, Mao goes further to define the material character of consciousness as "a form of matter in movement", as "a particular property of the material brain of humankind".[40] Moreover,

> ...this form of matter is composed of a complex nervous system.... These objective physiological processes of the nervous systems of human beings function in line with the subjective manifestation of the forms of consciousness that they adopt internally; these are themselves all objective things, are certain types of material process.[41]

The unrelenting materialism of *Dialectical Materialism* thus suggests as faulty the view that Mao juxtaposed thought and matter as separate ontological realms and attributed thought with analytical priority because it possessed an ontological character different from matter; rather, thought was matter. On the basis of this ontological unity Mao did, however, construct an epistemological dualism; but here again the reflection theory of epistemology articulated in *Dialectical Materialism* and the empiricist deference to experience elaborated in *On Practice* preclude the suggestion that Mao regarded thought as either independent of matter or was to be attributed analytical priority in the epistemological relationship between thought and matter. In *Dialectical Materialism,* Mao constructs the epistemological dualism on an ontological unity as follows:

> Accordingly, it is apparent that it is conditional when we make a distinction between matter and consciousness and moreover oppose the one to the other; that is to say, it has significance only for the insights of epistemology.[42]

It is thus only in the realm of epistemology, and not ontology, that one could speak of a distinction between thought and matter, and much of Mao's epistemology is concerned with the mechanism by which thought can have access to and come to know objectively the realm of reality. This dichotomy was made clear in an earlier article (1936) on military strategy; "everything outside of the mind (*tounao*) is objective reality".[43] Moreover, in *Dialectical Materialism*, Mao refers to the "knowability" (*kerenshixing*) of matter by consciousness,[44] and proceeds to argue that the theory of reflection of dialectical materialism has positively resolved the problem of "knowability" and is thus the "soul" of Marxist epistemology.[45] The suggestion that human thought is a reflection of objective reality permeates *Dialectical Materialism* and a short section (Section 9 of Chapter 2) is devoted to it. The formulation of reflection theory contained there is fundamentally similar to the epistemology contained in *On Practice*. Schram has, on the basis of sections 1-6 of Chapter 2, suggested a more profound epistemology to be found in *On Practice* than in *Dialectical Materialism*.

...the extraordinarily simplistic exposition of the "reflection" theory as the beginning and end of Marxist epistemology is a far cry from the sophisticated presentation of "On Practice".[46]

This judgement cannot, I would suggest, be borne out by a close comparison of the two documents. While it is true that *On Practice* devotes a good deal more space (and perhaps intellectual effort) explicitly to the issue of epistemology, the notions of knowledge as a reflection of natural and social realities, and of deepening knowledge through a process of progressive engagement with reality (i.e., practice) are present in both sources. For example, in *Dialectical Materialism,* Mao argues that:

Objective truth exists independently and does not depend on the subject. Although it is reflected in our sense perceptions and concepts, it achieves final form gradually rather than instantaneously ... in the process of cognition, the material world is increasingly reflected in our knowledge more closely, more precisely, more multifariously, and more profoundly.[47]

A good deal of *On Practice* is actually devoted to fleshing out the concept adumbrated in the quote above that, while knowledge is a reflection of objective reality, it only comes to reflect it accurately through a process of practice which may involve a considerable length of time and expenditure of energy as the subject of cognition grapples with reality and attempts to alter it. The suggestion that in either text Mao's epistemology is premised on a simple assumption of a mirror reflection in which thought exactly or immediately mirrors reality is quite wrong. The overly passive epistemology of a simple reflection theory is absent from both texts. Moreover, the notion of a complex reflection as spelt out in *Dialectical Materialism* logically precedes the elaboration of epistemology contained in *On Practice*, and it also precedes it textually. If the three essays on philosophy are indeed part of "a single intellectual enterprise", we would expect nothing less. It is also important to note that the epistemological judgements rendered in *Dialectical Materialism* and *On Practice* draw heavily on arguments already existing within Marxist philosophy and in particular those elaborated by Lenin and Engels. Lenin, in particular, had devoted a rather polemical book-length study to the issue of epistemology,[48] and as one would expect given the genealogy of Soviet Marxist philosophy discussed above, Lenin was in turn to draw heavily on the epistemological writings of Engels.[49] In drawing on Engels, Lenin articulates the conceptions of both reflection and practice as premises for the dialectical materialist approach to epistemology:

> Thus, the materialist theory, the theory of the reflection of objects by our mind, is here presented [in Engels' writings] with absolute clarity: things exist outside us. Our perceptions and ideas are their images. Verification of these images, differentiation between true and false images, is given by practice.[50]

This concatenation by Lenin of reflection and practice as elements of a unified dialectical materialist theory of epistemology indicates the orthodoxy of Mao's own elaboration of the problem of epistemology. In both *Dialectical Materialism* and *On Practice*, Mao drew on a position well established within Soviet Marxist philosophy, and his employment of these concepts was to persist well beyond the Yan'an Period. For example, in a speech in 1957, Mao asserted that "man's social being determines his consciousness", and spoke of the way in which the social changes in China had been "reflected in people's minds".[51]   Similarly, in 1960 he declared:

> Initiative ... originates in seeking truth from facts, in the true reflections of objective conditions in the minds (*tounao*) of the people, namely from the people's dialectical process of knowledge of the objective external world.[52]

The concept of reflection was also to appear in Mao's "Sixty Articles on Work Methods" of 1958:

The human brain can reflect the objective world, although it is not easy to do so correctly. Correct reflection or the reflection which is closest to reality can be arrived at only after thinking and rethinking.... However great a man may be, his thoughts, views, plans and methods are a mere reflection of the objective world....[53]

Moreover, it is very clear from numerous references in his writings of the post-Liberation period that Mao continued to view practice as a critical element of Marxist epistemology.[54] Perhaps his best known statement on this issue from this period is "Where do correct ideas come from?" of May 1963. In this short text, Mao reiterates his belief in the dialectical materialist position on epistemology, and again links reflection and practice as key elements in the process of knowing the objective world:

Countless phenomena of the objective external world are reflected in a man's brain.... Man's knowledge makes another leap through the test of practice. This leap is more important than the previous one. For it is this leap alone that can prove the correctness or incorrectness of the first leap, i.e., of the ideas, theories, policies, plans or measures formulated in the course of reflecting the objective external world. There is no other way of testing truth.... Such is the Marxist theory of knowledge, the dialectical materialist theory of knowledge.[55]

The persistence in Mao's thought of the epistemological concepts of reflection and practice and his continued linkage of the two indicates the significance of his employment of Soviet Marxist philosophical categories during the early Yan'an period.

The laws of dialectics and the "negation of the negation"

Another very significant example of this influence which can be drawn from *Dialectical Materialism* and subsequent writings is Mao's reference to and utilisation of the so-called "basic laws of materialist dialectics". Mao detailed these as follows in *Dialectical Materialism*:

> The law of the unity of contradictions; the law of the transformation of quality into quantity and vice versa; the law of the negation of the negation.[56]

The first of these "basic laws", the law of the unity of contradictions (or opposites), was (following the precedent established by orthodox Marxist philosophy) to become the most significant philosophical category in Mao's thought. While Mao had employed the concept of contradiction in writings prior to 1937,[57] his acceptance of this basic law in *Dialectical Materialism* and his lengthy elaboration of it in *On Contradiction* established the basis for his continued and increasing use of it. Indeed, from 1937 on, it is very clear that this law had become for Mao more than *primus inter pares*, and constituted the most fundamental of all laws in Marxism. For example, the opening sentence of *On Contradiction* states: "The law of contradiction in things, that is, the law of the unity of opposites, is the basic law (*zui genben de faze*) of materialist dialectics".[58] And some twenty years later, in his speech "On the Correct Handling of Contradictions Among the People", Mao was to reiterate the significance of the law of the unity of opposites:

> Marxist philosophy holds that the law of the unity of opposites is the fundamental law (*genben guilü*) of the universe. This law operates universally, whether in the natural world, in human society, or in man's thinking. Between the opposites in a contradiction there is at once unity and struggle, and it is this that impels things to

move and change. Contradictions exist everywhere, but their nature differs in accordance with the different nature of different things. In any given thing, the unity of opposites is conditional, temporary and transitory, and hence relative, whereas the struggle of opposites is absolute. Lenin gave a very clear exposition of this law.[59]

Mao's writings of the 1950s and 1960s are replete with references to this "most basic law", and he employed it not only in an abstract philosophical manner, but in analysis of social and political realities.[60]

Mao's derivation of the concept of the unity of opposites from orthodox Soviet Marxist philosophy was to have a profound impact on the subsequent development of his philosophical thought. As indicated in the quote given immediately above, Mao refers to and draws on Lenin's exposition of the law of the unity of opposites in elaboration and application of his own position. Both in this source, and in *On Contradiction*, Mao was to draw heavily on the fragments on philosophy which came to be incorporated in Lenin's *Philosophical Notebooks*. In these fragments, in particular "On the Question of Dialectics", the dialectical conception of the unity of opposites is expounded with considerable force, a factor which suggested to Mao its preeminence as the "most basic law" of Marxist philosophy. For example, in "On the Question of Dialectics", Lenin states:

The identity of opposites (it would be more correct perhaps, to say their "unity" - although the difference between the terms identity and unity is not particularly important here. In a certain sense both are correct) is the recognition (discovery) of the contradictory, mutually *exclusive*, opposite tendencies in *all* phenomena and processes of nature (*including* mind and society). The condition for the knowledge of all processes of the world in their "*self-movement*", their spontaneous development, in their real life, is the knowledge of them as a unity of opposites.[61]

Moreover, in this as in other aspects of his philosophical writing, Lenin draws heavily on Engels to legitimize his own position. In both *Anti-Dühring* and *Dialectics of Nature*, Engels had referred to the ubiquity of contradictions, pointing out that a dialectical conception of reality which considers "things in their motion, their change, their life, their reciprocal influence" immediately becomes "involved in contradictions".[62] In *Anti-Dühring*, Engels stresses this aspect of dialectics:

> If simple mechanical change of place contains a contradiction, this is even truer of the higher forms of motion of matter, and especially of organic life and its development.... Life is therefore also a contradiction which is present in things and processes themselves, and which constantly asserts and resolves itself....[63]

The view that the unity of opposites constituted the most fundamental law of dialectics was thus well established in Marxist philosophy prior to the 1930s, and the Soviet texts on philosophy which Mao was to draw on so heavily in his own writings on dialectical materialism were to further reinforce the centrality of this law. For example, the text by Mitin and others entitled *Dialectical and Historical Materialism* referred to the law of the unity of opposites as the "fundamental law (*jiben faze*) of materialist dialectics".[64] Similarly, Li Da's *Shehuixue dagang* described this law as the "basic law" (*genben faze*) of dialectics which incorporated all other laws, including the law of the "negation of the negation".[65] Mao could thus call on a well-established body of philosophical thought to assert the law of the unity of opposites to be the "most basic law" of materialist dialectics. It has been suggested, however, that evidence of Mao's divergence from orthodoxy is provided demonstration through his elevation of this law at the expense of the other two; indeed, both Western[66] and Chinese[67] scholars have argued that Mao eventually came to reject one of the three laws of dialectical materialism, that of the "negation of the negation". Let us pause to consider this charge, for it bears on the proposition being advanced here that categories of Soviet Marxist philosophy did constitute a significant and persistent influence on Mao's philosophical thought. If it is possible to find in Mao's subsequent writings a rejection of one of the philosophical laws embraced in his *Lecture Notes on Dialectical Materialism*, it could betoken a significant change of direction in Mao's thought and cast doubt on the degree of influence which Soviet philosophical categories exerted.[68]

On 18 August 1964, Mao held an informal conversation on various aspects of philosophy with several old comrades. Although it is not certain how many were present at this talk on philosophy, it appears that the group was a small one; only three other persons are actually identified as being in attendance with Mao - Kang Sheng, Chen Boda, and Lu Ping. In the course of the conversation, Mao made a number of provocative statements, but we will restrict our attention here to just one of these: his apparent rejection of the law of the "negation of the negation". On being asked by Kang Sheng if the Chairman would "say something about the problem of the three categories", Mao responded:

> Engels talked about the three categories, but as for me I don't believe (*xiangxin*) in two of those categories. (The unity of opposites is the most basic law, the transformation of quality and quantity into one another is the unity of the opposites quality and quantity, and the negation of the negation does not exist at all (*fouding zhi fouding genben mei you*).) The juxtaposition, on the same level, of the transformation of quality and quantity into one another, the negation of the negation, and the law of the unity of opposites is "triplism" (*san yuan lun*), not monism. The most basic thing is the unity of opposites. The transformation of quality and quantity into one another is the unity of the opposites quality and quantity. There is no such thing as the negation of the negation (*mei you shenme fouding zhi fouding*). Affirmation, negation, affirmation, negation ... in the development of things, every link in the chain of events is both affirmation and negation. Slave-holding society negated primitive society, but with reference to feudal society it constituted, in turn, the affirmation. Feudal

society constituted the negation in relation to slave-holding society but it was in turn the affirmation with reference to capitalist society. Capitalism was the negation in relation to feudal society, but it is, in turn, the affirmation in relation to socialist society.[69]

A number of points can be made about this passage. First, when called on to address the issue of categories of Marxist philosophy, Mao commences by invoking Engels. We made the point earlier that the genealogy of the philosophical concepts and categories employed by Mao could be traced back to Engels, rather than Marx, and here is provided further substantiation of that judgement. Second, this is, as far as I am aware, the only textual evidence available to support the proposition that Mao did reject the category of the "negation of the negation". It is possible to find many other positive references to this category in his writings from the 1930s to the 1960s, and the existence of these references calls into question the propriety of taking this one reference as final proof that Mao had cut his links with the orthodox Marxist philosophical tradition.[70] I will argue below that Mao's rejection of the "negation of the negation" was a rejection of the title, rather than the substance, of this philosophical category, that he was seeking a nomenclature more in keeping with his predilection to perceive a unity of opposites in all things and processes. To pursue this argument, let us first of all place Mao's 1964 statement in the broader context of his other textual references to the "negation of the negation".

In his *Lecture Notes on Dialectical Materialism*, Mao referred to the "negation of the negation" as one of the "three basic principles (*faze*) of materialist dialectics" and incorporated a quote from Engels to reinforce his position.[71] Similarly, the "negation of the negation" figures quite prominently in the pre-Liberation text of *On Contradiction*. In a section subsequently entirely excised from the official text, Mao analysed and critiqued the three basic laws of formal logic. In doing so, Mao employed the "negation of the negation" as a foil to formal logic's law of excluded middle:

Correct thought should not exclude the third factor, should not exclude the law of the negation of the negation.... The law of excluded middle in formal logic also supplements its law of identity, which only recognises the fixed condition of a concept, and which opposes its development, opposes revolutionary leaps, and opposes the principle of the negation of the negation.... Why do formal logicians advocate these things? Because they observe things separate from their continual mutual function and interconnection; that is, they observe things at rest rather than in movement, and as separate rather than in connection. Therefore, it is not possible for them to consider and acknowledge the importance of contradictoriness and the negation of the negation within things and concepts, and so advocate the rigid and inflexible law of identity.[72]

Although it is evident from this document that Mao was employing the concept of the "negation of the negation" in a positive way during the Yan'an period, it is also evident, as we have seen, that Mao had arrived at a position which perceived the unity of opposites as the most important of the philosophical categories; as Mao was to point out in the same section of the pre-Liberation text of *On Contradiction,* "the revolutionary law of contradiction (namely the principle of the unity of opposites) therefore occupies the principal position in dialectics".[73]

In the Mao texts of the 1950s and early 1960s, we find that Mao was still employing the concept of the "negation of the negation", and not by any means in a dismissive way. By the same token, this concept appears far less frequently than does the unity of opposites, and references to it are sometimes rather enigmatic. For example, in January 1957, Mao employed the concept of the "negation of the negation" to indicate Stalin's lack of ability as a dialectician; "Stalin made mistakes in dialectics. 'Negation of the negation'. The October Revolution negated capitalism but he refused to admit that socialism may be negated too".[74] In May 1958, Mao again employed the concept to explain and illustrate change and supercession in the historical process; "The dialectics of Greece, the metaphysics of the Middle Ages, the Renaissance.... It is the negation of the negation.... Lenin's dialectics, Stalin's partial metaphysics, and today's dialectics are also the negation of the negation".[75] Similarly, in his July 1957 criticism of *Wen Hui Bao*, Mao had perceived the "negation of the negation" at work in the rapid fluctuations which characterised the political situation at the time: "Two meetings were called by the Journalists' Association, the first a negation and the second a negation of the negation, and the fact that this took place in a little over a month indicates the swift changes in the situation in China".[76] A further reference occurs in a text of May 1958, in which Mao called for a "negation of the negation" in rectifying the Chinese attitude toward foreigners; "By the end of the Ch'ing dynasty, when the foreigners attacked and entered China, the Chinese were frightened, became slaves, and felt inferior. Arrogant before, now we are too humble. Let us have the negation of the negation".[77] In the same speech, Mao also referred cryptically to developments in the area of cooperativization as the "negation of the negation".[78]

As late as September 1962, Mao continued to employ this concept. In his important speech at the Tenth Plenum of the Eighth Central Committee, he referred to the "negation of the negation" as constituting an aspect of the transformation of opposites into one another:

> This kind of reversal is also possible in socialist countries. An example of this is Yugoslavia which has changed its nature and become revisionist, changing from a workers' and peasants' country to a country ruled by reactionary nationalist elements. In our country we must come to grasp, understand and study this problem really thoroughly ... otherwise a country like ours can still move towards its opposite. Even to move towards its opposite would not matter too much because there would still be the negation of the negation, and afterwards we might move towards our opposite yet again.[79]

It is evident, therefore, that one can find a good number of references to the concept of the "negation of the negation" in the Mao texts of the late 1950s and early 1960s. It would appear that Mao's August 1964 "rejection" of the concept is thus at odds with his otherwise relatively frequent and positive references to it. However, parallel to such references to the "negation of the negation" emerges a different appellation for the concept, one which suggests that Mao was seeking a label more in keeping with the more fundamental philosophical category of the unity of opposites. In his important "Sixty Articles on Work Methods" of January 1958, we discover that in referring to the three categories of Marxist philosophy, Mao did not actually employ the title of the "negation of the negation":

> The law of the unity of opposites, of quantitative to qualitative changes, and of affirmation and negation, will hold good universally and eternally.[80]

The formula used here to describe the third philosophical category - "affirmation" (*kending*) and "negation" (*fouding*) - is identical to that used by Mao in his August 1964 talk on philosophy; "affirmation, negation ... in the development of things, every link in the chain of events is both affirmation and negation".[81] What we have here is merely a change in title, for the substance of the concept remains unchanged. The concept of the "negation of the negation" assumes that the factor which negates the negative (for example, capitalism's negation of feudalism) will initially constitute a positive factor, the affirmative. Over time, however, its positive character will transform into its opposite, the affirmative becoming the negative, as a new and historically progressive force emerges to challenge it. This cycle, of negation, affirmation, negation as described by Mao in August 1964, is in essence no different from that described earlier by himself and other Marxist philosophers, including Lenin and Engels, under the rubric of the "negation of the negation".[82]   Mao's demonstrable predilection for linking and using oxymoronic categories (life and death, truth and falsehood, materialism and idealism, right and wrong, finite and infinite, advanced and backward, to name but a few) suggests that he would have been unsympathetic to a formula which described a contradictory process and yet appeared to link like to like: the negation of the negation. By renaming the concept "affirmation and negation", Mao could leave the substance of the concept unaltered while bringing its title into line with the pervasive idea that the unity of opposites exists in all things and processes.

At a speech in Hangzhou in December 1965, Mao was to return to the problem of the three categories and to the theme of the primacy of the law of contradiction; and here again, Mao was to describe the third category by the title "affirmation and negation":

> It was said that dialectics had three basic laws and then Stalin said there were four. But I think there is only one basic law - the law of contradiction. Quality and quantity, affirmation and negation, substance and phenomenon, content and form, inevitability and freedom, possibility and reality, etc., are all cases of the unity of opposites.[83]

Mao here restates his long-held position that the law of contradiction - the unity of opposites - is the most basic law of materialistic dialectics. What is even more significant, however, is that Mao does not overtly reject the law of the "negation of the negation"; rather, as in his "Sixty Articles on Work Methods" of 1958, Mao chooses to describe the law by the title "affirmation and negation", a title which immediately suggests a unity of opposites. It is also significant that Mao listed this law along with a number of other categories of materialist dialectics which appear in his *Lecture Notes on Dialectical Materialism.* This reinforces the point made throughout this Introduction: that the philosophy enunciated in the *Lecture Notes*, which derived largely from Soviet sources, was to have a marked and sustained influence on the development and structure of Mao's philosophical thought; and that it is thus illegitimate to dismiss this document as irrelevant to an understanding of Mao's philosophy because of its derivation from and reliance on Soviet sources.

As a postscript to this discussion of Mao's supposed rejection of the "negation of the negation" it is worth noting that its level of orthodoxy within Soviet philosophy has been far from static. As Marcuse points out, the concept "disappeared from the list of fundamental dialectical laws" following Stalin's example of 1938.[84] Wetter, too, comments on the "checkered history" of this concept,[85] noting that Stalin's omission of "the law of the negation of the negation" from *Dialectical and Historical Materialism* (1938) meant the disappearance of this law from Soviet philosophy until after Stalin's death.[86] It is also interesting that on its revival in the mid-1950s, Soviet philosophers turned to the writings of Mao Zedong, especially *On Contradiction*, as a basis from which to elaborate the "negation of the negation" from a fresh perspective,[87] one which concentrated on "preserving what is worthwhile of the old state and in elevating and transforming it to a higher positive level".[88]

At the very least, the "checkered history" of the law of the "negation of the negation" in Soviet philosophy calls into question the propriety of peremptory judgements regarding Mao's heterodoxy on the issue, particularly when such judgements are based only on a single textual reference to a transcript of a conversation never intended for publication.

Empiricism and rationalism: theory and practice

I have argued above that a fresh perspective on Mao's philosophical thought emerges if the philosophy contained in his better known essays *On Contradiction* and *On Practice* is examined in conjunction with the *Lecture Notes on Dialectical Materialism*. Nowhere is this judgement borne out more clearly than in the realm of epistemology. Basing their interpretations largely on the epistemology contained in *On Practice,* many Western Mao scholars have argued that Mao was an empiricist, that for Mao the process of knowledge production commenced with experience (practice) and that the development of theory emerged as a subsequent link in the chain of cognition and was therefore inevitably subordinate to the primacy of experience; it is held, in other words, that for Mao experience produced knowledge.[89] I referred earlier to Mao's stress on practice and reflection as elements of his epistemology, and there is indeed no gainsaying that these occupy a central position in *On Practice*. Yet if we widen our perspective to incorporate the philosophy contained in *On Contradiction*, a number of troublesome questions suggest themselves. For example, how are we to reconcile the supposedly rather naive empiricism of *On Practice* with the overarching theoretical framework of *On Contradiction*? In this latter essay, Mao elaborates a highly theoretical conception of the universe and its most basic natural law, that of the unity of opposites. Incorporated in this conception are *a priori* ontological assumptions about the nature of matter, and in particular the belief that all things contain contradictions and that it is the ceaseless emergence and resolution of contradictions which allow change and development. It appears that, at the very least, there exists a tension between this position, with its strident assertion of overriding assumptions about the nature of the universe, and the view that humankind can only come to know the world through a piecemeal process of experience and practice. This tension raises the following questions. Did Mao believe that experience alone could provide the basis for such theoretical generalizations? Did he really contemplate the possibility that experience devoid of any prior theoretical orientation was the foundation on which human knowledge was constructed, including "knowledge" of the nature of the universe?

These questions emerge as a result of widening our perspective from *On Practice* to include *On Contradiction*. If we broaden our perspective yet again to incorporate the philosophy contained in the *Lecture Notes on Dialectical Materialism*, doubts regarding the propriety of branding Mao an undiluted empiricist are redoubled. The reasons for such doubts are as follows. First, the philosophical framework elaborated in the *Lecture Notes* rests less on an empiricist deference to the category of experience as the basis of knowledge production than on a rationalist conception of a universe in which there exists a rational order of objects constituted in a manner appropriate to the access of human thought.[90] That Mao perceived the universe as a rational order is borne out, as we have seen, by his deference to a number of objectively existing universal laws capable of describing the nature and change of the universe. Such universal laws indicate a universe whose structure and development are not random; there is order, logic, progression, ontological uniformity. Such characteristics exist in the very nature of the universe and the objects which comprise it. Objects and the relationships between them are thus assumed to constitute a rational order whose governing principles can be articulated within a rational framework in thought which parallels the external rational structure of the universe. This framework is constituted of a series of concepts (laws, principles, categories) which provide the criteria by which the truth or falsity of statements about reality are to be evaluated. The criteria of truth, from this perspective, appear to be provided by reason much more so than experience.

This leads to a second and related point. In a number of places in the *Lecture Notes on Dialectical Materialism*, Mao insists that no ontological distinction can be made between matter and thought. As we noted in an earlier section, Mao believed thought to be a particular form of matter; that is, matter in motion. Given this insistence, it follows that thought must inevitably obey the same natural laws as does matter generally. It can do no other. Consequently, the conception of a universe possessed of a rational structure refers equally to mind and thought as it does to an external reality. Both thought and reality (in ontological terms the distinction is an artificial one) are ordered in the same way and governed by the same imperatives. It is thus entirely possible for the rational structure of the universe to be replicated in thought, a position which emerges in the pages of both *On Contradiction* and the *Lecture Notes on Dialectical Materialism.*

Third, in all of these philosophical essays we find references to the "essence" of objects. The conception of an "essence" of a phenomenon is one which is entirely foreign to the empiricist tradition to which Mao is so often purported to belong. From the empiricist (or positivist) perspective, no distinction is made, or can be made, between the surface appearance of a phenomenon and its "true" nature; the data apprehended by sensory perceptions (the visual character of a phenomenon, for example) is all that is available for the human subject of cognition to arrive at knowledge of a phenomenon, and indeed all that is necessary. If Mao had been a genuine empiricist, the concept of an "essence" would have been absent from his philosophical writings, and yet it is very clearly present. And the reason is that Mao did *not* subscribe to the empiricist assumption that it is possible to know an object of cognition on the basis of a sensory familiarity with its surface appearance. This latter position was guilty of superficiality and one-sidedness, he believed, and the subject of cognition had to move beyond this and progress in a dialectical process to a deeper and deeper understanding of the nature of a phenomenon until its "essence" was grasped; and only when this had been achieved was true knowledge created.

Fourth, we can find in a variety of the Mao texts an explicit rejection of empiricism (*jingyanzhuyi*). It must be noted, however, that Mao appeared to understand the epistemology of empiricism as one which limited the subject of cognition to a one-sided and superficial perception of its object. For example, in the *Lecture Notes on Dialectical Materialism* Mao attacks the "strident realism" of Machism for its view that "truth is already established in final form in sense perceptions".[91] This "narrow viewpoint"[92] was empiricist in preventing a dialectical progression from sense perceptions to rational knowledge and back again; it remained locked in the stage of sense perceptions. Mao's rejection of "empiricism" did not, therefore, betoken a rejection of experience, and it remained an important element of his epistemology.

Given the importance of the concept of experience in Mao's epistemology, on what basis is it possible to challenge the received view that Mao's epistemology was an undiluted empiricism? The answer lies in the elaboration in the *Lecture Notes on Dialectical Materialism* of a theoretical framework which could provide direction and focus to the process of experience. As we have noted, the most fundamental laws of the universe are articulated in these *Lecture Notes*, laws seemingly not capable of formulation through empiricism with its deference to experience. Such laws were of necessity posited *a priori*, as premises which constituted the foundation for the epistemological project. An example is Mao's insistence on the materiality of the universe:

The first condition of belonging to the materialist camp is the acknowledgement that the material world is separate from and exists independently of human consciousness - it existed prior to the appearance of humankind, and following the appearance of humankind it remained separate from and existed independently of human consciousness. The recognition of this point is the fundamental premise of all scientific research.[93]

The interesting point about this statement of philosophical premises is that Mao posits the existence of a material reality prior to the existence of humankind, a position incapable of validation through the agency of human experience for the simple reason that no humans existed. It is also very clear that Mao regarded the materialist "premise" as one which had to be "acknowledged", and although he does subsequently proceed to elaborate "proofs" for this premise, they are proofs ultimately grounded on the acceptance of the premise itself, namely, that a material reality exists independently of human consciousness.

Consequently, the epistemological picture which emerges from an evaluation of the philosophy contained in the three philosophical essays under question is one of a tension between a rationalist and an empiricist approach to epistemology.[94] On the one hand it is rationalist: the universe is a rational order; the relationships between objects in the universe constitute a rational structure; the universe and its constituent objects are ordered according to a series of objectively existing universal laws, these laws providing criteria of truth by which propositions about reality are to be evaluated; thought (as matter) is structured in a way which parallels external reality; phenomena possess "essences" not immediately apprehendable by sensory perceptions. Each of these rationalist dictums appears in these philosophical essays, and particularly so in *Dialectical Materialism*. On the other hand, however, it is empiricist: knowledge derives from experience; the first stage in the knowledge process is perceptual knowledge; perceptual knowledge is transformed into conceptual knowledge (how we are not told);[95] the criterion of truth for conceptual knowledge is practice; in the contradiction between theory and practice, practice is "under normal conditions" the principal aspect;[96] knowledge of reality is progressively deepened through a process of practice in which reality and the subject of cognition are transformed; and so on. Each of these empiricist propositions too can be located within these philosophical essays. How is this tension in Mao's epistemology to be reconciled? Is it possible to reconcile it?

In the final analysis, there can be no reconciliation of the conflicting imperatives within Mao's epistemology. One cannot at the same time elevate experience as the privileged site of knowledge production *and* defer to the primacy of thought in the rationalist mould (as Mao does in the pre-Liberation text of *On Practice*, for example)[97] without becoming entangled in a contradiction. The important point, it seems to me, is to recognise the significant rationalist element which exists in Mao's philosophical position, and abandon the myth so prevalent in Western Mao studies that Mao was a crude empiricist and that the analysis of his thought and action should therefore employ an empiricism equally as crude.[98] For the existence of a rationalist element in Mao's thought indicates that his actions were, contrary to empiricist expectations, driven by theory, often at a very abstract level.

The importance of a rationalist perspective to the activities of a Marxist revolutionary are obvious. In the first place, a concerted and protracted political struggle required more than the random and erratic insights which experience alone could provide. What was necessary was an elaborated theoretical framework which could allow questions to be asked about the nature of the historical process, which provided premises for an understanding of social structure, and which constructed criteria by which the effectivity of particular actions could be evaluated.[99] Secondly, a theoretical framework of the kind supplied by dialectical and historical materialism could provide motivation towards a future state of society hitherto unexperienced by humankind. No crude empiricist could talk, as Mao was wont to do during the Yan'an period, of an era of "perpetual peace" founded on communism as the inevitable future of humanity; for experience could not allow the possibility of such grand predictions.[100] It is very clear that the predictive element of Marxism was to exert a profound influence on Mao's approach to revolutionary struggle, a predictive element which derived from a largely abstract conception of the potentialities of humankind and human society. It is consequently no coincidence that one of Mao's favourite sayings is drawn from Lenin's *What is to be Done?*, a saying which nicely illustrates the importance he attached to theory in directing revolutionary struggle; "without revolutionary theory there can be no revolutionary movement".[101]

This challenge to prevailing interpretations of Mao's epistemology has implications beyond the narrow confines of philosophical debate. If it is once conceded that Mao's epistemology was not an undiluted empiricism, it raises a series of questions about the development of his political and philosophical thought, his adherence to Marxism, his relationship to and conception of the "reality" of Chinese society, his views on the future, the sources of his thought and action, and so on. At the very least, it calls into question the basic premise of the "*in vivo*" interpretation elaborated by Womack[102] and endorsed by Schram[103] which regards Mao's paradigm for political action emerging from his experience of pre-Yan'an days; for such an interpretation makes virtually no allowance for the orienting role of theory in the development of political strategies and tactics. And this in turn leads to the unfortunate tendency to give less than sufficient attention to the theory which drove Mao's practice and that of the Chinese revolution generally.

Reliance on Soviet sources and the issue of plagiarism

As stated earlier, one of the reasons for the generally dismissive treatment by Western Mao scholars of the *Lecture Notes on Dialectical Materialism* is its heavy reliance on translations of Soviet texts on philosophy of the 1930s. I have argued that an overemphasis on the issue of plagiarism and reliance on Soviet philosophy has resulted in a tendency to downplay the significant influence that the categories, concepts, and laws of Soviet Marxist philosophy was to have on the development of Mao's philosophical thought. The reasoning for this latter position runs as follows: if Mao did indulge, while writing the *Lecture Notes on Dialectical Materialism*, in a wholesale exercise of plagiarism and borrowing, then the philosophical content of these *Lecture Notes* cannot really be taken as equivalent to Mao's own philosophical thought, which is to be found rather in the essays *On Contradiction* and *On Practice*, essays apparently written by Mao himself. As suggested, this form of logic ignores the point that the issues of authorship of a document and that of influence are not synonymous; in other words, while there is no gainsaying that Mao *did* rely heavily on Soviet philosophical sources in the writing of this text, it is clear from his absorption of the philosophical categories contained in these sources and their persistent reemergence in his subsequent writings, that the exercise of reading (and in some cases, repeatedly reading) Soviet texts on philosophy had a major impact on his own thought at a critical juncture in its development. To deny this position on the basis of Mao's plagiarism is thus to deny the possibility of serious consideration of the relationship between Mao's philosophical thought (or for that matter, Chinese Marxism generally) and Soviet Marxist philosophy of the 1930s. This would constitute a serious analytical error, for *one* of the significant elements of the foundation of Mao's philosophy and Chinese Marxism is the form of Marxist philosophy which became formalised and legitimised as orthodoxy in the Soviet Union in the early 1930s. I emphasise that the Soviet philosophy of the 1930s was *one* of the influences on Mao's thought, for it is as equally erroneous to suggest that it was the *only* influence; Mao's philosophical thought drew on a number of sources (including some aspects of traditional Chinese philosophy and the Chinese proverbial tradition). But the totality of Mao's philosophical thought is more than the sum of its constituent influences; for he took these influences and created a synthesis of his own, a synthesis which, nevertheless, clearly exhibits parallels to its sources.

Stung by Wang Ming's criticism of "narrow empiricism" during the early 1930s, Mao made a personal commitment to study theory and philosophy when the historical context permitted.[104] The opportunity to indulge in a bout of extended philosophical study presented itself during the early years of the Yan'an period and culminated in the writing of *On Practice, On Contradiction*, and the *Lecture Notes on Dialectical Materialism* in July and August 1937. The timing of this exercise in philosophical study is significant also because it occurred just subsequent to a period in which a number of Soviet philosophical texts had been translated into Chinese.[105] According to Chinese scholars, three of the five or six sources so heavily employed by Mao during this period of intense study and writing were translations of Soviet texts on philosophy; the other two or three were volumes by the Chinese Marxist philosophers Ai Siqi and Li Da, whose influence we will examine in a subsequent section.[106]

Let us look a little more closely at these Soviet texts on philosophy. Our purpose is twofold. The first is to provide a brief description of the content of each volume. In so doing, the striking similarity of these volumes in their coverage of the philosophy of dialectical materialism will become evident. This similarity would suggest that each text was engaged in presenting a philosophy whose orthodoxy severely curtailed variation. In other words, each text was not merely metonymic, but representative of mainstream Soviet philosophy in a very real sense. Mao's search for comprehension of this intellectual tradition, while inevitably premised on a fairly narrow textual basis, was thus made more fruitful through the repetitive nature of the texts he employed.[107] Moreover, the intertextual congruence of these Soviet texts also serves to query the importance of establishing the exact textual source of Mao's plagiarism. Such an exercise has already been carried out for sections of the *Lecture Notes on Dialectical Materialism* by Wittfogel and Schram.[108] However, if Mao's sources are perceived as a constellation of interlocking and overlapping texts whose essential function was the same, then the issue of the direct appropriation of words, phrases, passages, even sections, assumes less significance than the general influence which these texts exercised on his thinking at that time and subsequently.

Secondly, we will briefly examine the information released recently in China about Mao's annotations on two of these three Soviet texts.

1.   *A Course on Dialectical Materialism* by M. Shirokov and A. Aizenberg et al., translated into Chinese by Li Da and Lei Zhongjian under the title *Bianzhengfa weiwulun jiaocheng*. This volume went through a series of editions, and it was the third edition published in June 1935 and the fourth edition published in December 1936 that Mao studied.[109] The volume contains 582 pages. The contents of *A Course on Dialectical Materialism* include *inter alia* sections on mechanistic materialism, knowledge and practice and the unity of subject and object, stages and causes of movement in the process of cognition, truth, the law of the mutual transformation of quantity into quality, the law of the unity and struggle of opposites as the essence of contemporary dialectics, the significance of the principal aspect of a contradiction, the movement of contradiction from the beginning to the end of a process, the relativity of identity and the absoluteness of struggle within the law of the unity of opposites, on equilibrium, the negation of the negation, essence and appearance, form and content, possibility and reality, chance and necessity, basis and condition, necessity and freedom, dialectical and formal logic, the fundamental laws of formal logic, and the function of experience and practice in knowledge.

According to recent Chinese commentaries on Mao's annotations and marginalia, it was this text, *A Course on Dialectical Materialism*, which was most heavily annotated by Mao in the period prior to writing his own three philosophical essays.[110] Between November 1936 and April 1937, Mao studied the third edition of this volume, covering its margins and any blank spaces with close to 13,000 characters of annotations and commentary, a selection of which is contained in the translations in this volume. The third chapter of the third edition, entitled "The basic laws of dialectics", attracted the most extensive commentary by Mao, the longest paragraph of the commentaries extending to almost one thousand characters. According to Mao specialists in China, the "overwhelming proportion of these marginal annotations were devoted to elaboration of Mao's own dialectical materialist and historical materialist philosophical viewpoint, including development of the ideas in the text and criticism of them".[111] In many places, they continue, Mao made connections between the history of China and other countries, including analysis of the experience and lessons of the Chinese Revolution. They are thus at pains to point out that Mao did not react to the philosophical content of *A Course on Dialectical Materialism* in a mechanical, uncritical manner; rather he reacted to the text critically, applying its abstract content to the historical situation of the Chinese Revolution.

Of particular interest here is the relationship between the content of this volume and Mao's *On Contradiction* and *On Practice*. In his annotations throughout this volume regarding the particular aspect of a contradiction, Mao developed this concept through its application to the concrete conditions of China. Mao noted that not only does the particular aspect of a contradiction play a determining role, but that under certain conditions, the principal and secondary aspects of a contradiction can undergo mutual transformation (*huxiang zhuanhua*); "In the situation of antagonism between China and Japan, the Chinese factors are at present changing from a secondary to a principal position; if the national united front can be extended and consolidated, and because of international factors (the Soviet Union, the Japanese masses, other peaceful nations), the superiority of the Japanese aspect will be transformed".[112] Elsewhere in this text, Mao wrote "in each process of the movement of a contradiction, identity is relative, struggle is absolute".[113] Similarly, the fourth edition contains the following annotation on the two processes of cognition: "In the process of cognition, the particular determines the universal; in the process of practice, the universal determines the particular".[114] These few examples suggest the importance of this volume in the preparation of Mao's *On Contradiction* and *On Practice*. We will turn to a more detailed analysis of the relationship between these two essays and Soviet philosophy in a subsequent section.

2. *Dialectical and Historical Materialism* by M.B. Mitin et al., translated Shen Zhiyuan, and published in China under the title *Bianzhengweiwulun yu lishiweiwulun* in December 1936. This volume, of 538 pages, contains sections on the two lines in philosophy, mechanistic materialism, the materiality of the world and the form of material existence, matter and thought and the reflection theory of dialectical materialism, truth, the law of the unity of opposites, the law of the mutual transformation of quantity into quality, the law of the negation of the negation, essence and appearance, form and content, chance and necessity, possibility and reality, and formal logic and dialectics.

According to Chinese sources, Mao read and annotated this volume prior to August 1937.[115] As with *A Course on Dialectical Materialism*, this volume has a "direct relationship" with *On Contradiction* and *On Practice*, both in terms of context and content.[116]

In their identification of Mao's plagiarism, both Wittfogel and Schram[117] have compared sections of Ai Siqi's translations of Mitin's 1933 work *Dialectical Materialism* which appear in a volume entitled *Zhexue xuanji* published in Shanghai in 1939 with Mao's *Lecture Notes on Dialectical Materialism*. While there can be no doubt that Schram and Wittfogel are correct in identifying Mitin as the author of these passages, it is highly probable that the exact textual source was the volume *Dialectical and Historical Materialism* under consideration here, and published in December 1936. Some textual comparisons are provided in the notes and in the tables appended to this Introduction.[118]

3. *Outline of New Philosophy*, edited by M.B. Mitin et al., translated by Ai Siqi and Zheng Yili, and published in Chinese as *Xin zhexue dagang* in June 1936.[119] This volume, of 454 pages, contains sections on the historical origins of dialectical materialism, the two tendencies in philosophy, the object of dialectical materialism, matter and motion, space and time, the law of the unity of opposites, the law of the mutual transformation of quantity into quality, the law of the negation of the negation, essence and appearance, basis and condition,

form and content, chance and necessity, possiblity and reality, a critique of formal logic, and the process of cognition.

Mao's personal copy of this volume has not survived, although Chinese Mao scholars believe it very likely that Mao did annotate it in the same manner as the two volumes previously discussed.[120] Indeed, it is largely on the basis of the similarity between *Outline of New Philosophy* and *Lecture Notes on Dialectical Materialism* that Schram and Wittfogel identified Mao's reliance on Soviet sources to an extent tantamount to plagiarism.

However, the point that emerges from our brief comparison of the content of these three Soviet philosophical texts is the similarity of the material presented. Expositions of the fundamental laws and basic categories of dialectical materialism and critiques of formal logic appear in each of these texts. Almost identical expositions and critiques appear in Li Da's *Shehuixue dagang* (Elements of Sociology), which Li modelled on Shirokov and Aizenberg's *A Course on Dialectical Materialism*, and also in Ai Siqi's *Sixiang fangfalun* (Methodology of thought) and *Dazhong zhexue* (Philosophy for the masses). These three texts by Chinese Marxist philosophers were also almost certainly employed by Mao in the preparation of his philosophical essays of 1937.[121] While it may be possible, therefore, to pinpoint passages in these texts which Mao inserted into his own writings on dialectical materialism, the importance of this exercise is overshadowed by the similarity of the content and style of language of all the sources employed, even when these were written by different authors. It is clear from a comparison of their writings that originality was not the issue, but the elaboration of the basic concepts and categories of dialectical materialism within the strict guidelines imposed by orthodoxy.

Let us pursue this issue of plagiarism a little further and explore how this might affect interpretation of Mao's philosophical writings of 1937. The first point to be made is that the concept of plagiarism in the English language implies not only the borrowing of textual material from a source written by another, it also suggests intent to deceive the reader into believing that the borrowed material is one's own. There can be no denying that the *Lecture Notes on Dialectical Materialism* do indeed use a significant amount of material lifted wholesale from Chinese translations of the Soviet philosophical texts previously mentioned. In this sense there can be no doubt that an act of plagiarism took place. But did Mao consciously intend an act of deception, one in which his readers would be deceived into accepting the material from Soviet philosophical texts as his own? There are a number of considerations which suggest against such an interpretation. First, in the classical Chinese tradition, it was not at all common for an author to attribute his sources. The educated person was expected to be able to identify the text from which the saying or quote had been extracted. This practice undoubtedly extended into early Marxist writings in China, and it is one of the frustrations of working with such documents that sources of quotes or precis of another author's views are not provided. It was a problem I encountered in the translation and annotation of not only the *Lecture Notes on Dialectical Materialism,* but also the pre-Liberation text of *On Contradiction.* The sources of quotes had to be tracked down by sifting through texts by Engels, Lenin, and other authors from which the quotes may have been taken; but in these cases, no intention to deceive was ever suspected. This failure to identify the source of quotes or information is certainly not acceptable in the Western academic tradition as it has developed, but the judgement reserved for a Western academic writer who indulged in such a practice may not be entirely appropriate to a Chinese author, even as late as the 1930s, who did so. My suggestion here is that a condemnation of Mao for plagiarism in the second sense outlined above may rest on something of a cultural misunderstanding, and a failure to appreciate different cultural norms of academic propriety.

Second, the point needs to be emphasised that the *Lecture Notes on Dialectical Materialism* were just that - lecture notes. The words "lecture notes" (*jiangshou tigang*) are clearly included in the title, and would warn the reader that the content of the document did not necessarily represent an original or highly polished contribution to the realm of intellectual inquiry of dialectical materialism. One also must recall the context within which these *Lecture Notes* were written. Mao was not, like Kant, involved in a lengthy period of isolated philosophical rumination. Rather, Mao was engaged in a protracted process of dialogue with colleagues and philosophers who were close to hand in the far from private world of Yan'an. A group of Party members with a bent toward philosophy developed around Mao, and Mao was later to institutionalise this study group (either towards the end of 1937 or the beginning of 1938),[122] meeting initially in Mao's own office on three nights a week. Seven or eight attended (probably including Ai Siqi, Zhou Yang, He Sijing, Ren Beigou, Pei Yuan, and Chen Boda),[123] and the subjects discussed were the various laws of dialectical materialism and aspects of dialectical materialism generally. In a context such as this, could Mao hope to get away with a conscious act of plagiarism in which deception was intended, when there were those present (like Ai Siqi) whose familiarity with the philosophy of dialectical materialism was far more advanced than Mao's, and who in fact had been responsible for translating into Chinese some of the texts which Mao relied on? It seems hardly likely.[124]

The *Lecture Notes*, and particularly the plagiarised sections, may well have constituted the raw material which Mao elaborated in the course of an oral explication of the basic tenets of dialectical materialism. It seems unlikely that the text of the *Lecture Notes on Dialectical Materialism* that is available to us in its various versions is the exact transcription of the lecture Mao presented to old cadres of the Red Army.[125] Although a record of the lecture was taken by the Political and Propaganda departments, it was subsequently tidied up by them and Mao himself before it was published in the journal of the Anti-Japanese Military and Political University in 1938. It is probable that Mao never regarded the published piece as anything more than a roughly edited version of his own lecture notes, useful as instructional material in a context where teaching materials on philosophy were notoriously scarce, but not pretending to any high degree of originality. His final words of the *Lecture Notes* display a becoming modesty which suggests as faulty the view that Mao was attempting to pass the document off as anything more than notes designed for a lecture, and hopefully of use to the novice in the subject:

The reason why people feel dialectics is difficult is that there exist no books which explain dialectics well. In China, there are many books on dialectics which, while not incorrect, are explained poorly or none too well, and which frighten people off. Books which are good at explaining dialectics employ everyday language and relate moving experiences. Sooner or later such a book must be put together. This talk of mine is far from adequate since I have myself only just begun to study dialectics. There has been no possibility of writing a useful book on the subject as yet, although perhaps the opportunity may present itself in the future. I wish to do so, but this will be decided by how my study proceeds.[126]

Such a passage would hardly have been included in the published version had Mao been consciously attempting to masquerade as an expert on dialectical materialism through an act of plagiarism intended to deceive his readers.

Third, the point needs to be made that the *Lecture Notes on Dialectical Materialism* have never, as far as I am aware, been officially published for general circulation and consumption in post-Liberation China. The versions of it which are available have been designated as *neibu* documents, and included in collections of material for study by academics and cadres. As study material for academics and cadres, the *Lecture Notes on Dialectical Materialism* were intended for exactly the same purpose in post-Liberation China as during the Yan'an period. And it is very obvious that Chinese philosophers and Mao specialists in post-Liberation China were and are well aware of Mao's textual debt to Soviet texts on philosophy, although this has not led them to reject the philosophy contained in the *Lecture Notes*.[127] Had Mao wished to pursue a conscious act of plagiarism in which there existed an intention to deceive, why were the *Lecture Notes* not substantially rewritten and re-edited, as many of his other works were prior to official republication, and published as a creature of his own intellect? The answer is, that because there existed no intention to deceive, the *Lecture*

Notes were neither revised nor published as part of Mao's officially sanctioned *oeuvre*.

On Contradiction and *On Practice* and the issue of plagiarism

The issue of plagiarism in the case of the *Lecture Notes on Dialectical Materialism* is also important as it raises the question of the degree of influence of Soviet philosophy on Mao's two better-known philosophical essays, *On Contradiction* and *On Practice*, and the extent of Mao's textual reliance on these sources in their writing. After all, the three essays are, as Schram has argued, part of a "single intellectual enterprise", written at the same time, under the same influences, and in the same historical context. If one chooses to look hard at the Soviet texts mentioned before and the works of philosophy created by Ai Siqi and Li Da during the early to mid-1930s, one is struck by the wealth of material there on the issues of dialectics, contradiction, and epistemology couched in terms remarkably similar to that employed by Mao in his own essays. However, if one pursues this line of reasoning to its apparently logical conclusion, what is the result? The result is that one ends with Wittfogel, asserting Chinese Marxism to be *nothing more* than an imitation and extension of Soviet and orthodox Marxism, and therefore entirely consonant with Soviet political ambitions;[128] or with Cohen, decrying any claim by Mao or Chinese Marxism to "originality", perceiving there *nothing* but second-hand ideas dressed up as new wares.[129] Both of these positions, I believe, prevent a constructive and sensitive approach to an understanding of the theoretical influences which gave rise to Mao Zedong's philosophical thought and Chinese Marxism, and to their subsequent development. For the point remains that influence and source are not the equivalent of subsequent development. Were they to be so, the realm of intellectual history would amount to nothing more than the reduction of a thinker to his or her sources and influences; the exercise would be limited to a compilation of these, and originality, innovation, and development would disappear from view. And yet there is more to the comprehension of thought, and particularly bodies of thought, than this.

My purpose is thus not to replicate the perspectives of Wittfogel and Cohen. Nevertheless, because of the exaggerated tendency within Western Mao studies to regard Mao's Marxism as having achieved a decisive break from more orthodox forms of Marxism,[130] I believe it essential to return to the issue of sources and to reopen the debate on Mao's own debt to Soviet philosophy of the 1930s; and part of this debate inevitably concerns the problem of plagiarism. Where does plagiarism start and where does it finish? Does it involve only the direct appropriation of words used in another source; does it extend (as Wittfogel implies) to summarising a passage in one's own words; or can it be applied more generally, to indicate a reliance on or utilisation of the ideas (if not the exact words) to be found in another source? These questions are not merely rhetorical, for if we are to bring *On Contradiction* and *On Practice* under the spotlight and submit them to the same critical scrutiny as the *Lecture Notes,* then we may find that these two essays, without doubt the cornerstone of Chinese Marxist philosophy, bear more than just a passing similarity to the sources Mao was employing in 1936-37. But does this imply that there is nothing original to be found in these essays? A balanced response to this question can be gained through a consideration of recent discussions of this issue by Mao specialists in China.

Since Mao's death, scholarship on his philosophical thought in China has pursued a more independently critical path than previously. While maintaining the overwhelming significance of Mao's writings on philosophy for the development of Chinese Marxist philosophy generally, Chinese Mao scholars have subjected his philosophical writings of 1937 to detailed and critical comparison with the texts on philosophy which constituted his major influence. This exercise has been facilitated by the publication of the annotations and marginal notes which Mao inscribed on these philosophical texts. In the context of looking closely at his sources of influence and his immediate response to them in the form of his annotations and marginalia, Chinese Mao scholars have inevitably posed the question I have raised above: to what extent were *On*

Contradiction and *On Practice* reliant on Soviet texts on philosophy and those of Li Da and Ai Siqi? The response to this question is instructive.

According to Shi Zhongquan,[131] there is a direct relationship of text and content between *On Contradiction* and *On Practice* and two of his sources - *A Course on Dialectical Materialism (Bianzhengfa weiwulun jiaocheng)* and *Dialectical and Historical Materialism (Bianzhengweiwulun yu lishiweiwulun)*. There is an indirect relationship - that of the absorption of ideas (*sixiang*) - between Mao's two essays and Mitin's *Outline of New Philosophy*. Shi argues that the relationship between Mao's essays and these Soviet texts on philosophy can be looked at from two perspectives. First, it should be acknowledged that Mao's two essays absorbed and employed the positive conclusions of the Soviet texts. Any major thinker must employ accumulated intellectual sources in the process of elaborating his theory, and Mao was no exception when he came to write *On Contradiction* and *On Practice*. Points of view and analysis from *A Course on Dialectical Materialism* and *Dialectical and Historical Materialism* were absorbed by Mao to become an organic component of his own essays on philosophy. In writing *On Practice*, Shi continues, Mao absorbed the viewpoint of *A Course on Dialectical Materialism* that, apart from practice, one could not come to know the external world, and that the process of cognition involved the stages of perception and cognition; and from *Dialectical and Historical Materialism*, Mao assimilated the concepts that practice could assume a multiplicity of forms, and that pre-Marxist materialism, in not stressing the social character of man, failed to comprehend the dependent relationship of knowledge to social practice. Similarly, concepts and ideas to be found in the Soviet text were to find their way into Mao's *On Contradiction*. In particular, Mao drew from *A Course on Dialectical Materialism* the following concepts and viewpoints: the restriction which the principal contradiction imposes on other contradictions and the determining role played by the principal aspect of a contradiction, the resolution of different contradictions requires different methods, there is mutual connection and interpermeation (*shentou*) between a pair of opposites, difference is contradiction, the analysis of the particularity of contradiction in each process and each aspect of a process, the struggle of opposites is absolute whereas the unity of opposites is relative, and the critique of the theory of equilibrium. From *Dialectical and Historical Materialism*, the following views and concepts found their way into *On Contradiction*: the two theories of development and the critique of the theory of external causation, the analysis of the various forms of motion and the particularity of contradiction in the various stages of development, and the model examples provided by Marx and Engels of concretely analyzing concrete conditions.

Anyone familiar with the content of Mao's *On Contradiction* and *On Practice* will recognise at once that this list of concepts and viewpoints cuts a broad swathe through the content of those essays. Given the degree of indebtedness to Soviet philosophical sources now acknowledged by Chinese Mao scholars, to what extent can *On Practice* and *On Contradiction* be regarded as independent creations of Mao's? In response to this, Shi insists that the acknowledgement of Mao's debt to Soviet philosophical texts must be balanced by recognition of a number of other considerations. In the first place, the content of these Soviet texts on philosophy were themselves based on the theories and concepts of Marx, Engels, and Lenin, their primary function being the elaboration and development of these theories and concepts into a philosophical system. As such, these texts on philosophy were to have a significant influence on Marxists in China and abroad and on the world of Marxist philosophy generally. It was *not* just Mao who was influenced by this systematization of Marxist philosophy in the Soviet Union during the 1930s.

A second consideration is that the substance of *On Practice* and *On Contradiction* involves the utilisation of the viewpoint of Marxist philosophy to sum up the experiences of the Chinese revolution, and to critique subjectivism and dogmatism in its conduct; threading through the two essays is a spirit of integrating Marxist theory and the reality of the Chinese Revolution, and they are the embodiment of "practical materialism", devoid of bookish and academic theorizing.

Consequently, Mao's two essays can still be regarded as a major development of the philosophical theories of Marxism, Shi contends, a development manifesting its own particular characteristics. The latter judgement is supported by Shi by reference to three major differences between *On Practice* and *On Contradiction* and the Soviet texts on philosophy.

First, Mao's two essays on philosophy were a model of the sinification and actualisation (*xianshihua*) of Marxism. Mao perceived Marxism as something more than an abstract body of principles, and *On Contradiction* and *On Practice* provide plentiful evidence of his attempt to integrate these principles with the concrete realities of the Chinese Revolution. Shi refers to Mao's marginal notes in *A Course on Dialectical Materialism* to illustrate this point. Mao wrote, when he read the section on different contradictions requiring different methods for their resolution, "the national contradiction between China and Japan requires for its resolution a united front with the bourgeoisie"; and further on Mao wrote, "In normal times, the contradiction between labour and capital requires a united front of the workers. And in the contradiction between correct practice and incorrect tendency within the party and revolutionary ranks, the method of ideological struggle must be employed to achieve resolution". Further examples of the kind appear to illustrate the manner in which Mao perceived the practical implications of this abstract principle.

Mao's philosophical essays also are illustrative of the process of the sinification of Marxism insofar as they integrate Marxist philosophical concepts and ideas and those of traditional Chinese philosophy. In so doing, such traditional concepts and ideas were endowed with a scientific quality. Shi points to Mao's employment in *On Practice* of the traditional philosophical category of knowledge and action (*zhixingguan*) and the way he linked this to knowledge (*renshi*) and practice. Similarly, in *On Contradiction*, Mao employed the traditional Chinese saying "things that oppose each other also complement each other" (*xiangfan-xiangcheng*) to explicate the concept of the identity of contradiction, and the law of the unity of opposites generally.

Second, not only is the philosophical framework employed by Mao in his two essays more tightly argued and complete than the Soviet sources, in terms of content many of his formulations, and much of his analysis and explanations, are clearer, more concise, systematic, and profound than the Soviet texts on philosophy. In making this claim, Shi refers to Mao's ability in his marginal notes to summarise with great clarity and even more profoundly sections of the Soviet text. This quality was to be reflected in *On Practice* and *On Contradiction*, which were able to present concisely and with great lucidity major areas of Marxist philosophy.

Third, Shi argues that on the basis of the positive conclusions of the Soviet texts absorbed by Mao, he raised a number of new ideas (*sixiang*), and developed the philosophical theories of Marxism. Original ideas in *On Practice* include the concept of the two leaps in the process of cognition, and the notion that knowledge is a concrete historical unity of subjective and objective, theory and practice, and knowledge and action (*zhi he xing*); Mao also expressed the general laws of the movement of knowledge in a way not to be found in the Soviet texts. In *On Contradiction*, Mao provided an elaboration of the abstract category of the universality of contradiction which went beyond that to be found in the Soviet sources; Mao also systematised the elaboration to be found there on the important issue of the particularity of contradiction, and most importantly employed analysis of the complex particular contradictions of the Chinese Revolution to explicate this principle in a way which was innovative. Shi goes on to assert that the Soviet texts on philosophy did not contain mention of the concepts of the relationship of the principal and non-principal contradiction, or the transformation of the principal and non-principal aspects of a contradiction. *A Course on Dialectical Materialism* did, he concedes, raise the issue of the determining role of the principal contradiction and the principal aspect of a contradiction, but these concepts were not elaborated. In his annotations on this Soviet text, Mao wrote the longest paragraph of any of his marginal notes on this issue (amounting to some 1200 characters), elaborating a position which was to find its way into *On Contradiction*; Mao's formulation on this problem can be regarded as a development of Marxist dialectics, according to Shi. He proceeds to list a series of categories whose elaboration by Mao constituted a development of the material contained in the Soviet texts; these include generality (*gongxing*) and individuality, the idea that the relationship of absolute and relative are central to the question of the contradiction in things, the two important meanings of the concept of identity (*tongyixing*) and also the difference between concrete and imaginery identity, and the mutual relation between conditional relative identity and unconditional absolute struggle.

Shi Zhongquan concludes by saying that the definite theoretical relationship between *On Contradiction* and *On Practice* and the Soviet texts on philosophy has been either not acknowledged or underemphasized in the past, and there has been a tendency to exaggerate (*bagao*) the achievements and significance of Mao's philosophical essays, something not in keeping with the current emphasis on "seeking truth from facts". Nevertheless, the opposite tendency, that of completely denying or underemphasizing the important position of *On Contradiction* and *On Practice* in the history of the development of Marxism, is also an unscientific attitude.

The position advanced by Shi Zhongquan is clearly of significance for the line of argument I have been pursuing throughout this introduction. On the one hand, it emphasizes the debt to the philosophy of the orthodox Marxist tradition by Mao, while on the other hand stressing the areas in which Mao can be perceived to have either made a contribution of some originality or to have applied the abstract principles of Marxism in a novel way which could function as a model in the subsequent development of the theories, strategies, and tactics which were to become part-and-parcel of the ideology of Chinese Marxism. The conclusion arrived at by Shi appears to me to be a balanced and persuasive one, avoiding as it does the extremes of Wittfogel and Cohen on the one side and the political culture school[132] on the other, with its view of overwhelming dominance of traditional Chinese philosophy and culture on the formation of contemporary Chinese thought. The adoption of this middle path allows a recognition of influence *and* originality, source *and* subsequent development in the philosophical thought of Mao Zedong.

Another important issue emerges as a result of Shi Zhongquan's discussion of the extent of Mao's reliance on Soviet philosophical sources in the writing of *On Contradiction* and *On Practice*, and that is the issue of the sinification of Marxism. Stuart Schram has argued that Mao denied altogether the existence of "a universally valid form of Marxism", and that his "preoccupation with the glory of China" led to a sinified Marxism which was "hermetic".[133] In opposition to this view, I have suggested that the sinification of Marxism was an attempt by Mao to establish a formula by which a universal theory such as Marxism could be utilised in a particular national context and culture without abandoning the universality of that theory.[134] The fact that *On Contradiction* and *On Practice* drew so heavily for inspiration on a number of Soviet texts on philosophy enhances the suggestion that one important component of a sinified Marxism - the philosophical component - was not "hermetic" and bore a clear genealogical relationship to a form of Marxism claiming to be, and widely accepted as, universal in its content and applicability. There can be no doubt that the content of *On Contradiction* and *On Practice* is in most important respects acceptably orthodox as judged by the standards of orthodoxy established by Soviet Marxism in the 1930s.[135] Consequently, it is just not logical to recognise, as Schram has done, Mao's reliance on Soviet sources in the compilation of his writings on dialectical materialism, while insisting that the sinified Marxism that Mao was largely responsible for creating was "hermetic". There was nothing "hermetic" about it; Mao's employment of concepts drawn from Soviet sources in all of his three philosophical essays ensured that his thought and Chinese Marxism generally contain significant elements which are not specifically Chinese in origin.

Moreover, a recognition of this dependent relationship on mainstream Marxism in Mao's philosophical writings is necessary if one is to have any hope of comprehending the world of philosophy in post-Liberation and especially contemporary China. Textbooks and primers on dialectical and historical materialism in contemporary China read like regurgitations of the Soviet philosophical texts employed by Mao in the 1930s;[136] and the connection clearly is Mao's endorsement of this reading of dialectical materialism in his writings on philosophy of 1937. Chinese Marxism *does* possess elements which are particular to the Chinese case; but it likewise incorporates concepts, categories, laws, and modes of thought and expression whose source obviously extends beyond the Chinese Marxist tradition itself.

The issue of Mao's plagiarism and reliance on Soviet philosophical sources thus raises questions beyond the confines of Mao studies, questions which extend to the problem of understanding the contemporary Chinese world view, of which philosophy is an important and integral part.

The origins of Mao Zedong's philosophical thought: perspectives from China

We have seen above that Mao scholars in China are subjecting Mao's philosophical thought - its sources, development, content - to more rigorous academic scrutiny and analysis than was possible before his death. Nevertheless, while the stature and influence of Mao have been very seriously eroded in the political arena and in everyday Chinese life, amongst professional philosophers and Mao scholars in China there is still a very high regard for his abilities as a philosopher and as the major architect of the intellectual edifice now recognisable as Chinese Marxism. This regard is, of course, tempered by the current Party line, but the current stress on "seeking truth from facts" and the more open intellectual atmosphere of the last decade have facilitated the emergence of a field of Mao studies in which, like its Western counterpart, there is disagreement, debate, and controversy. It is, therefore, no longer possible to talk of a single perspective on Mao's philosophical thought emanating from China; rather, a number of perspectives have emerged. And while the issue of Mao and his thought is likely to remain a politically sensitive one for many years to come, its study in the halls of Chinese universities and research institutes appears to be assuming an increasingly academic countenance. In this section I will look briefly at a number of themes and differences of opinion which have characterised the study of Mao's philosophical thought in China in recent years. These are particularly relevant to the concerns of this Introduction, for they take as their point of departure the issue of the origins of the philosophical thought of Mao Zedong. In the literature on this subject, three perspectives are discernible, although one is at present dominant.

In the first, Mao's philosophical thought is regarded as being overwhelmingly of Marxist origin.[137] From this perspective, Mao is considered to be above all a Marxist, his thought emerging in an almost natural progression from the development of the Marxist intellectual tradition. The structure of his thought, its concepts and categories, derived from Marxism, and not from the Chinese classics. The reason for the rejection of Chinese traditional philosophy as a source of influence runs along class lines.

This philosophy, the argument runs, was produced within a class society dominated by a feudal landlord class. According to basic Marxist tenets, such a philosophy was a reflection at a superstructural level of the economic interests of this class; it is thus inevitably coloured by a class characteristic, and it is therefore not possible to employ eclectically elements of it without at the same time absorbing its negative and deleterious class values. As a Marxist, Mao was thus constrained to reject the Chinese intellectual tradition, emerging as it did from and serving the interests of a largely stagnant feudal mode of production. This viewpoint appears to be very much in the minority, particularly as its rejection of traditional Chinese philosophy tends to undermine the claim that Chinese Marxism developed its own national form and characteristics while abiding by the universal principles of Marxism. A rejection *in toto* of the Chinese tradition is perceived by other scholars as leaving Chinese Marxism in something of a cultural no-man's-land, with no sense of historical continuity or cultural adaptation to provide it a form recognisable by and acceptable to the Chinese people.

The second perspective regards Mao's philosophical thought to be the product of both the Marxist and Chinese intellectual traditions, plus the influence of Soviet and Chinese texts on philosophy of the 1930s. The distinguishing characteristic of this perspective is that it highlights the immediate influence of texts on philosophy from the Soviet Union and China.

The third and dominant perspective does not distinguish such philosophical texts from the Marxist tradition generally, and avers that the origins of Mao's philosophical thought are to be found in Marxist philosophy and Chinese traditional philosophy. In terms of the weighting of influence between these two intellectual traditions, the emphasis is placed overwhelmingly on Marxism. Consequently, Mao was first and foremost a Marxist; his methodology, standpoint, and world view were constituted of dialectical and historical materialism, and in this respect Mao owed a considerable intellectual debt to the writings of the 1930s which elaborated the philosophical laws and categories of Marxism in a concise and accessible form. While Mao's philosophical thought drew largely on the Marxist tradition, he was also influenced by modes of dialectical thought which had been present in Chinese philosophy from very early times. Mao did not, however, draw on this tradition of thought in an undiscerning way, but critically inherited and continued (*pipan jicheng*) those positive aspects which were compatible with Marxism and which served to provide Marxism with a national form which was Chinese.[138]

The influence of Chinese philosophy and Mao's critical continuation of it, this perspective suggests, can be discerned in five areas. First, Mao directly utilised the correct principles and propositions of ancient Chinese dialectics. In particular, the concepts of *yin* and *yang* which appeared in the *Yi Jing* and were subsequently elaborated in the *Dao De Jing* created an intellectual predisposition to view the world as constituted of opposites - life and death, large and small, strength and weakness, difficulty and facility, above and below - which was further elaborated by philosophers such as Han Fei Zi. This dialectical approach within traditional Chinese philosophy was to facilitate Mao's development of the Marxist theory of contradictions, with its emphasis on the unity of opposites. Nevertheless, early Chinese dialectics was not based on a scientific foundation, was simplistic, and often mixed together materialism and idealism, and dialectics and metaphysics; it could not, therefore, be incorporated into modern Chinese Marxism without undergoing a process of critical scrutiny and selection, in which elements incompatible with dialectical materialism were sifted out and rejected.

Second, Mao took propositions from traditional Chinese philosophy and transformed or developed them to provide them with a new significance. For example, *xiangfan-xiangcheng* (things that are in opposition are also complementary) did not in the *Han Shu* extend the concept of the unity of opposites universally. Mao, however, was to take this idea and employ it in *On Contradiction* to illustrate the message that there is both struggle and identity between the two opposing aspects of a contradiction, and that this was a universally occurring phenomenon.[139] A further example is Mao's employment of Lao Zi's maxim that things that are in opposition undergo a process of mutual transformation, each changing into its opposite; here again, Mao could absorb this dialectical conception while excluding its metaphysical and idealist aspects, basing it on a materialist conception of the universe.

Third, Mao used propositions or categories from traditional dialectics which were readily understandable and lively in form to express the principles of dialectical materialism. A particular example is the concept of "one divides into two" (*yi fen wei er*), which appears in a large number of traditional sources. While being incorporated within an idealist and mystical system, it contained the dialectical conception of the two aspects of a contradiction and was expressed in a form which could be readily appreciated by all.

Fourth, Mao employed examples of dialectics which appear in classical Chinese stories and proverbs. Of particular importance here were the *Shui Hu Zhuan* (Water Margin), *Xi You Ji* (Journey to the West), *San Guo Yan Yi* (Romance of the Three Kingdoms), amongst others. These sources were well known amongst the masses of the people, and the use of material from them to illustrate his expositions of dialectical materialism would have the effect of making a rather abstruse and unfamiliar subject more accessible to ordinary Chinese people.

Fifth, Mao drew on the oral tradition of the Chinese people, a tradition replete with sayings with a dialectical flavour. Examples are "the east wind prevails over the west wind", and "failure is the mother of success".

It was the employment and incorporation of these aspects of traditional Chinese philosophy and culture which provided Mao's philosophical thought and his Marxism generally with a distinctly Chinese flavour. While this perspective on the origins of Mao's philosophical thought emphasises the influence of Chinese traditional concepts and categories on Mao's thought, it is emphatic in its assertion that this influence was never to become the dominant aspect. His achievement was to draw critically on the dialectical and materialist themes already present in an often undeveloped and confused form within traditional Chinese philosophy. Nevertheless, the basic categories, concepts, and principles which characterised Mao's philosophical thought were Marxist, and these formed the foundation which provided the standpoint and method from which the Chinese tradition could be evaluated. And of course, the foundation of Mao's philosophy was dialectical materialism, which he elaborated and developed in a systematic way in his essays of 1937.

It is worth pausing at this point to make some comparisons with the views of Western Mao scholars on the origins of Mao's thought. We notice at once that there is considerable overlap. At one pole of a continuum of interpretation, there are those scholars who approach Mao's thought and philosophy as Marxist.[140] From this perspective, Mao's writings are replete with the categories of Marxism - economic base/ideological superstructure, relations and forces of production, a teleological conception of history based on materialism, class and class struggle, revolution, etc. - and his sources of theoretical inspiration are taken to be those of the Marxist tradition. Scant if any attention is given to the Chinese cultural and philosophical tradition, for these were the product of a class-based society which Mao was determined to destroy and reconstruct on the basis of Marxist conceptions of a communist future. Further along the continuum of interpretation lies the bulk of Western views on the origins of Mao's thought.

This range of views perceives Mao as the product of two intellectual traditions, the Marxist and Chinese.[141] In such interpretations, however, there is considerable difference of opinion over the extent of influence of these traditions; in some, the resultant synthesis is one in which the Chinese aspect is dominant, the Marxist element representing a thin and rather insubstantial gloss; in others, there is something of a balance, the two traditions coexisting in uneasy juxtaposition; and finally, there is the view, similar to the Chinese position elaborated above, that, while Mao did draw on the Chinese intellectual tradition for sources of inspiration, his debt to Marxism was the more important. What links these apparently disparate approaches to the origins of Mao's thought is the willingness to entertain the view that Mao's thought was a combination, be it of whatever proportions, of both the Marxist and Chinese traditions.

The significant difference between Western and Chinese perceptions of the origins of Mao's philosophical thought lies in the fact that there are Western interpretations which do not recognise Marxism as a significant influence.[142] From this perspective, the breadth and longevity of China's philosophical and cultural tradition had an overwhelming influence, not just on the development of Mao's thought, but on the course of the Chinese Revolution before and after Liberation. In this respect, Mao was no different from other Chinese in the sense that his thought and political responses were dictated by the very fact of his being Chinese. Mao was first and last a Chinese, and the Marxist terminology which entered the vocabulary of his generation was nothing more than a transparent and largely unimportant veneer overlaying Chinese sources of thought and action.

As we have seen, no contemporary Mao scholar in China would entertain this latter notion. The dominant perspective is that Mao was firstly a Marxist, but he was also Chinese, and his particular contribution was the integration of Marxist theory and principles with the concrete conditions of the Chinese Revolution. The basis of Mao's philosophical thought was dialectical and historical materialism, and it was from this standpoint that he interpreted China's past and present. Indeed, it is significant that the bulk of books written on Mao's philosophical thought in contemporary China read like primers on dialectical and historical materialism. A short section within such volumes may be reserved for a discussion of parallels between Mao's philosophy and traditional Chinese philosophy, but it is evident that this source of influence is regarded as very much less important than the Marxism imbibed by Mao during the 1920s and particularly the 1930s.

It is for this reason, it seems, that Chinese Mao scholars are not overly exercised by the issue of Mao's plagiarism in his *Lecture Notes on Dialectical Materialism*. They point to Mao's reliance on Soviet sources to indicate why the text has never been openly published as part of Mao's officially sanctioned *oeuvre*. It does not, they contend, achieve the purpose of integrating abstract Marxist philosophical principles with the concrete conditions and problems of the Chinese Revolution; neither does Mao "sinify" (a word Chinese Mao specialists are *not* hesitant to use) Marxist principles through employment of illustrative material from traditional Chinese philosophy. Nevertheless, the philosophy contained in the *Lecture Notes on Dialectical Materialism* has never, as far as I am aware, been rejected as incorrect by Chinese philosophers and Mao scholars in post-Mao China. In this regard, it is instructive that this text has been reproduced in a number of *neibu* collections of study materials for academics and Party theorists, and it is quite widely and openly quoted in recent works on Mao's philosophy and thought.[143] It is obviously regarded as a concise and quite useful introduction to the fundamental themes and categories of dialectical materialism, one put together by the major architect of Chinese Marxism, and thus possessing some legitimacy if not the hallmark of originality.

And, lastly, it is worth noting that there is not agreement amongst Chinese Mao scholars as to the relative influence of the Soviet and Chinese texts on philosophy of the mid-1930s as compared to Mao's earlier exposure in the 1920s and early 1930s to currents of Marxist thought which were at that time penetrating Chinese intellectual circles. For example, Mao scholars at Wuhan and Sichuan universities object to the notion that Mao was entirely reliant in the writing of his philosophical essays on materials from Soviet sources that became available during the mid-1930s.[144] In the first place, they contend, Mao knew well in the 1920s a number of Chinese intellectuals who had already been influenced by and were elaborating dialectical materialist concepts in essays and letters which Mao read. In the second place, a significant number of books by Marx, Engels, Lenin, and other Marxists had become available in the 1920s and early 1930s, and Mao had read and studied these. Some examples from a lengthy list include Engels' *Ludwig Feuerbach and the End of Classical German Philosophy* (often translated into Chinese as *On Feuerbach), Dialectics of Nature* (extracts), and *Anti-Dühring*; Lenin's *Materialism and Empirio-Criticism*, and *Philosophical Notebooks* (extracts); Marx's *The Poverty of Philosophy*, and *Capital*, Volume One; and Stalin's *On Problems of Leninism*. They point to Mao's interest in the translation of Marxist classics and his personal use of these to broaden and deepen his understanding of dialectical materialism. For instance, Mao took a personal interest in the translation of *Anti-Dühring* into Chinese, and its translator, Wu Liping, has recorded that Mao did refer to this text in the writing of *On Contradiction*.[145] Similarly, Li Yongtai has pointed to Mao's study of *Capital* in the year prior to writing his three essays on philosophy, suggesting that Mao absorbed the dialectical materialist methodology contained therein.[146] Moreover, it is possible that Marxist texts on philosophy which Mao had not read in the original reached him via the writings of Ai Siqi and Li Da who had written extensively in the 1920s and early 1930s on problems of Marxist philosophy. The picture which emerges, these contemporary Chinese Mao specialists contend, is a much more complex one than might be assumed if excessive emphasis is placed on the Soviet texts on philosophy of the mid-1930s employed by Mao prior to and during the writing of his three philosophical essays of 1937. The translated works of Marx, Engels, Lenin, and Stalin, and their elaboration by Chinese Marxist philosophers such as Li Da and Ai Siqi "encouraged the spread and transmission of Marxist philosophy in China and helped the development and maturation of Mao Zedong's philosophical thought; all exerted an important influence and played an important role".[147] According to this view, the immediate influences on Mao's philosophical thought at the time he wrote his essays on philosophy were the translations of the Soviet texts on philosophy and writings by Li Da and Ai Siqi; but the concepts and viewpoints contained in these sources were employed by Mao to extend an already firmly established foundation of philosophical thought, a foundation created through a decade and a half of interest in and exposure to Marxist philosophy.

The influence of Li Da and Ai Siqi

While there exists significant disagreement amongst Mao scholars in contemporary China over the origins of Mao's philosophical thought, there is apparent consensus on the importance of the writings of Li Da (1890-1966) and Ai Siqi (1910-1966) to the development of Chinese Marxism. Both of these prolific philosophers were responsible for the systematization and popularization of the philosophy of dialectical materialism, and are widely regarded as the first of China's home-grown Marxist philosophers. Ai Siqi, in particular, took it upon himself to present the rather arcane formulations of dialectical materialism in forms accessible to students and interested laypersons, and his writings of the early-to-mid 1930s contributed to the philosophical background against which Mao's own views on philosophy were to develop. Li Da's writings on Marxist philosophy date from the early 1920s, and he, more than any other Chinese philosopher, was responsible for making accessible to the early Chinese Communist movement a wealth of sources and commentary. Through their translations of Marxist classics into Chinese, Li Da and Ai Siqi were instrumental in making available the new philosophy, and in the 1930s especially, their translations brought to China information on developments within the philosophical world of the Soviet Union, particularly its emerging orthodoxy.

How important was the influence of these philosophers on the development of Mao's philosophical thought? In terms of accessibility of Soviet philosophical sources, their translations brought to Mao material which, as we have seen, he employed heavily in the writing of his three philosophical essays. Two of these Soviet sources were translated by them; *A Course on Dialectical Materialism* was translated by Li Da and Lei Zhongjian; and *Outline of New Philosophy* was translated by Ai Siqi and Zheng Yili. Mao also thought extremely highly of their own philosophical writing, and it is probable that two of the five main texts used by Mao in 1937 were authored by Li Da and Ai Siqi.[148]

Li Da's *Shehuixue dagang* (Elements of Sociology) was completed in 1936, and published in May 1937. Immediately on its publication, Li sent Mao a copy. According to the diary Mao kept of his own reading activity (which he began to keep on 1 February 1938), he annotated this text between 17 January and 16 March 1938.[149] However, some Chinese Mao scholars now believe it possible that Mao read the text shortly after its publication, which would mean he had access to it during the months of writing his philosophical essays.[150] The recollections of Guo Huaruo, in Yan'an from August 1937, suggest that Mao did indeed read it at the time he was preparing lectures on philosophy in 1937,[151] and the fact that Mao claimed to have read the book ten times[152] (the book contains 430,000 characters) indicates a continuing and deepening familiarity with the work over a lengthy period of time. It is also possible that the annotated copy of *Shehuixue dagang* which survives is not the one Mao originally received from Li Da immediately on publication, for Mao wrote to Li asking him to send an additional ten copies for the Yan'an Anti-Japanese Military and Political University, and the annotated copy which survives may well be one of these.[153]

The contents of Li Da's *Shehuixue dagang* would obviously have been of great significance for Mao, attempting as he was to master orthodox Marxist philosophy and to prepare lectures on this subject for delivery at the Anti-Japanese Military and Political University.[154] The text is divided into five major sections: Materialist dialectics, historical materialism, the economic structure of society, the political structure of society, and social ideology.[155] Each section contains subject matter discussed by Mao in his own philosophical essays. For example, the section on materialist dialectics contains a chapter on the laws (*faze*) of dialectical materialism, in which Li Da not only discusses the three major laws discussed in a previous section of this Introduction, but also the categories of essence and appearance, form and content, chance and necessity, and possibility and reality, to which Mao refers in his *Lecture Notes on Dialectical Materialism*. In describing the unity of opposites, Li employs language remarkably similar to that which appears in both *On Contradiction* and the *Lecture Notes*. The law of the unity of opposites is the "basic law" of dialectics, it is its kernel; all of the things existing in the world contain contradictions, for without the struggle between contradictions, there would be no movement, development, or life.[156]   Virtually all areas covered by Mao in his own philosophical essays are covered in like fashion in Li's volume, and couched in language very similar to that employed by Mao.

Are we then to assume that Li Da's exposition of the philosophy of dialectical materialism constituted a major influence on Mao's thought at the time he was writing *On Contradiction, On Practice,* and the *Lecture Notes on Dialectical Materialism*? On the assumption that Mao did indeed have access to *Shehuixue dagang* in mid-1937 when he was writing these texts, there can be no doubt that the contents of this volume would have been extremely useful as source material. However, it would be wrong to exaggerate this work as an influence in its own right, for it is evident that one of Li Da's major purposes in writing the text was to systematise and explain the philosophy of dialectical materialism as this was emerging in the Soviet Union following the overthrow of the Deborin school in 1931. As such, *Shehuixue dagang*, while a massive tome and clearly a work of considerable scholarship, does not project an impression of originality. Li consciously employed the philosophy contained in the Soviet texts of the early to mid-1930s as the basis for his own exposition, and indeed took *A Course on Dialectical Materialism* (which he had translated) as the model for *Shehuixue dagang*.[157]   We know this Soviet text, *A Course on Dialectical Materialism*, was the one most heavily annotated by Mao in late 1936 and early 1937. It could be suggested, then, that the influence of Li Da's *Shehuixue dagang* was thus limited to that of reinforcing the views expressed in this and other Soviet texts on philosophy, and providing in one accessible volume discussion of the whole range of issues canvassed by Mao in his own writings on dialectical materialism. Consequently, Li Da's writings should not be seen as an influence separate from the influence of Soviet philosophy generally.

A similar judgement can be made on the influence of Ai Siqi on the development of Mao's philosophical thought. There can be no doubt that Ai was enormously important in making available through his translations Soviet texts on philosophy; he was also a prolific populariser and disseminator of the ideas of dialectical materialism. Nevertheless, as with Li Da, Ai Siqi's writings on philosophy added little that was original to the general corpus of concepts, categories, and ideas of orthodox Soviet Marxist philosophy. As Ai himself openly acknowledged, he was a "reteller and copier" of the basic theory of dialectical materialism.[158]

The volumes written by Ai to which Mao had access prior to and during the writing of his own philosophical essays included *Dazhong zhexue* (Philosophy for the Masses) and *Sixiang fangfalun* (Methodology of Thought).[159] The former had been first published in January 1936, and it is highly likely that Mao did read and annotate it, although his personal copy of the volume has not survived.[160] The latter was published in January 1937 (second edition), and Mao's annotated copy of this text has survived.[161] The annotations made by Mao on this text were of much less significance (in terms of text and content), Chinese specialists contend, in the writing of *On Contradiction* and *On Practice*, than were his annotations on the Soviet texts *Dialectical and Historical Materialism* and *A Course on Dialectical Materialism*.[162]

As with Li Da's *Shehuixue dagang*, the volumes by Ai Siqi referred to by Mao contained a wealth of material relevant to his philosophical project of comprehending and elaborating the basic concepts and categories of dialectical materialism. For example, Chapter Three of *Philosophy for the Masses* is entitled "The epistemology of dialectical materialism", and Chapter Four "The laws (*faze*) of materialist dialectics". This latter chapter contains individual sections on the laws of the unity of opposites, the mutual transformation of quantity and quality, and the negation of the negation. This chapter also includes discussion of several other of the categories referred to by Mao in his *Lecture Notes*, including appearance and essence, form and content, and chance and necessity. What is distinctive about the approach taken by Ai in this volume is that the abstruse subject matter of dialectical materialism is explained in a straightforward manner, and more importantly perhaps for Mao's own application of dialectical materialism to Chinese realities, the text contains numerous examples of dialectics taken from everyday life.

Ai Siqi's *Methodology of Thought* similarly contains a chapter on the laws (*faze*) of dialectical materialism with individual sections on each of the fundamental laws discussed in *Philosophy for the Masses*. There is also a section on formal logic, and epistemology (including sections on reflection theory and the process of development of cognition).

Mao also read and made notations on Ai Siqi's *Zhexue yu shenghuo* (Philosophy and Life)[163] in September 1937, that is, immediately following the writing of his other essays on philosophy. Mao thought highly of this text, as attested by a letter of congratulation he wrote to Ai.[164] Mao did, however, challenge Ai on the issue of whether a difference is a contradiction. Ai had argued that "different things are not in contradiction" but that "under certain conditions difference can become a contradiction". Mao thought this an incorrect way of putting it. "Differences exist in all things in the world, and under certain conditions are contradictions, and the reason is that difference is contradiction, is so-called concrete contradiction".[165] A translation of Mao's "Extracts" from Ai's *Philosophy and Life* appears in this anthology.

However, the point remains that the material contained in these volumes cannot be regarded as having an influence on the development of Mao's philosophical thought separate from the more general and pervasive influence of Soviet philosophy. A number of Western scholars have, through narrowing their focus to Ai's contributions to Chinese Marxism and intellectual relationship with Mao, exaggerated the influence that Ai's philosophy had on Mao. Ignatius Ts'ao, for example, suggests that Ai's own writings on contradiction and practice were "essentially identical" to Mao's essays on these subjects, and he considers Ai's influence on Mao to be such that Ai can be considered (along with Chen Boda) as a co-author of the thought of Mao Zedong.[166] Similarly, Joshua Fogel argues that "an examination of the language, ideas, and organization of his [Mao's] philosophical essays illuminates his enormous debt to Ai".[167] Where both of these scholars err is in failing to situate both Ai and Mao in the broader intellectual context of the development of Chinese Marxist philosophy during the early to mid-1930s with its overwhelming debt to and reliance on Soviet philosophy. It may very well be true that the style of language and philosophical content of Ai's writings are similar if not identical in parts to Mao's own philosophical essays; but if one broadens one's gaze to incorporate the Chinese translations of the Soviet texts discussed earlier and the writing of Li Da, one is struck by the essential similarity of *all* of these documents, both in terms of style and content. And the reason for this similarity is that Soviet and Chinese philosophers alike were constrained to operate within an emerging orthodoxy with its constraints on individuality or originality of thought. It is no mere accident that Ai Siqi occupied the role of popularizer of Marxist philosophy; for the possibility of innovation within the narrow circle of Soviet dialectical materialism was limited indeed. The function of the philosopher in such a context becomes less one of inquiry and more that of repetition, repetition of what is officially sanctioned, and avoidance of views which may be heterodox.[168]

Moreover, while it is true that Mao had access to the writings of Li Da and Ai Siqi, the material recently published in China concerning Mao's annotations and marginalia suggests that in many instances he proceeded directly to the Chinese translations of Soviet texts on philosophy for confirmation of the appropriate interpretation of dialectical materialism.[169] The works of Li Da and Ai Siqi thus contributed to the general constellation of texts dealing with dialectical materialism available at the time, and to the intellectual environment in which Mao's own essays on philosophy were written; but they should not be regarded as the starting point for an investigation of the origins of the philosophy contained in Mao's essays on dialectical materialism.

The translations

This anthology of Mao's philosophical writings of 1937 contains five separate translations. Some explanation is required regarding the forms that the translations take.

1.   *Lecture Notes on Dialectical Materialism*: The translation which appears below is of a composite text drawn from the two versions to be found in the *Mao Zedong ji* and its supplements. The construction of a composite text was found to be necessary as the text to be found in the *Mao Zedong ji* contained passages which were either obscure or marred by apparent typographical errors which in some instances altered the meaning of the text.[170]   The version of this document to be found in the supplements to *Mao Zedong ji* also suffers from a number of similar problems (problems in both texts, I hasten to add, in the original Chinese text and not due to the editorship of Takeuchi Minoru). The translation proceeded through a comparison of the two texts, identifying differences and points of interest, reference to which are contained in annotations appended to the translation. No attempt has been made to indicate in the translation itself those parts of the text which Mao appropriated from the Soviet and Chinese sources discussed in this Introduction. As I have argued in previous sections, Mao drew on a series of texts on philosophy, all extremely alike in terms of style and content matter. It would therefore be a problematic exercise to insist on any one text as the source of Mao's information or wording. Nevertheless, a table of possible sources has been appended to the notes following this Introduction. The reader wishing to pursue the issue of plagiarism further may use this as a guide.

The version of *Lecture Notes on Dialectical Materialism* contained in the supplements to the *Mao Zedong ji* also contains *On Contradiction* and *On Practice* as integral parts of that text. The decision to separate them for purposes of translation may thus be queried, particularly as I have stressed throughout this Introduction that these do, as Schram has argued, belong to "a single intellectual enterprise". However, the translations of *On Contradiction* and *On Practice* have a very different purpose to the translation of the *Lecture Notes*.

2.   *On Contradiction*: The availability of the pre-Liberation version of *On Contradiction* (discovered in the late 1970s by Takeuchi Minoru) allows textual comparison with the post-Liberation official version to determine the extent of revision and additions to the earlier text before it was deemed suitable for publication as part of Mao's *Selected Works*. This textual comparison has been performed in the translation of the pre-1949 text which appears in this anthology. A major purpose of this translation is to make as explicit as possible the points at which the pre-Liberation and official texts intersect and parallel each other, and where they diverge and differ. This has been achieved by two methods: (a) Points at which this text and the official text exactly parallel each other have been indicated by the use of bold type (for example, **the principal contradiction**). By this means, it is evident at a glance which sections of the pre-Liberation text have been incorporated into the official text. At such places where the two texts do exactly parallel each other, I have utilized without exception the official English translation.[171] This was felt necessary to facilitate comparison of the texts; moreover, the official English translation is, apart from a few minor exceptions, quite satisfactory and little would have been gained by its alteration. (b) Points at which the pre-Liberation text have been revised or added to on republication as the official text have been indicated by annotations appended to the end of the translation. The use of these two methods makes immediately evident the variations and similarities between the two texts.

3.   *On Practice*: The translation of the pre-Liberation version of *On Practice* included in this volume is of the text contained in the supplements to the *Mao Zedong ji*. This is the text originally incorporated in *Bianzheng weiwulun* (Dialectical materialism) and published by Dazhong Shudian (no date of publication, but almost certainly 1946). As with the translation of *On Contradiction,* the purpose of this translation is to make as explicit as possible points of similarity and difference between the pre-1949 version of *On Practice* and the official post-

Liberation text. Unlike the translation of *On Contradiction,* however, only sections *not* included in the official version have been indicated by the use of bold type. This reversal of the strategy used in the translation and annotation of *On Contradiction* was made necessary by the fact that there are far less differences between the pre- and post-Liberation versions of *On Practice* than is the case with *On Contradiction.* Annotations appended to the translation nevertheless disclose almost one hundred minor differences between the texts, a number of them of significant interest for an understanding of Mao's epistemology. A number of minor differences between the two existing pre-Liberation versions of *On Practice* have also been noted. The official English translation contained in Mao's *Selected Works* has been used as the basis for this translation.[172]

4.   "Extracts from Ai Siqi's *Philosophy and Life*" (September, 1937): This is not a coherent essay as are the three previous texts. The document is made up of a series of extracts taken from and notations on Ai Siqi's book *Philosophy and Life.* The extracts and notations in isolation thus have very little significance. The translator of these "Extracts", Dr John Hanafin, has therefore chosen to translate the extracts parallel to the sections of Ai Siqi's book from which they were taken. The extracts are thus placed in textual relationship to their original source. Dr Hanafin has employed the edition of *Zhexue yu shenghuo* (Philosophy and Life) published by Yunnan People's Publishing House in 1980 (the volume was first published in April 1937), which also employs this device. Ai Siqi's *Philosophy and Life* was comprised of a series of essays written in response to problems readers encountered in reading the journal *Dushu Shenghuo* (Intellectual Life) edited by Ai in Shanghai in the mid-1930s. The essays in the book from which Mao took extracts are those concerned with relativism and absolutism, formal and dialectical logic, and internal and external cause.

        Mao's extracts are shown in the left column and the corresponding section from *Zhexue yu shenghuo* in the right column. The left column (from a1 to a31) gives the complete

content of Mao's "Extracts", but the right column (from b1 to b31) only the relevant, corresponding sections of Ai's essays.
5.   *Philosophical Annotations and Marginalia*: From late-1936 to mid-1937 Mao annotated and wrote marginal comments on two Chinese translations of Soviet texts on philosophy. These were M. Shirokov and A. Aizenberg et al., *A Course on Dialectical Materialism* (third edition) and M.B. Mitin et al., *Dialectical Materialism and Historical Materialism* (Volume I). Limitations of space prevent a complete translation of these annotations and marginalia here, for to make sense of Mao's often cryptic comments would require reproduction of large sections of the original text which Mao annotated. This is the strategy employed by the editors of *Mao Zedong zhexue pizhuji* (The Philosophical Annotations of Mao Zedong), a strategy which required 189 pages. I have chosen rather to select those annotations and marginal comments which are of sufficient coherence and significance to stand alone. I have, nevertheless, included the page numbers of the two texts on philosophy on which the annotations appear, as well as the relevant page numbers of *Mao Zedong zhexue pizhuji*. The interested reader can therefore locate any annotation in its original textual context should the need arise.

Notes

1.   For the official versions of these essays, see *Selected Works of Mao Tse-tung* (Peking: FLP, 1965), Vol. I, pp. 295-309, and pp. 310-347.   For discussion of the pre-Liberation versions of *On Contradiction* and *On Practice*, see Nick Knight, "Mao Zedong's *On Contradiction* and *On Practice*:   Pre-Liberation Texts", *China Quarterly* 84 (December 1980), pp. 641-668;   also Nick Knight, "Mao Zedong's *On Contradiction*:   An annotated translation of the pre-Liberation text", *Griffith Asian Papers* No. 3 (Nathan: School of Modern Asian Studies, Griffith University, 1981), esp. pp. 3-11;   also Nick Knight (ed.), *Philosophy and Politics in Mao Texts of the Yan'an Period, Chinese Studies in Philosophy*, Vol. XIX, No. 2 (Winter 1987-88), esp. pp. 3-19;   also Takeuchi Minoru, "Mo Takuto mujunron no genkei nitsuite" [The original form of Mao Zedong's "On Contradiction"], *Shisō*, April 1969;   also Takeuchi Minoru, "'Mujunron' no genkei hosetsu", [The original form of "On

Contradiction": supplementary hypotheses], *Zoho Mo Takuto noto* (Tokyo: Shinsensha, 1978), pp. 256-276; also Gong Yuzhi, "'Shijianlun' san ti" ["On Practice": three problems], in *Lun Mao Zedong zhexue sixiang* [On Mao Zedong's philosophical thought] (Beijing: Renmin chubanshe, 1983), pp. 66-86.

2. The exact date of composition and publication of the *Lecture Notes on Dialectical Materialism* remained uncertain after the text was generally accepted as having been written by Mao. On this point, see Takeuchi Minoru, "'Mujunron' no genkei hosetsu". See also Stuart R. Schram, *The Political Thought of Mao Tse-tung* (Harmondsworth: Penguin, 1969, second edition), pp. 86-87, 180. Schram's quite accurate estimate was that Chapter 1 of "Dialectical Materialism" must date from late 1936 or early 1937. However, a publication of the *Lecture Notes* published as a *neibu* document in China gives the date of composition as July, August 1937, and its initial publication in the journal *Kangri junzheng daxue,* Vol. I, Nos. 6, 7, and 8 in the year 1938. See Song Yixiu, Sun Kexin, and Su Houzhong (eds.), *Mao Zedong zhexue sixiang ziliao xuanji* [A collection of materials on Mao Zedong's philosophical thought] (Beijing: Beijing University philosophy department, October, 1982), pp. 208-245.

3. For the text of *Lecture Notes on Dialectical Materialism*, see Takeuchi Minoru (ed.), *Mao Zedong ji* [Collected Writings of Mao Zedong] (Tokyo: Hokubasha, 1970-72), Vol. VI, pp. 265-305; also Takeuchi Minoru (ed.), *Mao Zedong ji bujuan* [Supplements to Collected Writings of Mao Zedong] (Tokyo: Sososha, 1983-6), Vol. V, pp. 187-280.

4. See footnotes 21, 22, 23 below.

5. The phrase is Edgar Snow's, see *The Long Revolution* (London: Hutchinson & Co., 1971, 1972), p. 206.

6. See *Ibid.*, p. 207. Snow asked Mao if he had written "Dialectical Materialism": "Mao asked for the question to be repeated. He replied that he had never written an essay entitled 'Dialectical Materialism'. He thought that he would remember it if he had". See, however, Edgar Snow, "Interview with Mao", *New Republic*, February 1965, p. 21, for a somewhat different version.

7. Dennis J. Doolin and Peter J. Golas, "On Contradiction in the Light of Mao Tse-tung's essay on Dialectical Materialism", *China Quarterly* 19 (July-September 1964), pp. 38-64.

8. Karl A. Wittfogel, "Some Remarks on Mao's Handling of Concepts and Problems of Dialectics", *Studies in Soviet Thought*, Vol. III, No. 4 (December 1963), pp. 251-269.

9. Arthur A. Cohen, *The Communism of Mao Tse-tung* (Chicago and London: University of Chicago Press, 1964), p. 26.

10. John E. Rue, "Is Mao Tse-tung's 'Dialectical Materialism' a forgery?", *Journal of Asian Studies*, Vol. XXVI, No. 3 (1967), pp. 464-468.

11. Stuart R. Schram, "Mao Tse-tung as Marxist Dialectician", *China Quarterly* 29 (January-March 1967), pp. 157-158.

12. Schram, *The Political Thought of Mao Tse-tung*, p. 87.

13. Doolin and Golas, "On Contradiction in the Light of Mao Tse-tung's essay on Dialectical Materialism"; Wittfogel, "Some Remarks".

14. Schram, *The Political Thought of Mao Tse-tung*, pp. 86-88, 180. For Schram's more recent comments based on the entire text of the *Lecture Notes*, see his contribution to John K. Fairbank and Albert Feuerwerker (eds.), *The Cambridge History of China* (Cambridge: Cambridge University Press, 1986), Vol. XIII, pp. 837-846.

15. See footnote 3 above.

16. See footnote 2 above.

17. See footnote 2 above. Although the text cited in footnote 2 contains all sections of the *Lecture Notes*, it does not contain *On Practice* and *On Contradiction*. According to one Chinese source, the *Lecture Notes on Dialectical Materialism* were first "published" in September 1937 as a mimeographed (*youyin*) and thread bound volume whose title page (*fengmian*) bore this date. See Wu Jun, "Mao Zedong shengping, sixiang yanjiu gaishu" [comment on research on Mao Zedong's life and thought], in *Mao Zedong zhexue sixiang yanjiu dongtai*, No. 1 (1987), pp. 52-58. The *dongtai* is a *neibu* journal published in Shanghai.

18. See Schram, *The Political Thought of Mao Tse-tung*, p. 180, note 1; also *Mao Zedong ji*, Vol. VI, pp. 303-304.

19. This judgement is based on the difference between the text of the *Lecture Notes* which appears in the Supplements to the *Mao Zedong ji* and the texts from 1938 and 1940 which the *Mao Zedong ji* draws on. These differences have been highlighted in the annotations to the translation which appears below.

20. See *Mao Zedong ji bujuan*, Vol. V, pp. 278-279.

21. Reference is made to this publication in Song Yixiu et al. (eds.), *Mao Zedong zhexue sixiang ziliao xuanji*, p. 245. The text referred to is a volume published by Tianjin Publishing House in 1958. I have not been able to obtain a copy of this volume.

22. Reference to this text, *Mao Zedong zhexue sixiang* (*zhailu*) [Extracts of Mao Zedong's philosophical thought] edited and published by the philosophy

department of the University of Beijing, appears in Schram's contribution to Fairbank and Feuerwerker (eds.), *The Cambridge History of China*, Vol. XIII, p. 838, note 108. I have not been able to obtain a copy of this volume.

23. *Weiwubianzhengfa* [Dialectical Materialism] (np: np, July 1972). This volume contains only the pre-Liberation text of *On Contradiction*. What is particularly interesting about this volume is that it makes very clear that philosophers and theorists in China have had access to this pre-Liberation text since at least 1972. It is also interesting that the text not only provides the month of composition of the text, but the very day that Mao completed writing it - the 9th of August 1937. See this text, p. 38.

24. See footnote 2 above.

25. See Schram's contribution to Fairbank and Feuerwerker (eds.), *The Cambridge History of China*, Vol. XIII, p. 837; also Takeuchi Minoru, "'Mujunron' no genkei hosetsu", pp. 257 ff.

26. John Bryan Starr, "'Good Mao', 'Bad Mao': Mao Studies and the re-evaluation of Mao's political thought", *The Australian Journal of Chinese Affairs* 16 (July 1986), pp. 5-6.

27. See *Mao Zedong ji bujuan*, Vol. V, pp. 220-234, and 240-278.

28. Schram, *The Political Thought of Mao Tse-tung*, p. 87.

29. *Ibid.*, pp. 84-88; also Stuart R. Schram, "Mao Tse-tung and the Theory of the Permanent Revolution, 1958-69", *China Quarterly* 46 (April-June 1971), pp. 223-224, note 5; also Wittfogel, "Some Remarks", pp. 251-277.

30. Wittfogel, "Some Remarks", p. 264.

31. See, for example, T.A. Bisson, *Yenan in June 1937: Talks with Communist Leaders* (Berkeley: University of California Press, 1973), p. 37. Bisson comments that Mao and his colleagues were "severely handicapped by a shortage of books, even to the works of Marx and Lenin. Little in the way of a library had survived the Long March".

32. Schram, *The Political Thought of Mao Tse-tung*, p. 88.

33. See Lucio Colletti's "Introduction" to Karl Marx, *Early Writings* (Harmondsworth: Penguin, 1975), pp. 14-16; see also Gustav A. Wetter, *Dialectical Materialism: A Historical and Systematic Survey of Philosophy in the Soviet Union* (New York: Praeger, 1958), pp. 280 ff, and passim; see also Terrel Carver, *Marx and Engels: The Intellectual Relationship* (Brighton: Wheatsheaf Books, 1983), esp. pp. 52, 96-98, 107, 115, 117, 125-126, 129 and passim; also Norman Levine, *The Tragic Deception: Marx Contra Engels* (Oxford and Santa Barbara: Clio Books, 1975); also Richard T. de George, *Patterns of Soviet Thought* (Ann Arbor: University of Michigan Press, 1966),

esp. 107-108. However, for a contrary view, see E.P. Thompson, *The Poverty of Theory and other Essays* (Merlin, 1978).

34. Colletti, "Introduction", p. 15.

35. See in particular, the famous "Preface" to *A Contribution to the Critique of Political Economy* (London: Lawrence and Wishart, 1971), pp. 19-23.

36. Colletti, "Introduction", p. 14.

37. *Ibid.*, p. 16.

38. See, for example, Schram, *The Political Thought of Mao Tse-tung*, p. 79; also Stuart R. Schram, *Mao Zedong: A Preliminary Reassessment* (Hong Kong: The Chinese University Press, 1983), pp. 15-17, 79; see also Maurice Meisner, "Utopian Socialist Themes in Maoism", in John W. Lewis (ed.), *Peasant Rebellion and Communist Revolution in Asia* (Stanford: Stanford University Press, 1974), pp. 207-252; also Maurice Meisner, "Leninism and Maoism: Some populist perspectives on Marxism-Leninism in China", *China Quarterly* 45 (January-March 1971), pp. 2-36.

39. *Mao Zedong ji*, Vol. VI, p. 268; *Mao Zedong ji bujuan*, Vol. V, p. 189.

40. *Mao Zedong ji*, Vol. VI, p. 282; *Mao Zedong ji bujuan*, Vol. V, p. 204.

41. *Mao Zedong ji*, Vol. VI, pp. 290-291; *Mao Zedong ji bujuan*, Vol. V, p. 212.

42. *Mao Zedong ji*, Vol. VI, pp. 282-283; *Mao Zedong ji bujuan*, Vol. V, p. 204.

43. *Selected Works of Mao Tse-tung*, Vol. I, p. 190; also *Mao Zedong xuanji* (Beijing: Renmin chubanshe, 1966), Vol. I, pp. 165-166; also *Mao Zedong ji*, Vol. V, p. 97.

44. *Mao Zedong ji*, Vol. VI, p. 292; *Mao Zedong ji bujuan*, Vol. V, p. 214.

45. *Mao Zedong ji*, Vol. VI, p. 293; *Mao Zedong ji bujuan*, Vol. V, p. 215.

46. Schram, *The Political Thought of Mao Tse-tung*, p. 87.

47. *Mao Zedong ji*, Vol. VI, pp. 293-294; *Mao Zedong ji bujuan*, Vol. V, p. 215.

48. V.I. Lenin, *Materialism and Empirio-Criticism* (Peking: FLP, 1972).

49. See Frederick Engels, *Dialectics of Nature* (Moscow: FLPH, 1954); also *Anti-Dühring* (Peking: FLP, 1976).

50. Lenin, *Materialism and Empirio-Criticism*, p. 119.

51.   *Selected Works of Mao Tse-tung* (Peking: FLP, 1977), Vol. V, p. 422.

52.   *Mao Zedong sixiang wansui* [Long live the thought of Mao Zedong] (n.p.:   n.p., 1967), p. 253.

53.   Jerome Ch'en (ed.), *Mao Papers: Anthology and Bibliography* (London: OUP, 1970), pp. 71-2.

54.   See for example Joint Publication Research Service, *Miscellany of Mao Tse-tung Thought* (1949-1968) (Arlington, Virginia: February 1974), Part I, pp. 104, 231, also Part II, pp. 303, 384, 398;   Mao Tse-tung, *A Critique of Soviet Economics* (New York and London: Monthly Review Press, 1977), pp. 72-73, 113.

55.   Mao Tse-tung, *Four Essays on Philosophy* (Peking: FLP, 1968), pp. 134-136.

56.   *Mao Zedong ji*, Vol. VI, p. 300; *Mao Zedong ji bujuan*, Vol. V, p. 237.

57.   See Nick Knight, "Mao Zedong's *On Contradiction* and *On Practice*: pre-Liberation Texts", pp. 644-647.

58.   *Selected Works of Mao Tse-tung*, Vol. I, p. 311; *Mao Zedong xuanji*, Vol. I, p. 274.

59.   *Selected Works of Mao Tsetung*, Vol. V, pp. 392-393.

60.   For an extensive list of Mao's references to the law of the unity of opposites and discussion of the formulation of laws (guilü) in Mao's thought, see N.J. Knight, *Mao and History: An interpretive essay on some problems in Mao Zedong's Philosophy of History* (Unpublished Ph.D. thesis, University of London, 1983), pp. 411-416, esp. note 333.

61.   V.I. Lenin, *Collected Works* (Moscow: FLPH, 1963), Vol. XXXVIII, pp. 359-360. Emphases in original.

62.   Engels, *Anti-Dühring*, p. 152.

63.   *Ibid.*, p. 153.

64.   M.B. Mitin et al., *Bianzhengweiwulun yu lishiweiwulun* [Dialectical and historical materialism], translated by Shen Zhiyuan (n.p.:   Shangwu yinshuguan, 1936), pp. 212-213.

65.   *Li Da wenji* (Beijing: Renmin chubanshe, 1981), Vol. II, p. 132. On this point, see also *Mao Zedong zhexue pizhuji* [The philosophical annotations of Mao Zedong] (Beijing: Zhongyang wenxian chubanshe, 1988), pp. 6, 161, 169.

66.   John Bryan Starr, *Continuing the Revolution: The Political Thought of Mao* (Princeton: Princeton University Press, 1979), p. 24;   also Stuart R. Schram, *Mao Tse-tung Unrehearsed* (Harmondsworth: Penguin, 1974),

p. 26; also Stuart Schram, 'The Marxist', in Dick Wilson (ed.), *Mao Tse-tung in the Scales of History* (Cambridge: Cambridge University Press, 1977), p. 63; also Schram, *Mao Zedong: A Preliminary Reassessment*, p. 66.

67. "Mao Zedong lun 'fouding zhi fouding'" [Mao Zedong on the "negation of the negation"] *Mao Zedong zhexue sixiang yanjui dongtai* [Developments in the research of Mao Zedong's philosophical thought] No. 2 (1982), pp. 1-9. The *dongtai* is a *neibu* journal. See also Wang Shubai, "'Shijielun' 'Maodunlun' yu Zhongguo chuantong zhexue" ["On Practice" and "On Contradiction" and Chinese traditional philosophy], *Mao Zedong zhexue sixiang yanjiu dongtai* 4 (1987), pp. 1-7. See also He Zuorong, "Zai Mao Zedong zhexue sixiang zhong youwu 'fouding zhi fouding' de diwei" [The status of the "negation of the negation" in Mao Zedong's philosophical thought], *Mao Zedong sixiang yanjiu* 3 (1984), pp. 122-124.

68. From Schram's perspective, Mao's "rejection" of the law of the "negation of the negation" is associated with the fact that Mao turned back to his Chinese roots during the 1960s. See Schram, *Mao Tse-tung Unrehearsed*, p. 26.

69. Schram, *Mao Tse-tung Unrehearsed*, p. 226; for the original, see *Mao Zedong sixiang wansui* [Long live the thought of Mao Zedong] (n.p.: n.p. August 1969), p. 558.

70. Schram has argued that Mao's ideas on the issue of the "negation of the negation" raise "serious problems about the conformity of his thinking as a whole to the basic logic of Marxism, and of Leninism". See "The Marxist", p. 64.

71. *Mao Zedong ji*, pp. 300, 302.

72. *Mao Zedong ji bujuan*, pp. 245-246.

73. *Ibid.*

74. *Miscellany of Mao Tse-tung Thought*, Part I, p. 50.

75. *Ibid.*, p. 98.

76. *Selected Works of Mao Tse-tung*, Vol. V, p. 453.

77. *Miscellany of Mao Tse-tung Thought*, Part I, p. 123.

78. *Ibid.*, p. 122.

79. Schram, *Mao Tse-tung Unrehearsed*, pp. 189-190.

80. Ch'en, *Mao Papers*, p. 65.

81. Schram, *Mao Tse-tung Unrehearsed*, p. 226.

82. For a description and evaluation of the law of the "negation of the negation", see Wetter, *Dialectical Materialism*, pp. 355-365; also De George, *Patterns of Soviet Thought*, pp. 89-90. See also *Mao Zedong zhexue pizhuji*, pp. 113-127. From Mao's annotations in this source, some of which are

reproduced in translation in this volume, it is very clear that he perceived the concept of "affirmation" as central to the law of the "negation of the negation". He moreover invokes Lenin to reinforce his position.

83.   Schram, *Mao Tse-tung Unrehearsed*, p. 240.

84.   Herbert Marcuse, *Soviet Marxism: A Critical Analysis* (New York: Vintage Books, 1961), p. 137.

85.   Wetter, *Dialectical Materialism*, p. 355.

86.   *Ibid.*, p. 312; also De George, *Patterns of Soviet Thought*, pp. 193, 210.

87.   Wetter, *Dialectical Materialism*, p. 359.

88.   De George, *Patterns of Soviet Thought*, p. 213.

89.   See, for example, Rip Bulkeley, "On 'On Practice'", *Radical Philosophy*, No. 18 (Autumn 1977); also Brantly Womack, *The Foundations of Mao Zedong's Political Thought*, 1917-1935 (Honolulu: University Press of Hawaii, 1982), pp. 32, 77.

90.   See also Mao's views in the post-Liberation period.   Mao commented on the unified (*tongyi*) and mutually linked *(huxiang lianxi de)* nature of the world and the universe. See *Miscellany of Mao Tse-tung Thought*, Part I, p. 152.

91.   *Mao Zedong ji*, Vol. VI, p. 293; also *Mao Zedong ji bujuan*, Vol. V, p. 214.

92.   *Mao Zedong ji*, Vol. VI, p. 294; also *Mao Zedong ji bujuan*, Vol. V, p. 216.

93.   *Mao Zedong ji*, Vol. VI, p. 281; *Mao Zedong ji bujuan*, Vol. V, p. 202.

94.   I am indebted to Dr Paul Healy for his views on this subject. For his brilliant analysis of the tension between rationalist and empiricist epistemologies in Mao's post-1955 writings, see his doctoral dissertation. *Mao and Classical Marxism: Epistemology, Social Formation, Classes and Class Struggle in Mao Zedong's Post-1955 Thought* (Griffith University, 1988).

95.   Mao was to comment in 1964 that "as to the reasons for the leaps from practice to perception, and from perception to reasoning, neither Marx nor Engels discussed it very clearly.   Nor did Lenin discuss it very clearly". *Miscellany of Mao Tse-tung Thought*, Part II, p. 397.

96.   See the pre-Liberation text of *On Contradiction*. See Knight, "Mao Zedong's *On Contradiction* and *On Practice*: pre-Liberation texts", p. 651.

97.   See *Ibid.*, p. 654; "each of man's actions (practice) is guided by his thought (*sixiang*), so naturally without thought there can be no action whatsoever".

98. For my critique of empiricism in the field of Mao studies, see "The Marxism of Mao Zedong: Empiricism and Discourse in the Field of Mao Studies", *The Australian Journal of Chinese Affairs* 16 (July 1986), pp. 7-22; also "Mao and History: Who Judges and How?", *The Australian Journal of Chinese Affairs* 13 (January 1985), pp. 121-136.

99. Arif Dirlik has come closest to grasping the importance of theory in Mao's thought. See "The Predicament of Marxist Revolutionary Consciousness: Mao Zedong, Antonio Gramsci, and the Reformulation of Marxist Revolutionary Theory", *Modern China* Vol. 9, No. 2 (April 1983), pp. 182-211.

100. See *Mao Zedong ji*, Vol. V, p. 88, and Vol. VI, p. 93. For an analysis of Mao's conception of the historical future, see Knight, *Mao and History: An Interpretive Essay*, pp. 166-199.

101. This quote from Lenin appears in the pre-Liberation texts of both *On Contradiction* and *On Practice*. See Knight, "Mao Zedong's *On Contradiction* and *On Practice*: pre-Liberation Texts", p. 657.

102. Womack, *The Foundations of Mao Zedong's Political Thought*, pp. xi-xii.

103. Stuart R. Schram, "Mao Studies: Retrospect and Prospect", *China Quarterly* 97 (March 1984), p. 109.

104. Guo Huaruo, "Mao zhuxi kangzhan chuqi guanghui de zhexue huodong" [The glorious philosophical activities of chairman Mao during the early stage of the War of Resistance], in *Zhongguo zhexue* [Chinese philosophy], Vol. I (1979), p. 32.

105. For a lengthy list of the Soviet and Chinese philosophical sources read by Mao during the Yan'an period, see "Mao Zedong dushu shenghuo" [Mao Zedong's life as a reader] in *Mao Zedong zhexue sixiang yanjiu dongtai* No. 2 (1982), p. 12. This extensive list suggests that Mao was quite well versed in contemporary Soviet and Chinese Marxist philosophy.

106. Tian Songnian, "Dui ji ben zhexue shuji de pizhu [On the annotations on several texts on philosophy]", in Gong Yuzhi et al. (eds), *Mao Zedong de dushu shenghuo* [Mao Zedong's life as a reader] (Beijing: Sanlian shudian, 1986), pp. 70-71.

107. On the issue of the repetitive nature of Soviet texts on philosophy, see De George, *Patterns of Soviet Thought*, p. 193; also Eugene Kamenka, "Soviet Philosophy, 1917-67", in Alex Simirenko (ed.), *Social Thought in the Soviet Union* (Chicago: Quadrangle Books, 1969), p. 95.

108. Wittfogel, "Some Remarks"; Schram, "Mao Tse-tung and the Theory of Permanent Revolution", pp. 223-224.

109. Tian Songnian, "Dui ji ben zhexue shuji de pizhu", p. 70; however, cf. Ran Changuang's chapter in Sichuan daxue Mao Zedong zhexue sixiang yanjiu shi (ed.), *Mao Zedong bianzhengfa sixiang yanjiu* [Research on Mao Zedong's dialectical thought] (Chengdu: Sichuan daxue chubanshe, 1985), pp. 93-94. Ran states that it was the second and fourth editions of this volume that Mao used. See also *Mao Zedong zhexue pizhuji*, pp. 1-136.

110. Tian Songnian, "Dui ji ben zhexue shuji de pizhu", pp. 70-71; also Shi Zhongquan, "Yanjiu Mao Zedong zhexue sixiang de xin wenxian" [New Documents for the study of Mao Zedong's philosophical thought], *Hongqi* [Red Flag] No. 17 (1987), pp. 3-4. This judgement is borne out by an examination of *Mao Zedong zhexue pizhuji*, passim.

111. *Mao Zedong bianzhengfa sixiang yanjiu*, pp. 93-94.

112. Tian Songnian, "Dui ji ben zhexue shuji de pizhu", pp. 73-74. See also *Mao Zedong zhexue pizhuji*, pp. 87-90.

113. *Ibid.*, p. 76.

114. *Ibid.*, p. 77.

115. *Ibid.*, p. 71. See *Mao Zedong zhexue pizhuji*, pp. 137-189. A selection of Mao's annotations on Mitin's book appears in translation in this volume.

116. *Ibid.*, p. 72.

117. Wittfogel, "Some Remarks", esp. p. 276; Schram, "Mao Tse-tung and the Theory of the Permanent Revolution", pp. 223-224.

118. A few examples of Mao's direct appropriation of sections of this text appear below:

Mao Zedong ji bujuan, Vol. V	188	188	189	189	192	199
Dialectical and Historical Materialism	47	48	50	51	156-7	158-9

119. Tian Songnian, "Dui ji ben zhexue shuji de pizhu", p. 71.

120. *Ibid.*

121. *Ibid.* Also Gong Yuzhi, "Cong 'Shijianlun' tan Mao Zedong de dushu shenghuo" [A discussion of Mao Zedong's life as a reader from the perspective of "On Practice"] in Gong Yuzhi et al. (eds.), *Mao Zedong de dushu shenghuo*, p. 46.

122. Guo Huaruo, "Mao zhuxi kangzhan chuqi guanghui de zhexue huodong", p. 36.

123. *Ibid.* Also personal discussions with Chinese Mao scholars at a number of research institutes and universities, December 1987, January 1988.

124. It is also interesting that Ai Siqi's translation of Mitin's *Outline of New Philosophy (Xin zhexue dagang)* was widely advertised for sale in the Communist press at the time. This would make the possibility of a successful act of plagiarism even more remote. See, for example, *Qunzhong* [the masses], Vol. 1, Nos. 2 and 3 (December 1937).

125. Guo Huaruo, "Mao zhuxi kangzhan chuqi guanghui de zhexue huodong", pp. 34-35.

126. *Mao Zedong ji,* Vol. VI, p. 303; *Mao Zedong ji bujuan,* Vol. V, p. 239.

127. Personal discussions with Chinese Mao scholars, December 1987, January 1988.

128. Wittfogel, "Some Remarks". See also Karl A. Wittfogel, "The Legend of 'Maoism'", *China Quarterly* 1 (January-March 1960), pp. 72-86, and 2 (April-June 1960), pp. 16-34.

129. Cohen, *The Communism of Mao Tse-tung.* See also Arthur A. Cohen, "How Original is 'Maoism'?", *Problems of Communism,* Vol. X, No. 6 (November-December 1961), pp. 34-42.

130. Particularly in the writing of Stuart Schram, Maurice Meisner, Benjamin Schwartz and Frederic Wakeman, Jr. For Schwartz's contribution to Mao studies, and his views on the "disintegration" or "decomposition" of Marxism, see Benjamin I. Schwartz, "On the 'Originality' of Mao Tse-tung", *Foreign Affairs* Vol. 34, No. 1 (October 1955), pp. 67-76; also "The Legend of the 'Legend of "Maoism"'", *China Quarterly* 2 (April-June 1960), pp. 35-42; also "China and the West in the 'Thought of Mao Tse-tung'", in Ping-ti Ho and Tang Tsou (eds.), *China in Crisis* (Chicago: University of Chicago Press, 1968), Vol. I, Book 1, pp. 365-379; also *Chinese Communism and the Rise of Mao* (New York: Harper, 1951, 1958); also "The Essence of Marxism Revisited: A Response", *Modern China* Vol. II, No. 4 (1976), pp. 461-472. See also Frederic Wakeman, Jr., *History and Will: Philosophical Perspectives of Mao Tse-tung's Thought* (Berkeley: University of California Press, 1973).

131. Shi Zhongquan, "Yanjiu Mao Zedong zhexue sixiang de xin wenxian", pp. 3-9. See also Shi Zhongquan, "'Mao Zedong zhexue pizhuji' zhong guanyu fandui 'zuo' you qing cuowu de zhexue sikao" [Philosophical reflections in "Mao Zedong's philosophical annotations" on opposing incorrect "left" and right tendencies], in *Lilun yuekan* 9 (1987), pp. 38-42. See also Li Junru, "Xiangxi di zhan you cailiao" [Collect all the available material], *Mao*

Zedong sixiang yanjiu 4 (1984), p. 58. See also "Mao Zedong zhexue pizhuji" [Mao Zedong's philosophical annotations], *Renmin Ribao*, 23rd August, 1987.

132. See Richard H. Solomon, *Mao's Revolution and the Chinese Political Culture* (Berkeley: University of California Press, 1971); also Lucien W. Pye, *Mao Tse-tung: The Man in the Leader* (New York: Basic Books, 1976).

133. Schram, *The Political Thought of Mao Tse-tung*, pp. 112-116.

134. Nick Knight, "The form of Mao Zedong's 'Sinification of Marxism'", *The Australian Journal of Chinese Affairs* 9 (January 1983), pp. 17-34; see also Nick Knight, "Mao Zedong and the 'Sinification of Marxism'", in Colin Mackerras and Nick Knight (eds.), *Marxism in Asia* (London and Sydney: Croom Helm, 1985), pp. 62-93.

135. For a detailed analysis of the Soviet Marxist philosophy of the 1930s by a Soviet philosopher, see W.N. Kohosokov, *Sulian Makesi Lieningzhuyi zhexueshi gangyao (sanshi niandai)* [An outline of the history of Marxist-Leninist philosophy in the Soviet-Union (the 1930s)], translated by Xu Xiaoying and Wang Shuqin (Beijing: Qiushi chubanshe, 1985). The original Russian text was written in 1978.

136. See, for example, Xiao Qian et al. (eds.), *Bianzhengweiwuzhuyi yuanli* [Principles of Dialectical Materialism] (Beijing: Renmin chubanshe, 1981); also Li Deyang et al. (eds.), *Bianzhengweiwuzhuyi yu Lishiweiwuzhuyi* [Dialectical and Historical Materialism] (Wuhan: Hubei renmin chubanshe, 1983); and *Bianzhengweiwuzhuyi yanjiu* [The study of dialectical materialism] (Beijing: Qiushi chubanshe, 1986).

137. "Dangqian Mao Zedong zhexue sixiang de yanjiu qingkuang" [The current situation of research on Mao Zedong's philosophical thought], in *Mao Zedong sixiang yanjiu tongxun* [Newsletter on Research on Mao Zedong's Thought], 5 May 1986, pp. 10-11. The *Tongxun* is a *neibu* journal. There are numerous articles on this subject also in the *neibu* journal *Mao Zedong zhexue sixiang yanjiu dongtai* and also in the open *(gongkai)* journal *Mao Zedong sixiang yanjiu*. See in particular, Xu Suhua, "Mao Zedong zhexue sixiang lilun laiyuan de tanjiu" [An investigation of the theoretical origins of Mao Zedong's philosophical thought], *Mao Zedong sixiang yanjiu* 2 (1984), pp. 107-110; also Tian Huang, "'Yi yuan shuo' hai shi 'liang yuan shuo' - Mao Zedong zhexue sixiang yu Zhongguo youxiu zhexue chuantong guanxi de tanjiu" ["A theory of a single source" or "a theory of two sources" - an investigation of the relationship between Mao Zedong's philosophical thought and China's fine philosophical tradition], *Mao Zedong sixiang yanjiu* (1984), pp. 123-128. See also Li Ke et al., *Mao Zedong zhexue sixiang yanjiu* [Research on Mao Zedong's

philosophical thought] (Jiangxi: Renmin chubanshe, 1983), pp. 16-22. My summary is also based on numerous discussions with Mao scholars, at a number of research institutes and universities in China in December 1987 and January 1988.

138. See also Sichuan daxue Mao Zedong zhexue sixiang yanjiu shi (ed.), *Mao Zedong bianzhengfa sixiang yanjiu*; also Chang Ruisen, Zhang Wenru, and Ran Changuang, *Mao Zedong zhexue sixiang gailun* [An introduction to the philosophical thought of Mao Zedong] (Beijing: Zhongguo renmin daxue chubanshe, 1985).

139. *Mao Zedong xuanji*, Vol. I, p. 308.

140. See, for example, Michael Dutton and Paul Healy, "Marxist Theory and Socialist Transition: the construction of an Epistemological relation", in Bill Brugger (ed.), *Chinese Marxism in Flux 1978-84: Essays on Epistemology, Ideology and Political Economy* (Armonk, New York: M.E. Sharpe, 1985), pp. 13-66; also Andrew G. Walder, "Marxism, Maoism and Social Change", *Modern China*, Vol. III, No. 1 (January 1977), pp. 101-118 and Vol. III, No. 2 (April 1977), pp. 125-159; also Steve Chin, *The Thought of Mao Tse-tung: Form and Content* (Hong Kong: Centre of Asian Studies Papers and Monographs, 1979); also P. Corrigan, H. Ramsay, and D. Sayer, *For Mao: Essays in Historical Materialism* (London: Macmillan, 1979).

141. See, for example, Vsevolod Holubnychy, "Mao Tse-tung's Materialist Dialectics", *China Quarterly* 19 (1964), pp. 3-37; also John M. Koller, "Philosophical aspects of Maoist thought", *Studies in Soviet Thought* 14 (1974), pp. 47-59; also Stuart R. Schram, "Chinese and Leninist Components in the Personality of Mao Tse-tung", *Asian Survey* Vol. III, No. 6 (1963), pp. 259-273.

142. See Solomon, *Mao's Revolution and the Chinese Political Culture*; also Pye, *Mao Tse-tung: The Man in the Leader*.

143. See notes 2, 21, 22, 23 above. See also Sichuan daxue Mao Zedong zhexue sixiang yanjiu shi (ed.), *Mao Zedong bianzhengfa sixiang yanjiu*, pp. 62, 63, 76, 81, 307, 308, 312, 320.

144. Li Yongtai, "Mao Zedong tongzhi dui zhexue de xuexi he changdao" [Comrade Mao Zedong's initiatives in and study of philosophy], *Xinan Shifan xueyuan xuebao* 2 (1985), pp. 9-16; also Wuhan daxue zhexuexi, Mao Zedong zhexue sixiang yanjiushi [The institute of the Philosophical thought of Mao Zedong at the philosophy department of Wuhan University], *Mao Zedong zhexue sixiang yanjiu* [Research on the philosophical thought of Mao Zedong] (Wuhan: Wuhan daxue zhexuexi, 1983), esp. pp. 22 ff.

145.   Wu Liping, "Mao zhuxi guanxin 'Fan Dulin Lun' de fanyi" [Chairman Mao's interest in the Translation of "Anti-Dühring"], in *Zhongguo zhexue,* Vol. I, p. 44.

146.   Li Yongtai, "Mao Zedong tongzhi dui zhexue de xuexi he changdao", pp. 12 ff.   See also Li Ji, "Mao Zedong you gemingjia zhuanbian wei gemingjia jian zhexuejia de biaozhi" [The watershed between Mao as revolutionary and Mao as revolutionary and philosopher], *Mao Zedong zhexue sixiang yanjui dongtai* 4 (1987), pp. 37-43.   This article provides a long list of texts on philosophy in the early to mid-1930s available for study, and those which Mao had read by 1937, including *Capital, Anti-Dühring,* and many of Lenin's writings.

147.   Chang Ruisen et al. (eds.), *Mao Zedong zhexue sixiang gailun,* p. 4.

148.   Gong Yuzhi et al. (eds.), *Mao Zedong de dushu shenghuo,* pp. 70-2.

149.   *Ibid.,* p. 46.   See also *Mao Zedong zhexue pizhuji,* pp. 279-283.

150.   *Ibid.,* p. 71;   also Li Yongtai, "Mao Zedong tongzhi dui zhexue de xuexi he changdao", p. 13;   also Sichuan daxue Mao Zedong zhexue sixiang yanjiu shi (ed.), *Mao Zedong bianzhengfa sixiang yanjiu,* pp. 93-94.   Another view expressed to me by a Chinese Mao scholar (in December 1987) was that Mao did not use *Shehuixue dagang* during the writing of *On Contradiction* and *On Practice,* but employed it to revise these essays when he read it in 1938.   See also *Mao Zedong zhexue pizhuji,* pp. 279-282.   For an evaluation of the importance of Li Da's *Shehuixue dagang* to Chinese philosophy in the 1930s, see Zhao Dezhi, "Li Da de 'Shehuixue dagang' zai Zhongguo Makesizhuyi zhexue fazhan shi shang de diwei" [The position of Li Da's "Elements of Sociology" in the history of the development of Marxist philosophy in China], in *Shehui kexue jikan* 4 (1987), pp. 25-29.   See also O. Briere, S.J., *Fifty Years of Chinese Philosophy, 1898-1950,* translated by Laurence G. Thompson (Westport, Connecticut: Greenwood Press, 1956), pp. 75-79.

151.   Guo Huaruo, "Mao zhuxi kangzhan chuqi de zhexue huodong", p. 34.

152.   *Ibid.*

153.   *Ibid.*

154.   According to one Chinese source, Mao's lecturing involved quite a heavy teaching load.   From May (perhaps April) 1937, Mao presented lectures to two classes every Tuesday and Thursday mornings.   This lasted until August, and Mao gave a total of more than 110 lectures.   He was unable to finish his series of lectures due to problems associated with the Anti-Japanese War.   See Wu Jun, "Mao Zedong shengping, sixiang yanjiu gaishu" [Comment on research on Mao Zedong's life and thought], in *Mao Zedong zhexue sixiang yanjiu dongtai* No. 1 (1987), pp. 52-58.

155. *Shehuixue dagang* now constitutes volume two of Li Da's *Collected Works*. See *Li Da Wenji* (Beijing: Renmin chubanshe, 1981).

156. *Ibid.*, pp. 128-130.

157. Li Qiju et al., "Li Da yijiusijiu nian qian lilun huodong ji zhuzuo biannian" [A chronology of Li Da's theoretical activities and compositions prior to 1949], in *Zhongguo zhexue* Vol. I, pp. 363-364.

158. Ignatius J.H. Ts'ao, "Ai Ssu-ch'i: the Apostle of Chinese communism", *Studies in Soviet Thought* 12 (1972), p. 244, note 6.

159. Gong Yuzhi et al. (eds.), *Mao Zedong de dushu shenghuo*, pp. 70-71.

160. *Ibid.*

161. *Ibid.* For Mao's annotations, see *Mao Zedong zhexue pizhuji*, pp. 447-452.

162. *Ibid.*, p. 72.

163. Ai Siqi, *Zhexue yu shenghuo* [Philosophy and Life] (Shanghai: Dushu shenghuo chubanshe, April 1937).

164. *Zhongguo zhexue*, Vol. I, pp. 3-4; also in *Mao Zedong shuxin xuanji* [Selected letters of Mao Zedong] (Beijing: Renmin chubanshe, 1983), pp. 112-113.

165. *Zhongguo zhexue*, Vol. I, pp. 5-30. This quote is from p. 29. See also *Mao Zedong zhexue pizhuji*, p. 175. Mao wrote there, "every difference contains contradiction".

166. T'sao, "Ai Ssu-ch'i", pp. 15-16.

167. Joshua A. Fogel, *Ai Ssu-ch'i's Contribution to the Development of Chinese Marxism* (Cambridge, Mass. and London: Harvard Contemporary China Series, No. 4, 1987), p. 70.

168. On the issue of repetition in Soviet philosophical writings, see De George, *Patterns of Soviet Thought*, p. 193; also Kamenka, "Soviet Philosophy, 1917-1967", p. 95.

169. Gong Yuzhi et al. (eds), *Mao Zedong de dushu shenghuo*.

170. A point confirmed by Takeuchi Minoru, "'Mujunron' no genkei hosetsu".

171. *Selected Works of Mao Tse-tung*, Vol. I, pp. 311-347.

172. *Ibid.*, pp. 295-309.

POSSIBLE SOURCES OF MAO ZEDONG'S
WRITINGS ON DIALECTICAL MATERIALISM

Key:

XZXDG	-	Mitin (ed.), *Xin Zhexue dagang*
BZWWL	-	Mitin et al., *Bianzhengweiwulun yu lishiweiwulun*
JC	-	Shirokov and Aizenberg et al., *Bianzhengfa weiwulun jiaocheng*
SHXDG	-	Li Da, *Shehuixue dagang*
SXFFL	-	Ai Siqi, *Sixiangfangfalun*
DZZX	-	Ai Siqi, *Dazhong zhexue*

TABLE ONE

LECTURE NOTES ON DIALECTICAL MATERIALISM (Bujuan edition)	SOURCES	
	DIRECT	INDIRECT
pp. 187-188		BZWWL, pp. 47-60 XZXDG, pp. 183-189
p. 187	BZWWL, pp. 47, 48	
p. 188	BZWWL, p. 48 XZXDG, pp. 183, 189	
pp. 189-192		JC, pp. 48-75
p. 189	BZWWL, pp. 50-51	
p. 190	BZWWL, pp. 55-56 JC, pp. 56-57	
p. 191	JC, p. 60 BZWWL, p. 56	
pp. 192-194		BZWWL, pp. 61-70 JC, pp. 76-99

LECTURE NOTES ON DIALECTICAL MATERIALISM (*Bujuan* edition)	SOURCES	
	DIRECT	INDIRECT
p. 192	JC, p. 50	
p. 193	JC, pp. 50, 51, 52	
p. 194	BZWWL, p. 155	
p. 195	BZWWL, p. 156	
p. 196	Deals with Chinese issues	
p. 197	BZWWL, p. 156 XZXDG, p. 191	BZWWL, p. 157
p. 198	XZXDG, pp. 192, 193, 194	
p. 199	BZWWL, pp. 158-159 XZXDG, p. 194	
p. 200	XZXDG, pp. 194, 195, 196	
p. 201	XZXDG, pp. 197, 198, 200, 201	
p. 202	BZWWL, p. 160 XZXDG, p. 202	XZXDG, pp. 201-203 SHXDG, pp. 84-85
pp. 203-204		BZWWL, pp. 161-163 XZXDG, pp. 203-205

LECTURE NOTES ON DIALECTICAL MATERIALISM (*Bujuan* edition)	SOURCES	
	DIRECT	INDIRECT
p. 203	XZXDG, p. 205	
pp. 205-210		SHXDG, pp. 87-88 XZXDG, pp. 213-215 SXFFL, pp. 117-122 BZWWL, pp. 165-169
p. 210	BZWWL, p. 169	SHXDG, pp. 89-90 XZXDG, pp. 205-212
p. 211	BZWWL, pp. 170-171	SHXDG, pp. 89-90
pp. 212-213	BZWWL, p. 174	BZWWL, pp. 172-186 SHXDG, pp. 208-215
pp. 214-216		SXFFL, pp. 39-44 BZWWL, pp. 174-186
p. 215	BZWWL, p. 177	
p. 216	BZWWL, p. 178	
p. 217	BZWWL, p. 179	
pp. 217-220		BZWWL, pp. 186-194 JC, pp. 232-252 DZZX, pp. 96-106
p. 218	BZWWL, p. 189	

TABLE TWO

ON PRACTICE (*Bujuan* edition)	POSSIBLE SOURCES
pp. 220-234	SXFFL, pp. 39-94 DZZX, pp. 60-88 JC, pp. 193-221 XZXDG, pp. 341-405 BZWWL, pp. 195-211 SHXDG, pp. 208-268

TABLE THREE

ON CONTRADICTION (*Bujuan* edition)	POSSIBLE SOURCES
pp. 235-278	BZWWL, pp. 212-238, 323-342 SHXDG, pp. 123-134, 267-280 JC, pp. 277-311, 486-494, 510-515 XZXDG, pp. 231-245, 413-420 DZZX, pp. 116-123, 154-165 SXFFL, pp. 123-131, 94-105

2 Lecture Notes on Dialectical Materialism

(p. 265) [p. 187]¹ *Chapter One: Idealism and Materialism*
1938²

This chapter will discuss the following questions:
(1) The two opposed forces within philosophy;
(2) The differences between idealism and materialism;
(3) The origins of the emergence and development of idealism;
(4) The origins of the emergence and development of materialism.³

1. *The Two Opposed Forces within Philosophy*

(p. 266) The entire history of philosophy is the history of the struggle and development of the two mutually opposed philosophical schools of idealism and materialism. All philosophical trends of thought and schools are disguised forms of these two fundamental schools.

Sources: Takeuchi Minoru (ed.), *Mao Zedong Ji* (Tokyo: Hokubasha, 1970-72), Vol. VI, pp. 265-305; and Takeuchi Minoru (ed.), *Mao Zedong Ji Bujuan* (Tokyo: Sososha, 1984), Vol. V, pp. 187-239. Translated and annotated by Nick Knight.

The various forms of philosophical theories are all created by persons who belong to definite social classes. The consciousness of these persons is historically determined by a particular social life. All of the theories of philosophy express the needs of certain social classes, and reflect the level of development of society's forces of production and the historical stage[4] of mankind's knowledge of nature. The fate of a philosophy is determined by the extent to which it satisfies the requirements of a social class.

[p. 188] The social origins of idealism and materialism are to be found in the contradictory social structure of class. The occurence of the earliest idealism was a product of the ignorance and confusion of a primitive and barbaric humankind. The development of the forces of production which followed acted as a spur to the subsequent development of scientific knowledge, and idealism should have declined and materialism should have emerged to replace it. However, to the present day idealism has not only not declined but has developed, to compete vigorously with materialism on an equal footing; and the reason for this is that society has had class divisions. On the one hand, an oppressing class cannot but, in the pursuit of its own interests, develop and consolidate its idealist theories; on the other, the oppressed class, similarly in pursuit of its own interests, can do no other than develop and consolidate its materialist theories. Idealist and materialist theories both exist as instruments of the struggle between classes, and prior to the elimination of classes, the opposition between idealism and materialism cannot be eliminated. In the process of its own historical development, idealism has represented the consciousness of the exploiting classes, thus performing a reactionary function. Materialism, the world view of the revolutionary classes, has grown and developed in class society in the ceaseless battles with the reactionary philosophy of idealism. Consequently, the struggle in philosophy between idealism and materialism has consistently reflected the struggle of interests between the reactionary classes and the revolutionary classes. Whether philosophers are conscious of it or not, their particular philosophical tendency invariably approximates the political orientation of their own class. All tendencies within philosophy always directly or indirectly[5] fosters the fundamental political interests of their class. In this sense, the particular form taken by the policies of their class can be seen as the implementation of a particular tendency within philosophy. (p. 267) The specific features of the Marxist philosophy of dialectical materialism are its ability to explain clearly the class characteristic of all social consciousness (philosophy included), its open declaration of its proletarian character, and its resolute struggle with the idealist philosophy of the propertied classes; and moreover, these specific tasks are subordinate to the general task of overthrowing capitalism, organizing and establishing a proletarian dictatorship, and constructing a socialist society.

The tasks of philosophy during the current stage in China are subordinate to the general tasks of overthrowing imperialism and the semi-feudal system, the thorough achievement of bourgeois democracy, the establishment of a completely new Chinese democratic republic[6] and also to prepare through peaceful means[7] for the transformation to socialism and communism. Philosophical theory and political practice should be intimately connected.

[p. 189] 2. *The Differences between Idealism and Materialism*

What is the fundamental difference between idealism and materialism? It is the opposite answers that each provides to the basic question of philosophy, namely the question of the relationship between spirit and matter (the question of the relationship between consciousness and existence). Idealism considers the world to have its sole origins in spirit (consciousness, concepts, the subject), and matter (the natural world, society, the object) to be dependent on it. Materialism considers matter exists independently of spirit, and spirit to be dependent on it. A confusing variety of opinions on all questions grows from the opposite answers given to this basic question.

According to idealism, the world is either a synthesis of the entirety of consciousness, or the spiritual process created by our reason or the world's reason; it regards the external material world as either a completely fabricated illusion or the material external trapping of spiritual elements. Idealism regards the knowledge of humankind as emanating spontaneously from the subject, and the product of spirit itself.

(p. 268) Materialism, on the other hand, considers the unity of the universe to derive from its materiality, and that spirit (consciousness) is one of the natural characteristics of matter which emerges only when matter has developed to a certain stage. Nature, matter and the objective world exist apart from spirit and are independent of it. Human knowledge is a reflection of the objective external world.

3. *The Origins of the Emergence and Development of Idealism*

What are the origins of the emergence and development of idealism, a philosophy which considers matter to be a product of spirit and which has inverted the position of the real world? [p. 190] As previously stated, the emergence of the earliest idealism was a product of the ignorance and confusion of a primitive and barbaric humankind. However, following the development of production, the division of manual and mental labour created the primary conditions under which idealism became a philosophical trend. The result of the development of society's forces of production was the emergence of division of function, and with the development of this division of function were created persons who specialized in mental labour. But during periods when the forces of production were poor and undeveloped the degree of separation between the two remained incomplete. However, a major transformation occurred when classes appeared, private property emerged and exploitation became the basis of the existence of the dominant class; at that time mental labour became the prerogative of the dominant class and manual labour became the fate of the oppressed class. The dominant class began to observe the relationship between themselves and the oppressed class in an inverted fashion, perceiving that it was not the workers who provided the dominant class with the means of livelihood, but themselves who provided the workers with it. Because of this, they disdained manual labour and there emerged the idealist view. The elimination of the distinction between mental and manual labour is one of the conditions for the elimination of idealist philosophy.

Of the social origins of the development of idealist philosophy, the principal one was the conscious representation of ruling class interest by that philosophy. The dominance of idealist philosophy in all spheres of culture must be explained by reference to this. If there were no exploiting class idealism would lose its social basis. The final elimination of idealist philosophy must follow the elimination of classes and the establishment of communist society.

(p. 269) The reason why idealism has deepened, developed and had the capacity to struggle against materialism, must be sought in the process of knowledge of humankind. When humankind employs concepts to think, there exists the possibility of drifting into idealism. Humankind cannot but use concepts when thinking and this facilitates the division of our knowledge into two aspects; the one deals with individual and particular things, the other incorporates generalized concepts (such as the judgement that "Yan'an is a city"). The particular and the general are actually indivisibly connected, for to divide them is to depart from objective truth. Objective truth is expressed in the unity of the general and particular; without the particular, the general could not exist; and without the general, there could be no particular. To separate the general from the particular, that is, to treat the general as an objective entity and to regard the particular only as a form of existence of the general, is the method adopted by all idealists. All [p. 191] idealists substitute consciousness, spirit or concepts for objective entities which exist independently of human consciousness. Commencing from this premise, idealism stresses the dynamic role of human consciousness in social practice; it cannot point out the materialist truth that consciousness is limited by matter, maintaining instead that only consciousness is dynamic and that matter is nothing but an inert ensemble of objects. In addition, driven by inherent class characteristics, idealists utilize every possible means to exaggerate the dynamic role of consciousness, one-sidedly developing and limitlessly

expanding it so that it becomes the dominant aspect of intelligence. They conceal the other aspect, leaving it subordinate. This artificially expanded role for consciousness is established as a general world view to the extent of transforming it into a god or an idol. Idealism in economics greatly overstates one non-essential aspect of exchange by elevating the principle of supply and demand to the extent that it becomes the basic principle of capitalism. Many people have observed the active role that science plays in the life of society; but they fail to realise this role is determined and limited by definite social relations of production, and come to the conclusion that science is the motive force of society. Idealist historians perceive heroes as the creators of history, idealist statesmen see politics as an omnipotent entity, idealist military strategists wage all-out war regardless of the costs, idealist revolutionaries advocate Blanquism, and there are those who advocate revival of the national character and restoration of the old morality;[8] all are the result of an excessive exaggeration of the dynamic role of the subjective. Our thought cannot reflect a phenomenon in its entirety at one stroke, but is constituted of knowledge which, in a dialectical process, approximates reality, and is lively and (p. 270) infinitely variegated. Idealism is founded on the specific properties of thought and has exaggerated this individual aspect; it is thus unable to achieve a correct reflection of this process and only succeeds in distorting it. Lenin said: "Human knowledge is not a straight line, but a curve. Any segment of this curve can be transformed into an independent, complete, straight line and this straight line may lead to confusion. Rectilinearity and one-sideness, to see the trees and not the wood, woodenness and petrification, subjectivism and subjective blindness - voilà the epistemological roots of idealism". "Philosophical idealism is a one-sided, exaggeration of one of the fragments or aspects of knowledge until it becomes a deified absolute, divorced from matter, from nature. Idealism is thus a religious doctrine. This is very true."[9]
[p. 192] Pre-Marxist materialism (mechanistic materialism) did not emphasise the dynamic role of thought in knowledge, attributing it only with a passive role, and perceiving it as a mirror which reflected nature. Mechanistic materialism adopted

an unreasonable attitude towards idealism, ignoring the causes of its epistemology, and consequently was incapable of overcoming it.

Only dialectical materialism has correctly pointed out the dynamic role of thought while at the same time pointing out the limitations which matter imposes on thought, has pointed out that thought emerges from social practice, and at the same time that it actively guides practice. Only the dialectical theory of the "unity of thought and action" can thoroughly overcome idealism.

4. The Origins of the Emergence and Development of Materialism

The foundation of materialism is the recognition that matter exists independently of thought in the external world, and was acquired by humanity through practice. Through the practice of productive labour, class struggle, and scientific experiment, humankind gradually broke away from superstition and wishful thinking (idealism), gradually recognised the essence of the (p. 271) world, and in so doing arrived at materialism.

Primitive humans, yielding before the force of nature and capable only of using simple tools, were unable to explain change in the environment and so turned to the gods for help. This was the origin of religion and idealism.

However, during a lengthy process of production, humans came into contact with the surrounding natural world, acted on it and changed it; and in producing the basic necessities of life, made the natural world conform to their interests, and allowed them the firm belief that matter exists objectively.

In the social life of humankind, there emerges relations and influence between people, and in class society class struggle also occurs. The oppressed class evaluates the situation, makes an estimation of its own strength, formulates a programme, and when its struggle succeeds, it becomes confident that its own views are not merely the product of an illusion, [p. 193] but a reflection of the objectively existing material world. The failure of the oppressed class because it has adopted an incorrect programme, and the success resulting from a correction of that programme, allows the oppressed class to comprehend that only correct knowledge in which a subjective programme relies on the materiality and law-like regularity of the objective world can achieve its purpose.

The science of history has proved to humankind the materiality and law-like regularity of the world, and given rise to a consciousness of the uselessness of the fantasies of religion and idealism, and resulted in humankind's arrival at materialism.

In summary, the history of humankind's practice - the history of the struggle with nature, the history of class struggle, the history of science over a protracted period - has, through the necessity of life and struggle, led to a consideration of material reality and its principles, and so testified to the correctness of the materialist philosophy. Consequently, humankind has found the ideological instrument for its own struggle - the philosophy of materialism. As the development of production advances to a higher level, as the class struggle becomes more developed, and as scientific knowledge reveals even more 'mysteries' of nature, so does the philosophy of materialism develop and become consolidated; and humankind is increasingly able to liberate itself gradually from the two-fold oppression of nature and society.

The bourgeoisie, during the period of its struggle against the feudal classes and at a time when the proletariat did not yet constitute a threat, had already discovered and moreover employed (p. 272) materialism as an instrument in its own struggle; it was already convinced that objects in the environment were material products and not spiritual products. It was only when the bourgeoisie itself became the ruling class and the struggle of the proletariat threatened it that it abandoned this 'useless' instrument and took up once again another - the philosophy of idealism. Evidence of this is the change in thought from before to after 1927 - from materialism to idealism - on the part of the spokesmen of the Chinese bourgeoisie Dai Jitao and Wu Zhihui.[10]

The proletariat, which is the gravedigger of capitalism, "is intrinsically materialist". However, because the proletariat is historically the most progressive class, its materialism is different from the materialism of the bourgeoisie, is more thorough and profound; in character, it is completely dialectical, and not mechanistic.

Dialectical materialism was created by the spokesmen [p. 194] of the proletariat Marx and Engels as a result of the practice of the proletariat[11] and at the same time because the proletariat had assimilated all the results[12] of the entire history of humanity. Dialectical materialism not only maintains that matter is divorced from human consciousness and exists independently of it, it also asserts that matter changes. Dialectical materialism became a thoroughly systematic and completely new world view and methodology. This is the philosophy of Marxism.

Chapter Two: *Dialectical Materialism*

The problems which emerge from this subject and which will be discussed are:[13]

(1)   The revolutionary weapon of the proletariat - dialectical materialism;
(2)   The relationship between dialectical materialism and the philosophical legacy of the past;
(3)   The unity of the world view and methodology within dialectical materialism;
(4)   The question of the object of philosophy; (p. 273)
(5)   On matter;
(6)   On motion;
(7)   On time and space;
(8)   On consciousness;
(9)   On reflection;
(10)   On truth;
(11)   On practice.

My viewpoint on these problems is stated briefly in the following sections.[14]

1. *Dialectical Materialism Is the Revolutionary Weapon of the Proletariat*

I have already referred to this problem in Chapter One, but will discuss it again here in simple terms.

Dialectical materialism is the world view of the proletariat. The proletariat, which has been given the task by history of eliminating classes,[15] utilises dialectical materialism as a spiritual weapon in its struggle and as the philosophical basis for its various viewpoints. Only when we adopt the standpoint of the proletariat to gain an understanding of the world can we correctly and completely grasp the world view of dialectical materialism. Only if we set out from that standpoint can the real world be truthfully and objectively known. This is because, on the one hand, only the proletariat is the most progressive and revolutionary class; and on the other, because only dialectical materialism, which closely integrates advanced and rigorous (p. 274) scientificity with a thorough and uncompromising revolutionary quality, is the most correct and revolutionary world view and methodology.

The Chinese proletariat, which is at present[16] shouldering the historical task of the bourgeoise-democratic revolution in order to arrive at socialism and communism,[17] must adopt [p. 195] dialectical materialism as its spiritual weapon. If the Chinese proletariat, Chinese Communist Party, and the broad revolutionary elements of all those people who wish to take the standpoint of the proletariat adopt[18] dialectical materialism, they will have gained[19] a most correct and most revolutionary world view and methodology, and they will be able to correctly understand the development and change of the revolutionary movement, put forward revolutionary tasks, unite their own and their allies' forces, triumph over reactionary theories, adopt correct courses of action, avoid errors in work, and achieve the goal of liberating and transforming[20] China. Dialectical materialism is an especially indispensible subject for cadres and personnel who lead the revolutionary movement. This is because subjectivism and a mechanistic outlook, both of which are incorrect theories and methods of work, frequently exist amongst cadres and personnel; and this often causes them to act contrary to Marxism, to take the wrong path in the revolutionary movement. This weakness can only be avoided and corrected through conscious study and an understanding of dialectical materialism, and in so doing, arming their minds anew.

2. The Relationship between Dialectical Materialism and the Old Philosophical Legacy

Modern materialism is not a simple inheritance of the various philosophical theories of the past. It was engendered and matured in the struggle to oppose previous dominant philosophies and in the struggle of science to rid itself of idealism and mysticism. The Marxist philosophy of dialectical materialism not only inherited the supreme result of idealism - the achievements of Hegelian theory - it also simultaneously overcame the idealism of that theory and by the application of materialism transformed its dialectics. Marxism is likewise not merely the continuation and completion of the development of all past materialisms, it is also at the same time in opposition to the limitations and narrowness of all past materialisms, (p. 275) namely mechanistic and intuitive materialism (of which French materialism and the materialism of Feuerbach are the most important). The Marxist philosophy of dialectical materialism inherits the scientific legacy of past cultures, while at the same time giving this legacy a revolutionary transformation, thus forming an historically unprecedented [p. 196] science of philosophy, one which is most correct, most revolutionary, and most complete.

After the May Fourth Movement in China in 1919 and following the Chinese proletariat's conscious entrance onto the political stage and the heightening of its scientific standard, there emerged and developed the Marxist philosophical movement. However, during its first stage, the understanding of materialist dialectics within Chinese materialist thought was still poorly developed; bourgeois influenced mechanical materialism and the subjectivist trends of the Deborin clique constituted its principal ingredients. After the defeat of the 1927 revolution, Marxist-Leninist understanding took a step forward and dialectical materialist thought gradually developed. In very recent times, because of the gravity of the national and social crisis, and because of the influence of the movement to expose and criticise within Soviet philosophy, there has developed an extensive movement of materialist dialectics within the Chinese intellectual world. It can be seen from the extensiveness of this movement that, while it is at present still in its youthful stage, it will develop along with the revolutionary struggles of the proletariat and revolutionary peoples of China and the world; and with a strength that sweeps all before it, it will establish its own authority, guide the Chinese revolutionary movement's courageous and large-scale advance, and lay the foundation for the path along which China's proletariat will lead the Chinese revolution to victory.[21]

Because of the backwardness of the evolution of Chinese society, the philosophical trend of dialectical materialism which is presently developing in China has not resulted from inheriting and transforming its own philosophical legacy, but from the study of Marxism-Leninism. However, if the dialectical materialist trend of thought is to deepen and develop throughout China and, moreover, is definitely to lead the Chinese revolution along the road to complete victory, then it is necessary to struggle against the various existing outworn[22] philosophies, and raise the flag of criticism on the ideological front throughout the entire country. It is also necessary to expose and criticise the ancient philosophical legacy of China. Only thus will the objective be achieved.

3. *The Unity of the World View and Methodology within Dialectical Materialism*

(p. 276) [p. 197] Dialectical materialism is the world view of the proletariat. It is at the same time the method by which the proletariat gains knowledge of the surrounding world and a method for carrying out revolution. The world view and methodology of dialectical materialism constitute a unified system. Idealist Marxist revisionists consider the entire essence of dialectical materialism to be only its "method". They separate the method from the world view within the general philosophy, and separate dialectics from materialism. They do not understand that the Marxist methodology of dialectics is not the same as the idealist dialectics of Hegel, but is materialist dialectics; or that the methodology of Marxism cannot depart from its world view in the slightest degree. On the other hand, mechanical materialists only perceive in the philosophy of

Marxism the world view of a general philosophy, removing its dialectical element. Moreover, they consider this world view to be nothing more than the conclusions drawn from mechanical natural science. They do not comprehend that Marxist materialism is not simply materialism, but is dialectical materialism. Both of these viewpoints which dissect Marxist philosophy are incorrect. The world view and methodology of dialectical materialism are a unified system.

4. The Question of the Object of Materialist Dialectics - What Is It that Materialist Dialectics Studies?

Lenin (as an observer of Marxist philosophical science) regarded materialist dialectics as learning concerned with the principles of development of the objective world and the principles of the development of knowledge (in which the objective world is reflected within the various categories of dialectics). He said: "Logic is not learning concerned with the external form of thought, but learning concerned with the principles of development of all material, natural and spiritual things; namely, learning concerned with the principles of development of all of the concrete content of the world and knowledge of it. In other words, logic is concerned with the sum total and conclusion of the history of the world's knowledge".[23] Lenin emphasised the significance of materialist dialectics as a general scientific methodology, and this was because of the conclusions [p. 198] arrived at by the system of dialectics from the history of world knowledge. (p. 277) It was because of this that he said: "Dialectics is the history of knowledge".

The meaning of the definition, given above, which Lenin gave to scientific materialist dialectics and its object is as follows: firstly, materialist dialectics, as with any other science, has its object of study, and this object is the most general principles of development of nature, history and human thought. Moreover, the task of materialist dialectics when studying is not to arrive, through thought within the brain, at the relationship which exists between various phenomena, but to arrive at that relationship through investigation of the phenomena themselves. There exists a fundamental distinction between this view of Lenin's and that of the Menshevik idealists (who in fact depart from concrete science and concrete knowledge) over the categories of study which function as the object of materialist dialectics. Because the Menshevik idealists have attempted to establish a philosophical system whose various categories have become dissociated from the actual developments of the history of knowledge, social science and natural science, they have in fact abandoned materialist dialectics. Secondly, all of the various sciences (mathematics, mechanics, chemistry and physics, biology, economics and other natural sciences and the social sciences) study the various aspects of the development of the material world and its knowledge. Because of this, the principles of the various sciences are restricted in a narrow and one-sided way[24] by concrete realms of study. Materialist dialectics is however quite different; it is the universalisation, the totality, the conclusions and the finished product of all the general content of value from all of the concrete sciences and all of humankind's other scientific knowledge. In this way, the concepts, judgements, and principles of materialist dialectics constitute exceedingly extensive laws and formulations (incorporating the most general principles of all of the sciences, and consequently incorporating the essence of the material world). This is one side of the picture and from this perspective, materialist dialectics is a world view. From the other perspective, materialist dialectics is the logical and epistemological foundation for genuine scientific knowledge liberated from all idle speculation, fideism[25] and metaphysics; hence it is at the same time the only true, objectively reliable methodology for the study of concrete science. This further adds to our comprehension of what we mean when we speak of materialist dialectics or dialectical materialism as a unified system of world view and methodology. In this way can also be understood the errors of the vulgarisers and distorters of Marxist philosophy who deny its philosophical right of existence.

(p. 278) [p. 199] In relation to the problem of the object of philosophy, Marx, Engels, and Lenin all opposed the separation of philosophy from concrete reality and allowing philosophy to be transformed into various independent entities. They pointed out the necessity of a philosophy which grew out of analysis founded on real life and real relations, and opposed the approach of formal logic[26] and Menshevik idealism in which logical concepts and a natural world of logical concepts are the object of study.[27] The so-called philosophy which grew out of analysis founded on real life and real relations is none other than the theory of development[28] of materialist dialectics. Marx, Engels, and Lenin all explained that materialist dialectics was a theory of development. Engels described materialist dialectics as the theory "of the general principles of development of nature, society and thought".[29] Lenin regarded materialist dialectics as "the theory of development which is most profound, multi-faceted and richest in content". They all consider that[30] "the forms of all principles of development stated by all other philosophical theories beside this theory, in their narrowness and lack of content cut in two the actual process of development of nature and society". (Lenin) And the reason why materialist dialectics has been described as the theory of development which is most profound, multi-faceted, and richest in content, lies in the fact that materialist dialectics reflects, in a manner which is most profound, multi-faceted, and rich in content, the contradictoriness and leaps within the process of change of nature and society; there is no other reason.

One further problem must be resolved in this question of the object of philosophy, and that is the problem of the unity of dialectics, logic, and epistemology.

Lenin emphatically pointed out the identity of dialectics, logic, and epistemology, stating this is "an extremely important question" and that "the three terms are superfluous, they are one and the same thing". He fundamentally opposed those Marxist revisionists whose approach involves treating the three terms as completely distinct and independent theories.

Materialist dialectics is the only scientific epistemology and it is also the only scientific logic. Materialist dialectics studies the emergence and development of our knowledge of the external world, studies how we move from a state of ignorance to one of knowledge and the transformation of incomplete knowledge to more complete knowledge; it studies the increasingly profound and extensive reflection of the principles of development of nature and society in the mind [p. 200] of humankind. This is the unity of materialist dialectics and epistemology. Materialist dialectics studies the most general principles of (p. 279) development of the objective world, and studies the form reflected in thought of the most developed behaviour and characteristics of the objective world. In so doing, materialist dialectics studies the principles of emergence, development, passing away and mutual transformation of each process and phenomenon of material reality; at the same time, it studies the forms in which the principles of development of the objective world are reflected in human thought. This is the unity of materialist dialectics and logic.

To gain a thorough understanding of the reasons why dialectics, logic, and epistemology constitute a single entity, we will turn now to an examination of how materialist dialectics resolves the problem of the mutual relations between the logical and the historical.

Engels said: "In relation to the method of thought of the various philosophers,[31] the strong point of the Hegelian method of thought resides in the extremely rich historical sensitivity which permeates its foundations. Although its form is abstract idealist, the development of its thought nevertheless frequently parallels the development of world history. Moreover, history was actually taken as the verification of thought. History frequently progresses through leaps and in a confused manner. Consequently, if history is to be complied with, not only must a mass of insignificant data be given attention, but thought must be allowed to pursue a discontinuous path. At such a moment, the only appropriate method was the logical method. However, this logical method was basically still an historical method, but one which had abandoned its historical form and accidental character". Marx, Engels, and Lenin paid ample attention to this concept of "the unity of the development of logic and history". "The categories of Logic are abbreviations for the 'endless multitude' of 'particulars of external existence and of action'". "Categories constitute divided compartments which help us comprehend the dividing line between classes of things". "The practical activity of man had to lead his consciousness to the repetition of the various logical figures thousands of millions of times in order that these figures could obtain the significance of axioms". "Man's practice, repeating itself a thousand million times, becomes consolidated in man's consciousness by figures of logic. Precisely (and only) on account of this thousand-million-fold repetition, these figures have the stability [p. 201] of a prejudice, an axiomatic character".[32] These words of Lenin's demonstrate clearly the distinguishing characteristic of materialist dialectical logic which is dissimilar to formal logic which regards (p. 280) its principles and categories as empty, divorced from content and autonomous, and whose form is unconcerned with content. It is also unlike Hegel, who regarded logic as estranged from the material world, an independently developing conceptual essence, reflected and transplanted in our minds; moreover, he perceived the manifestation of the movement of matter as being dealt with via a process of creation in the mind. Basing himself on the identity of existence and thought, Hegel saw the identity of idealism in the identity of dialectics, logic, and epistemology. In contrast, the identity of dialectics, logic, and epistemology within Marxist philosophy is founded on a materialist basis. Only when materialism is employed to resolve the question of the relationship of existence and thought, and only when one adopts the position of reflection theory, can the problems of dialectics, logic, and epistemology be completely resolved.

Marx's *Capital* must be regarded above all others as the finest model of the utilisation of dialectical materialism to resolve the mutual relationship between things logical and things historical. *Capital* contains firstly an understanding[33] of the historical development of capitalist society, and simultaneously incorporates the logical development of that society. What *Capital* analyses is the dialectics of the development of the various economic categories which reflect the emergence, development and passing away of capitalist society. The materialist character of the solution to this problem resides in the fact that it takes material objective history as its basis, resides in taking concepts and categories as reflections of this actual history. The identity of the theory and history of capitalism, of the logic and epistemology of capitalist society, is expressed in model form in *Capital*. From it we can gain access to some understanding of the identity of dialectics, logic, and epistemology.

What has been discussed above is the question of the object of dialectical materialism.

[p. 202]   5. *On Matter*

(p. 281) Marxism continued and developed the materialist line within philosophy, and correctly resolved the question of the relationship between thought and existence; that is, it thoroughly and in a materialist manner indicated the materiality of the world and objective reality, and the material origins of thought (or, the dependent relationship of thought to existence).

The recognition that matter is the origin of thought has as its premise the materiality of the world and its objective existence. The first condition of belonging to the materialist camp is the acknowledgement that the material world is separate from and exists independently of human consciousness - it existed prior to the appearance of humankind, and following the appearance of humankind it remained separate from and existed independently of human consciousness. The recognition of this point is the fundamental premise of all scientific research.

How can this point be verified? There are numerous proofs. At the very moment humankind comes in contact with the external world, it must employ harsh means to cope with the oppression and resistance of the external world (the natural world and society); humankind not only should but can overcome such oppression and resistance. All of the actual conditions of human social practice manifested in the historical development of human society are the best proof of this point. Throughout the course of the ten-thousand *li* Long March, the Red Army had no doubts about the objective existence of the regions it traversed, the Yangtze and Yellow Rivers, the snow-covered mountains, and the grasslands, or the enemy armies which did battle with it, etc.; neither did it doubt the objective existence of the Red Army itself.[34] China[35] does not doubt the objective existence of an invading Japanese imperialism, nor of the Chinese people themselves; neither do students of the Anti-Japanese Military and Political University doubt the objective existence of this university and the students themselves. These are all material things which exist independently and are separate from our consciousness; this is the fundamental viewpoint of all materialism, it is the materialist viewpoint of philosophy.

The philosophical materialist viewpoint and the materialist viewpoint of natural science are not identical. If we say that the philosophical material viewpoint resides in its pointing out the objective existence of matter, that what is described as [p. 203] so-called matter is the entire world which is separate from human consciousness and exists independently (this world acts on the sense organs of humans which produces human sense perceptions, and from these sense perceptions reflection is achieved), then that way of portraying it is permanent and unchangeable, it is absolute. The material viewpoint of natural science resides in its study of material structures, for example, previous atomic theory and subsequent electron theory, etc; and the way in which this is described changes in line with progress in natural science; it is relative.

The distinction, based on the insights of dialectical materialism, between the materialist viewpoint of philosophy and the materialist viewpoint of natural science, is a necessary condition for thoroughly implementing the orientation of the philosophy of materialism, and is of great significance in the struggle with idealism and mechanical materialism.

(p. 282) Materialists[36] were not aware of scientific knowledge of material structures, such as electron theory which demolished the erroneous theory of the elimination of matter and which clearly bears out the correctness of the materialism of dialectical materialism. Through the discoveries of modern natural science, such as the discovery of electron theory, certain material properties which appeared in old material concepts (weight, hardness, impermeability, inertia, etc.) were shown to exist only in certain material forms and not in others. Facts like these eradicated the one-sideness and narrowness of old materialism's approach to material concepts and nicely demonstrated the correctness of materialism's recognition of the world.[37] The materialist viewpoint of former dialectical materialism perceived the unity of the material world through diversity, that is the unity of the diversity of matter; and there is not the slightest contradiction between this materialist viewpoint and the fact that the movement and change involved in the transformation of matter from one form to another are eternal and universal. Ether, electrons, atoms, molecules, crystals, cells, social phenomena, phenomena of thought - these are various stages of the development of matter, are various temporary forms in the history[38] of the development of matter. The deepening of scientific research, and the discovery of all manner of forms of matter (the discovery of the diversity of matter) only serves to enrich the content of the materialist viewpoint of dialectical materialism; and is there any contradiction in that? It is necessary to make a distinction between the materialist viewpoint of philosophy and the materialist viewpoint of natural science, and this is so because the two do have differences which range from minor to extensive; however, [p. 204] they are not mutually contradictory, for matter in the broad sense incorporates matter in the narrow sense.

The materialist viewpoint of dialectical materialism does not acknowledge that there are so-called non-material things in the world (independent spiritual things). Matter exists eternally and universally and is limitless in both time and space. If there is something in the world which has "always been thus" and "everywhere is the same" (like its unity) then that something is so-called objectively existing matter referred to by philosophy. If things such as consciousness are observed employing the thoroughgoing insights of materialism (that is, the insights of materialist dialectics), then so-called consciousness is no different; it is only[39] a form of matter in movement, it is a particular property of the material brain of humankind. It allows material processes external to consciousness to be reflected in consciousness, which is a particular property of the material brain. Accordingly, it is apparent that it is conditional when we make a distinction between matter and (p. 283) consciousness and moreover oppose the one to the other; that is to say, it has significance only for the insights of epistemology. Because consciousness and thought are only properties of matter (brain), the opposition of knowledge and existence, that is, the opposition between matter that knows and matter that is known,[40] cannot be sustained. In this way, the opposition of subject and object departs from the realm of epistemology and is without any significance. If, beyond epistemology, consciousness and matter are still placed in opposition, this is tantamount to foresaking materialism. In the world there is only matter and its various manifestations; and signified by this are the following - the subject itself is matter, the so-called materiality of the world (matter is eternal and universal), the objective reality of matter, and matter as the origin of consciousness. In a word, matter encompasses everything in the world. The saying goes, "Unity belongs to Si-ma Yi"; but we say, "Unity belongs to matter". This is the principle of the unity of the world.

What has been discussed above is the theory of matter of dialectical materialism.

6. On Motion (On Development)

[p. 205] The first fundamental principle of dialectical materialism is its theory of matter; namely, the recognition of the materiality of the world, the objective reality of matter, and that matter is the origin of consciousness. This principle of the unity of the world has already been explained in the previous section "On Matter".

The second fundamental principle of dialectical materialism is its theory of motion (or theory of development): that is, the recognition that motion is a form of the existence of matter, that it is an intrinsic property of matter, and that it is a manifestation of the diversity of matter; this is the principle of the development of the world. The principle of development of the world and the principle of the unity of the world referred to above are linked one to the other to become the complete world view of dialectical materialism. The world is none other than a material world of limitless development (or, the material world is one whose development is without limit).

(p. 234) The theory of motion of dialectical materialism cannot tolerate (1) thoughts on motion separate from matter;

(2) thoughts on matter separate from motion; and (3) the simplification of matter in motion. The theory of motion of dialectical materialism has instituted an unequivocal and resolute struggle with these idealistic, metaphysical, and mechanical viewpoints.

The theory of motion of dialectical materialism is first and foremost in opposition to the idealism and religious deism of philosophy. The essence of all idealisms and religious deisms resides in their refusal to recognise the material unity of the world; they assume that the world's motion and development are non-material, or were at the very beginning non-material, and are the consequence of the operation of spirits or God's supernatural power. The German idealist philosopher Hegel believed that the contemporary world had developed out of the so-called "World Idea"; and in China, the philosophy of the *Book of Changes* and the moral theories of Song and Ming neo-Confucianism all engendered views of the development of the world which were idealist. Christianity asserts God created the world, and in Buddhism and the various Chinese fetishisms the motion and development of the world's myriad things is put down to the supernatural. All of these explanations which contemplate motion divorced from matter are fundamentally incompatible with dialectical materialism. Besides idealism and religion, all pre-Marxist materialism and all present-day anti-Marxist mechanistic materialism, are proponents of materialist theories of motion when it comes to discussing natural phenomena, but the moment social phenomena are mentioned, they cannot but become [p. 206] divorced from material causes[41] and revert to spiritual causation.

Dialectical materialism resolutely refutes all of these incorrect views on motion and points out their historical limitations - the limitations of class status and the limitations of the degree of development of science - and constructs its own view of motion on a thoroughgoing materialism which takes the standpoint of the proletariat and the most advanced level of science as its basis. Dialectical materialism first of all points out that motion is a form of the existence of matter, it is an intrinsic attribute of matter (and not a function of some external impetus); to imagine motion without matter and matter without motion is

equally incomprehensible. Materialism's view of motion is in intense opposition to the views on motion espoused by idealism and deism.
(p. 285) The observation and study of matter divorced from motion results in a metaphysical theory of a static universe or a theory of absolute equilibrium. These consider matter to be eternally unchangeable, and that within matter there is no such thing as development; they also consider absolute immobility to be matter's general or original state. Dialectical materialism resolutely opposes these viewpoints, and regards motion as the most universal form of the existence of matter and an inseparable property intrinsic to matter. All immobility and equilibrium have only relative significance, and motion is absolute. Dialectical materialism recognizes that all forms of matter possess the possibility of relative immobility or equilibrium, and moreover considers this differentiates matter, and consequently that it is the most important condition for distinguishing life (Engels).[42] However, it considers the condition of immobility or equilibrium to be only one of the essential aspects of motion, it is a particular condition of motion. The error of observing and studying matter separate from motion resides in overstating the importance of the factors of immobility or equilibrium, in concealing their limitations and substituting these partial factors for the whole, in generalizing a particular condition of motion, and in presenting them in absolute terms. The saying beloved of China's ancient metaphysical thinkers, "Heaven changeth not, neither does the *Dao*",[43] is indicative of this theory of a static universe; and although these thinkers recognised change in the phenomena of the universe and society, they refused to recognise it as change in their essence. From their perspective, the essence of the universe and society remained eternally unchangeable. And the principal reason that they thought like this was the limitations of their class; for if the feudal landlord class admitted that the essence of the universe and society is in motion and develops, then theoretically this was tantamount to signalling the [p. 207] death sentence of their own class. The philosophy of all reactionary forces is the theory of immobility. The revolutionary classes and masses have perceived the principle of

the development of the world, and therefore advocate the transformation of society and the world - and their philosophy is dialectical materialism.

In addition, dialectical materialism does not recognise the theory of the simplification of motion which lumps all motion in one particular form, namely, mechanical motion; this is the distinguishing feature of the world view of old materialism. Although old materialism (seventeenth and eighteenth century French materialism, and the nineteenth century German materialism of Feuerbach) did recognise the permanence of the existence and motion of matter (recognised the limitlessness of motion), it still had not broken free of the metaphysical world view. Needless to say, the explanations of their social theories were still idealist in their views on development; in their approach to the theory of nature, they also restricted the unity of the material world (p. 286) to a certain one-sided attribute, namely one form of motion - mechanical motion. The cause of this motion is an external force, like a machine which moves when externally impelled. They do not explain, by reference to essences or internal causes, matter or motion or the interrelated diversity of things. Rather, they are explained by reference to simple forms found externally, and to external force as a cause. In so doing, the diversity of the world is actually lost. They explain all of the world's motion as movement in place and an increase or decrease in quantity; an object at a certain place at a particular moment, and at another at a different moment, is thus described as motion. If there is change, it is only change involving an increase or decrease in quantity, not qualitative change; motion is cyclical, a repeated production of the same result. Dialectical materialism takes a contrary position to this view; it does not perceive motion as simple movement in place and as cyclical, but as limitless and qualitative in its diversity. Dialectical materialism regards motion as transformation from one form to another, and the unity of the world's matter and the motion of matter as the unity and motion of the limitless diversity of the world's matter.[44] Engels said: "Each of the higher forms of motion is necessarily connected with mechanical (external or molecular) forms of motion. For example, just as chemical action is not possible without change of temperature and electric changes, so too is organic life without mechanical (molecular), thermal, electric, chemical, etc. changes. This naturally cannot be denied. But the presence of these subsidiary forms does not exhaust [p. 208] the essence of the main form in each case".[45] These words absolutely and truthfully correspond to the facts. Even simple mechanical motion cannot be explained by the metaphysical viewpoint. It must be understood that all forms of motion are dialectical, although there are enormous differences between them in the depth and diversity of their dialectical content. Mechanical motion is still dialectical motion. And as for the view that an object "occupies" a point in space at a certain moment: in actuality, it both "occupies" that point while simultaneously not occupying it. The so-called "occupation" of a point and "immobility" are only particular conditions of motion; the object is still fundamentally in motion. While an object moves within the confines of time and space, it invariably and unceasingly overcomes such confines; it moves beyond the definite and limiting bounds of time and space to become an unbroken stream of motion. Moreover, mechanical motion is only one form of the motion of matter; in the real world, it has no absolutely independent (p. 287) existence and is always related to other forms of motion. Heat, chemical reaction, light and electricity, right through to organic and social phenomena, are all qualitatively particular forms of the motion of matter. The great and epoch-making contribution rendered by natural science at the turn of the nineteenth and twentieth centuries resides in its discovery of the principle of the transformation of motion, in pointing out that the motion of matter is always via the transformation of one form into another, and that the new form produced by this transformation is in essence different from the old form. The reason for the transformation of matter is not external but internal; it is not due to the impulsion of an external mechanical force, but to the struggle of the two mutually contradictory and qualitatively different elements which exist internally, and it is these which impel the motion and development of matter. Because of this discovery of the principle of the transformation of motion, dialectical materialism was able to extend the principle of the material unity of the world to natural and social history, not only to observe and study the world as matter in unceasing motion, but also to observe and study the world as matter in motion involving limitless advance from lower to higher forms; namely, to observe and study the world both as developmental and as a process. The following saying makes this point: "The unified material world is a process of development".[46] The cyclical theory of old materialism is thus exploded. Dialectical materialism has profoundly and comprehensively observed the forms of motion of nature and society. It considers the process of development of the entire observed world as eternal (without beginning or end). At the same time it regards each historically progressing concrete form of motion [p. 209] as temporary (having a beginning and an end); that is to say, it comes into being under definite conditions and passes away under definite conditions. Dialectical materialism considers that the process of the development of the world whereby lower forms of motion give rise to higher forms of motion expresses the historical and temporary character of motion; simultaneously, any one form of motion is a part of the eternal flow of motion (a flow without beginning or end) and therefore never the very first or last. According to the principle of the struggle of opposites (the reason for motion itself), each form of motion invariably arrives at a higher stage than that which preceded it and makes a real advance; however, at the same time, when considering the various forms of motion (the various concrete processes of development), there can occur motion which alters or reverses its direction. Forms of motion which advance and retreat are linked one to the other, so that in entirety they become a complex spiral motion. This principle also considers that a new form of motion occurs as the opposite of (or in antagonism to) an old form of motion; however, that at the same time the new form of motion necessarily preserves many essential elements of the old form of motion (p. 288), that new things grow out of old things. It considers that the new forms, characteristics, and properties of things are produced in leaps through successive ruptures, namely through conflict and division; but also that the connection and mutual relationship of things cannot be absolutely destroyed. Finally, dialectical materialism suggests that the world is infinite (limitless); not only is it so in its totality, but also in its parts. Are not electrons, atoms, and molecules[47] manifestations of a complex and infinite world?

The fundamental form of the motion of matter also determines the various subjects of the basic natural and social sciences. Dialectical materialism observes and studies the development of the world as a progressive motion which passes through the inorganic world to the organic world to arrive at the highest form of the motion of matter (society); the subordinate and related components of forms of motion constitute the foundations of the subordinate and related components of their corresponding sciences (inorganic science, organic science, social science). Engels said: "*Classification of the sciences,* each of which analyzes a single form of motion, or a series of forms of motion that belong together and pass into one another, is therefore the classification, the arrangement, of these forms of motion themselves according to their inherent sequence, and herein lies its importance".[48]

[p. 210] The entire world (including human society)[49] adopts qualitatively different and varying forms of matter in motion. Consequently, we cannot forget the question of the varying concrete forms of matter in motion; there is no such thing as so-called "matter in general" and "motion in general". In the world there is only motion or matter which is different in form and which is concrete. "Words like matter and motion are nothing but *abbreviations* in which we comprehend many different sensuously perceptible things according to their common properties" (Engels).[50]

Narrated above is the dialectical materialist theory of motion of the world or the principle of development of the world. These theories are the quintessence of Marxist philosophy, the world view and methodology of the proletariat. If all proletarian revolutionaries grasp the weapon of this thoroughgoing science, they will be able to understand and transform this world.

(p. 289) 7. *On Time and Space*

Motion is a form of the existence of matter, and space and time are also forms of the existence of matter. Matter in motion exists in space and time, and moreover, the motion of matter is itself the premise for these two forms of existence of matter, space and time. Space and time cannot be separated from matter. The sentence "matter exists in space" says that matter itself possesses the capacity of expansion; the material world is a world in which the capacity of expansion exists internally. It does not suggest that matter is situated in a space which is a non-material void. Neither space and time are independent non-material things; neither are they subjective forms of our perceptions. They are forms of existence of the objective material world; they are objective, have no existence apart from matter, and neither does matter exist apart from them.

The view that sees space and time as forms of the existence of matter is the thoroughgoing materialist viewpoint. This conception of time and space is in fundamental opposition to the [p. 211] various idealist conceptions of time and space listed below:[51]

(1)   The Kantian conception of time and space, which considers time and space are not objective realities, but forms of intuition of humankind.[52]

(2)   The Hegelian conception of time and space, which incorporates a conception of time and space as developing, increasingly approaching the absolute Idea.

(3)   The Machist conception of time and space, which considers time and space are "categories of sense perception", and "instruments for the harmonization of experience".[53]

None of these idealist viewpoints recognizes the objective reality of time and space, or recognizes that, in their own development, the concepts of time and space reflect materially existing forms. These incorrect theories have all been refuted one by one by dialectical materialism.

On the question of time and space, dialectical materialism not only struggles against these idealist theories listed above, it also struggles against mechanical materialism. Of particular note[54] (p. 290) is Newtonian mechanics, which treats space and time as unrelated and static insubstantial entities, and which situates matter within this insubstantial context. Dialectical materialism, in opposition to this theory of mechanics, points out that our conception of time and space[55] is a developmental one. "There is nothing in the world but matter in motion, and matter in motion cannot move otherwise than in space and time. Human conceptions of space and time are relative, but these relative conceptions go to compound absolute truth. These relative conceptions, in their development, move towards absolute truth and approach nearer and nearer to it. The mutability of human conceptions of space and time no more refutes the objective reality of space and time than the mutability of scientific knowledge of the structure and forms of matter in motion refutes the objective reality of the external world". (Lenin)[56]

This is the conception of time and space held by dialectical materialism.

[p. 212] 8. *On Consciousness*

Dialectical materialism considers consciousness to be a product of matter, that it is one form of the development of matter, and a specific characteristic of a definite form of matter. The theory of consciousness of materialism and the historical approach[57] is in fundamental opposition to the viewpoint of all idealisms and mechanical materialisms on this question.

According to the Marxist viewpoint, consciousness originated in the development from the inorganic world without consciousness to the animal world possessing rudimentary forms of consciousness; there then developed humankind which possessed high-level forms of consciousness. Such high-level forms of consciousness not only cannot be separated from the advanced nervous systems which came with physiological development, they cannot be separated from the labour and production which comes with the development of society. Marx and Engels have emphatically pointed out the dependent relationship which consciousness has to the development of material production, and the relationship between consciousness and the development[58] of human language.

So-called consciousness is a particular characteristic of a

definite form[59] of matter; this form of matter is composed of a complex nervous system, and this type of nervous system can only occur (p. 291) at a high stage in the evolution of the natural world. The entire inorganic world, plant kingdom, and rudimentary animal kingdom - none of these has the ability to comprehend those processes which occur either within or without them; they are without consciousness.[60] It is only the animal being that possesses an advanced nervous system that has the ability to comprehend processes;[61] that is, which has the ability to reflect internally or comprehend these processes. The objective physiological processes of the nervous system of human beings function in line with the subjective manifestation of the forms of consciousness that they adopt internally; these are themselves all[62] objective things, are certain types of material process; however, these simultaneously also constitute subjective psychological functions in the substance of the brain.

There is no mind comprised of thought which is in essence distinct, there is only ideational matter - the brain. This ideational matter is matter of a particular quality [p. 213], matter which has developed to a high degree following the development of language in human social life. This matter possesses the particular characteristic of thought, something possessed by no other type of matter.

However, vulgar materialists consider thought to be matter secreted from within the brain; this viewpoint misrepresents our conception of this problem. It must be understood that the behaviour of thought, emotion, and will is weightless, neither does it possess the capacity to expand; and yet consciousness, together with weight, and the capacity to expand (*shenzhangxing*), and so on, are all matter with different characteristics. Consciousness is an intrinsic condition of matter in motion; it reflects the particular characteristics of the physiological processes which occur with matter which is in motion. These particular characteristics cannot be separated from the objective processes of nerve function, but they are not[63] identical with such processes. The confusion of these two and the repudiation of the particularity of consciousness - this is the viewpoint of vulgar materialists.

Similarly, the mechanistic theory of sham Marxism echoes the viewpoint of certain bourgeois right-wing[64] schools of thought within psychology; this in actuality has also completely overturned consciousness. They consider the processes of the physiology and comprehension of consciousness to be a particular characteristic of the nature of advanced material substance, and do not recognise that consciousness is a product of the social practice of humankind.[65] For the concrete historical identity of object and subject, they substitute the equality of object and subject, and the one-sided mechanistic objective world. These viewpoints which confuse consciousness with a physiological process are tantamount to the abolition of the fundamental question of philosophy of the relationship[66] between thought and existence. (p. 292) The idealism of the Mensheviks attempts to employ a compromise theory, one which reconciles materialism and idealism, as a substitute for Marxist epistemology. They oppose the principle of dialectics through the principles of[67] the "synthesis"[68] of objectivism and subjectivism and the "mutual assistance" of these two methods.[69] However, this principle of dialectics is both non-mechanistic objectivism and non-idealist subjectivism, and represents the concrete historical identity[70] of objective and subjective.

However, there is also the unusual theory of Plekhanov's animist view on the problem of consciousness, which is fully expressed in his celebrated dictum "a stone also possesses consciousness". [p. 214]. According to this viewpoint, consciousness does not occur in the process of development of matter, but exists in all matter from the very beginning; there is only a difference of degree between the consciousness of humans, low-level organisms, and a stone.[71] This anti-historical viewpoint is fundamentally opposed to the viewpoint of dialectical materialism which considers consciousness to be the ultimately occurring particular characteristic of matter.[72]

Only dialectical materialism's theory of consciousness is the correct theory on problems of consciousness.

9. On Reflection

To be a thoroughgoing materialist, it is insufficient simply to acknowledge the material origins of consciousness; the knowability of matter by consciousness also must be acknowledged.

The question of whether or not matter can be known is a complex one; it is a question which all philosophers of the past have felt powerless[73] to deal with. Only dialectical materialism is able to provide the correct solution. On this question, the standpoint of dialectical materialism has been in opposition to agnosticism and is different to strident realism.

The agnosticism of Hume and Kant isolates the subject of knowledge from the object, and considers that it is not possible to transcend the limits which isolate the subject; between the "thing-in-itself" (p. 293) and its outward form exists an impassable chasm.

The strident realism of Machism equates the object with sense perceptions, and considers that the truth is already established in final form in sense perceptions. At the same time, Machism not only does not understand that sense perceptions are a result of the effects of the external world, it moreover does not understand the active role of the subject in the process of cognition, namely, [p. 215] the transformative work of the sense organs and thinking brain of the subject,[74] on the effects of the external world (such that two forms - impressions and concepts - are made manifest).

It is only the theory of reflection of dialectical materialism which has positively answered the problem of knowability to become the "soul" of Marxist epistemology. This theory has clearly demonstrated that our impressions and concepts not only arise from objective things, but also reflect them. It demonstrates that impressions and concepts are neither a product of the spontaneous development of the subject as the idealists suggest, nor the label given objective things as suggested by the agnostics; they are rather the reflection of objective things, a photographic image and sample copy of them.

Objective truth exists independently and does not depend on the subject.[75] Although it is reflected in our sense perceptions and concepts, it achieves final form gradually rather than instantaneously. The viewpoint of strident realism, which considers objective truth achieves final form in sense perceptions and that we gain it thus, is a mistaken one.

Although objective truth does not achieve final form at once in our sense perceptions and concepts, it is not unknowable. The reflection theory of dialectical materialism opposes the viewpoint of agnosticism, and considers that consciousness can reflect objective truth in the process of cognition. The process of cognition is a complex one; in this process, when the as yet unknown "thing-in-itself"[76] is reflected in our sense perceptions, impressions, and concepts, it becomes a "thing-for-us". Sense perceptions and thought certainly do not, as Kant has stated, isolate us from the external world; rather, they are what links us with it. Sense perceptions and thought are reflections of the objective external world. Mental[77] things (impressions and concepts) can be no other than "material things, altered (p. 294) and transformed, within the brain of humankind". (Marx) In the process of cognition, the material world is increasingly reflected in our knowledge more closely, more precisely, more multifariously, and more profoundly. It is the task of Marxist epistemology to carry on a struggle on two fronts against Machism and Kantianism, and to expose the errors of strident realism and agnosticism.

[p. 216] The reflection theory of materialist dialectics considers that our capacity to know the objective world is limitless; this view is in fundamental opposition to the viewpoint of the agnostics who consider the human capacity for knowledge to be limited. However, there are definite historical limits on each approach we make[78] to absolute truth. Lenin referred to it thus: "The *limits* of approximation of our knowledge to objective, absolute truth are historically conditional, but the existence of such truth is *unconditional* and the fact that we are approaching near to it is also unconditional. The contours of the picture are historically conditional, but the fact that this picture depicts an objectively existing model is unconditional".[79] We acknowledge that human knowledge is subject to the limitations of historical conditions, and that truth cannot be achieved at once. But we are not agnostics, and[80] recognise that truth becomes complete in the historical movement of human knowledge. Lenin also stated: "The *reflection* of nature in man's thought must be understood not 'lifelessly', not 'abstractly', *not devoid of movement, not without contradictions*; but in the eternal *process* of movement, the arising of contradictions and their solution".[81] The movement of knowledge is complex and replete with contradictions and struggle. This is the viewpoint of the epistemology of dialectical materialism.

The anti-historical standpoint of all those philosophies which, epistemologically, do not treat knowledge as a process consequently lacks breadth of view. This narrow viewpoint in the empiricism of sensationalism[82] has created a deep chasm between sense perceptions and concepts; in the rationalist school, it has caused concepts to become divorced from sense perceptions. It is only the epistemology of dialectical materialism (reflection theory) which treats knowledge as a process, and in so doing thoroughly eliminates this narrow viewpoint; it does so by attributing knowledge with a material and dialectical status.

Reflection theory points out: The process of reflection is not limited to sense perceptions and impressions, and exists in thought (in abstract concepts); knowledge is a process of motion from sense perceptions to thought. As Lenin has said: "Knowledge is the reflection of nature. But this is not a simple, not an immediate, not a complete reflection, but the process of a series of abstractions, (p. 295) the formation of concepts, laws, etc".[83]

[p. 217] At the same time, Lenin has pointed out: "The process of knowledge involving a movement from sense perceptions to thought is accomplished through a leap".[84] Lenin, here, has clearly expounded the dialectical materialist viewpoint of the interrelation between experiential and rational elements in cognition. Many philosophers do not comprehend the sudden change that occurs within the process of the movement of knowledge, that is, the process of movement from sense perceptions to thought (from impressions to concepts).

Consequently, to understand this transformation, which is produced by contradiction and adopts the form of a leap, namely, to comprehend that the identity of sense perceptions and thought is a dialectical identity, is to have comprehended the most important element of the essence of Lenin's reflection theory.

10. *On Truth*

Truth is objective and relative; it is also absolute - this is the viewpoint on truth of materialist dialectics.

Truth firstly is objective. Having recognised the objective existence of matter and the origin of consciousness in matter is to recognise the objective character of truth. The so-called objective truth, that is to say, the objectively existing material world, is the only source of the content of our knowledge or concepts; there is no other source. It is only idealists who deny that the material world exists independently of human consciousness - this fundamental principle of idealism maintains that knowledge or concepts emerge subjectively and spontaneously, and without any objective content.[85] Because of this, it acknowledges subjective truth and rejects objective truth. However, this is at odds with reality, for any knowledge or concept which fails to reflect the laws of the objective world is not scientific knowledge or objective truth; it is superstition or wishful thinking which subjectively engages in self-deception and the deception of others. All practical activity of humankind which has as its purpose the transformation of the environment is subject to the direction of thought (knowledge), regardless of whether it be productive activity, activity involving class struggle or national struggle,[86] or any other forms of activity. If this thought does not conform to objective laws, that is, if objective laws (p. 296) are not reflected in the brain of the person undertaking the action and do not constitute [p. 218] the content of his thought or knowledge, then that action will certainly not be able to achieve its purpose. The errors made by so-called subjective guidance[87] within the revolutionary movement is indicative of this sort of situation. Marxism became revolutionary scientific knowledge precisely because it correctly reflected the actual laws of the objective world; it is objective truth.[88] All thought that opposes Marxism is therefore incorrect, and this because it is not founded on correct objective laws and is completely subjective wishful thinking. There are those who say that what is universally accepted is objective truth (the subjective idealist Bogdanov stated this view). According to this viewpoint, then, religion and prejudice are also objective truth, because, although religion and prejudice are in fact erroneous views, they are frequently widely accepted by a majority of people; and sometimes correct scientific thought cannot overturn these erroneous widely held beliefs.[89] Materialist dialectics is fundamentally opposed to this viewpoint; it considers that it is only scientific knowledge which correctly reflects objective laws which can be designated as truth. All truth must be objective. Truth and falsity are absolutely in opposition. The only way to determine whether any knowledge is truth is to see if it does or does not reflect objective laws. If it does not conform to objective laws, even though it is acknowledged by the general populace or by certain wildly extravagant theories within the revolutionary movement, it can only be treated as erroneous.

The first problem[90] of the theory of truth of materialist dialectics is the question of subjective and objective truth. Its response is to deny the former and recognise the latter. Its second problem is the question of absolute and relative truth. Its response is, while recognising both, it does not one-sidedly accept or reject either aspect; moreover, it points out that the mutual relationship between them is correct, that it is dialectical.

It is absolute truth it acknowledges when materialist dialectics acknowledges objective truth. This is because, when we say the content of knowledge is a reflection of the objective world, that is the same as acknowledging the object of our knowledge is that external absolute world. "All true knowledge of nature is knowledge of the eternal, the infinite, and hence essentially absolute". (Engels)[91] However, objective absolute truth does not instantaneously and completely become the knowledge that we have; rather, through the introduction of countless relative truths in the limitless process of development of our thought, absolute truth is arrived at. [p. 219] The sum total of these countless relative truths is the manifestation of absolute truth. By its very nature, human thought can provide us with absolute truth. Absolute truth can only come about from the accumulation of many relative truths. Each stage of the development of science adds a new dimension to the sum total of absolute truth. However, the limits of the truth of each scientific principle are invariably relative; absolute truth is only manifest in countless relative truths; and if it is not so manifest through relative truth, absolute truth could not be known. (p. 297) Materialist dialectics certainly does not deny the relativity of all knowledge; but in doing so it is only indicating the historically conditional character of the limits of our knowledge's approximation to objective absolute truth, and not suggesting that knowledge itself is only relative. All inventions of science are historically limited and relative.[92] But scientific knowledge is different from falsehood; it displays and depicts objective absolute truth. This is the dialectical viewpoint on the interrelationship between absolute and relative truth.

There are two viewpoints, both of which are incorrect on the question of the interrelationship between absolute and relative truth. One is metaphysical materialism, the other is idealist relativism.[93]

On the basis of their fundamental metaphysical principle of "the unchangeable material world", metaphysical materialists consider that human thought is also unchanging; that is, they consider that this unchanging objective world can instantaneously and in its entirety be absorbed in human consciousness. That is to say, they acknowledge[94] absolute truth, but for them it is acquired only once by humans; they regard truth as immobile and lifeless, something that does not develop. Their error resides not in acknowledging that there is absolute truth - to acknowledge this point is correct. It is rather in their failure to understand the historical character of truth, and in their not perceiving the acquisition of truth as a knowledge process. It resides also in their not understanding that absolute truth can only come to fruition little by little in the process of development of human knowledge and that every step forward in knowledge expresses the content of absolute truth; that, in relation to complete truth, however, such knowledge possesses

only relative significance and certainly cannot instantaneously achieve the completeness of absolute truth. The viewpoint on truth of metaphysical materialism is an expression of one extreme of epistemology.
[p. 220] The other extreme within epistemology on the question of truth is idealist relativism. This denies that knowledge is characterised by absolute truth, only acknowledging its relative significance. It considers all scientific inventions contain no absolute truth; they are thus not objective truth. Truth is only subjective and relative. Consequently, all erroneous viewpoints have the right to exist. Where imperialism invades a weak and small nation, where a ruling class exploits the labouring masses, this doctrine[95] of invasion and system of exploitation are also truth, since truth is anyway only subjective and relative. The result of the rejection of objective and absolute[96] truth inevitably leads to this conclusion. Moreover, the purpose of idealist relativism is actually to present the case for the ruling class; for example, the purpose of relativist (p. 298) pragmatism (or experimentalism) is just that.

It can therefore be seen that neither metaphysical materialism nor idealist relativism can correctly solve the problem of the interrelationship between absolute and relative truth. Only materialist dialectics can provide the correct answer to the problem of the relationship between thought and existence, and consequently determine the objectivity of scientific knowledge; furthermore, it at the same time provides a correct understanding of absolute and relative truth. This is the theory of truth of materialist dialectics.

11. *On Practice* - [Refer the second translation in this volume - Ed.]

[p. 234] (p. 298) *Chapter 3: Materialist Dialectics*

The two questions of "Idealism and Materialism" and "Dialectical Materialism" have been briefly dealt with above. We come now to a systematic discussion of the problem of dialectics which has only been mentioned in outline.[97]

[p. 235] The Marxist world (or universal) view is dialectical materialism; it is not metaphysical materialism (also called mechanistic materialism). This distinction is a major issue of the utmost importance. What is the world? From ancient times until the present, there have been three major responses to this question. The first is idealism (either metaphysical or dialectical idealism), which states that the world is created by mind, or through extension, by spirit. The second is mechanistic materialism which denies that the world is a product of mind; the world is a material world, but matter (p. 299) does not develop and is unchanging. The third is the Marxist response which has overturned the two previous responses; it states that the world is not created by mind, and neither is it matter which does not develop; rather, it is a developing material world. This latter position is dialectical materialism.[98]

Is not this Marxist conception of the world, which has revolutionised the perception of the world previously held by humanity, a discourse of earth-shaking significance? There were those in the West's ancient Greece who espoused the view that the world is a developing material world; but because of the limitations of the era, it was only discussed in simple and general terms, and their view is described as naive materialism. It did not have (indeed, could not have had) a scientific base. However, its viewpoint was basically correct. Hegel created dialectical idealism, stating that the world is developmental, but is created by mind. He was a developmental idealist. His theory of development (that is, dialectics) was correct, but his developmental idealism was erroneous. In the West during the three centuries of the seventeenth, eighteenth, and nineteenth centuries, the bourgeois materialism[99] of Germany, France, and other countries was mechanistic materialism.[100] They asserted that the world is a material world, and this is correct; however, they stated that the world is machine-like in its movement, with only changes involving quantitative increase and decrease or in place, there being no qualitative change - an incorrect view. Marx inherited the naive dialectical materialism of Greece, transformed mechanistic materialism and dialectical idealism, and created dialectical materialism which hitherto had not been placed on a scientific basis, and which became the revolutionary weapon of the entire world proletariat and all oppressed peoples.

Materialist dialectics is the scientific methodology of Marxism, it is the method of knowledge and logic,[101] and yet it is a world view. The world [p. 236] is actually a developing material world: this is a world view. This world view becomes a method if used to observe the world, to study, think about, and resolve the problems of the world,[102] to lead a revolution, to do work, to engage in production, to direct warfare, and to discuss[103] a person's strengths and weaknesses; this is a methodology. There is no other single methodology apart from this; therefore in the hands of Marxists,[104] world view and methodology are a single entity, and so too are dialectics, epistemology, and logic.

We will systematically discuss materialist dialectics and its many issues - its numerous categories, laws, and principles (these several terms have one meaning).

(p. 300) What actually are the laws[105] of materialist dialectics? And of these, what are the fundamental laws and which are the subordinate laws which constitute the aspects, features, and issues of the theory of materialist dialectics which are indispensable and must be resolved?[106] Why is it that all of these laws are laws inherent in the objective world and not created subjectively? Why study and understand these laws?

The complete revolutionary theory of materialist dialectics was created by Marx and Engels, and developed by Lenin. To the present, with the victory of socialism[107] in the Soviet Union and the period of world revolution, this theory has entered a new stage of development which has enhanced and enriched its content. The following categories included in this theory are, firstly:

The law of the unity of contradictions;

The law of the transformation of quality into quantity and vice versa;

The law of the negation of the negation.[108]

These are the basic laws of materialist dialectics. Apart from the naive materialism of ancient Greece which simply and unsystematically pointed out some of the significance of these laws, and Hegel who developed these laws in an idealist manner, they have been repudiated by all metaphysical philosophies (the so-called metaphysical philosophies are theories opposed to the theory of development). It was only with Marx and Engels who transformed these laws of Hegel in a material way, that they became the most fundamental part of the Marxist world view [p. 237] and methodology.

Besides the basic laws outlined above and related to these laws are the following categories of materialist dialectics:

Essence and Appearance

(p. 301)   Form and Content

Cause and Effect

Basis and Condition

Possibility and Reality

Chance and Necessity

Necessity and Freedom[109]

Chain and Link, and so on.

Of these categories, some were previously studied in depth by metaphysical philosophies and idealist dialectics, some were studied only one-sidedly by philosophy, and some were put forward for the first time by Marxism. In the hands of Marxist revolutionary theorists and practitioners, these categories have stripped away the idealist and metaphysical husk of former philosophies, overcome their one-sidedness, and discovered their authentic form; moreover, as the era progressed, they greatly enriched their content to become an important component of revolutionary scientific methodology. The combination of these categories and the basic categories mentioned above forms a complete and profound system of materialist dialectics.

None of these laws and categories is created by human thought itself; they are the actual laws of the objective world. All idealisms assert [p. 238] spirit creates matter, and from this perspective, the tenets of philosophy, its principles, laws, and categories, are naturally created by mind. Hegel, who developed the system of dialectics, perceived dialectics in this manner. He saw the laws of dialectics not as being abstracted from the history of nature and society, but as a logical system in pure thought. After human thought has created this system, it imposes it on nature and society. Marx and Engels stripped away Hegel's mystical shell, discarded his idealism, and placed his dialectics on a material basis. Engels stated (p. 302): "It is, therefore, from the history of nature and humankind that the laws of dialectics are abstracted. For they are nothing but the most general laws of these two aspects of historical development. And indeed they can be reduced to three fundamental laws: the transformation of quality into quantity and vice versa, the unity of contradictions, and the negation of the negation".[110] While being laws of the objective world, the laws of dialectics are also laws of subjective thought, and that is because the laws of human thought are none other than the laws of the objective world reflected in the brains of humans through practice. As was discussed previously, dialectics, epistemology, and logic are one and the same.

Why do we study dialectics? We study it for no other reason than to change this world, to change the age-old relationships in this world between humans, and humans and matter. The lives of the vast majority of this world's humanity are filled with misery and suffering as a result of the oppression of the political and economic systems dominated by a minority. The people who live in China suffer a twofold cruel and inhuman oppression - national and social oppression. We must change these age-old relationships and strive for national and social liberation.

Why is it necessary to study dialectics to achieve the objective of changing China and the world? It is because dialectics is made up of the most general laws of development of nature and society; when we comprehend dialectics, we have gained a scientific weapon, and in the revolutionary practice of changing nature and society possess a theory and method suited to this practice. Materialist dialectics is itself a science (a philosophical science); it is the starting point for all sciences, and it is also a methodology. Our revolutionary practice[111] is itself also a science, called social or political science. If we don't understand dialectics, our [p. 239] affairs will be badly handled; mistakes made within the revolution are those that violate dialectics. However, if dialectics is understood, immense results can be achieved; and if all things done correctly are investigated, it will be found they conform with dialectics.

Consequently, all revolutionary comrades, and above all cadres, should diligently study dialectics.

There are those who say: many people understand practical dialectics, and moreover are practical materialists; and although they have not read books on dialectics, things that they do are done correctly, and in fact conform with materialist dialectics. They surely have no particular need to study dialectics. This sort of talk is incorrect. (p. 303) Materialist dialectics is a complete and profound science. Although revolutionaries who really do possess materialist and dialectical minds learn a great deal of dialectics from practice, it is not systematized and lacks the completeness and profundity already achieved by materialist dialectics. Therefore, they are unable to see clearly the long-term future of the movement, unable to analyse a complex process of development, unable to grasp important political links, and unable to handle the various aspects of revolutionary work. Because of this, they still need to study dialectics.

There are others who say that dialectics is abstruse and difficult to fathom, and that ordinary people have no possibility of mastering it. This is also incorrect. Dialectics encompasses the laws of nature, society and thought. Anyone with some experience of society (experience of production and class struggle) actually understands some dialectics. Those with even more experience of society actually have a greater understanding of dialectics, although their understanding remains in the chaotic state of common sense and is neither complete nor profound. It is not difficult to bring order to this commonsense dialectics and deepen it through further study. The reason why people feel dialectics is difficult is that there exist no books which explain dialectics well. In China, there are many books on dialectics which, while not incorrect, are explained poorly or none too well, and which frighten people off. Books which are good at[112] explaining dialectics employ everyday language and relate moving experiences. Sooner or later such a book must be put together. This talk of mine is also far from adequate since I have myself only just begun to study dialectics. There has been no possibility of writing a useful book on the subject as yet, although perhaps the opportunity may present itself in the future. I wish to do so, but this will be decided by how my study proceeds.

In the next section various laws of dialectics will be discussed. [There follows *On Contradiction* in the *Bujuan* text; see the third translation in this volume - Ed.]

Notes

1. Pagination in round brackets refers to the text published in *Mao Zedong Ji,* Volume VI, pp. 265-305 (hereafter *Ji*). Pagination in square brackets refers to the text published in *Mao Zedong ji bujuan,* Volume V, pp. 187-280 (hereafter *Bujuan*).

2. "(Lecture Notes)" in *Ji* only. The date 1938 appears in both *Ji* and *Bujuan*. However, this date almost certainly refers to the date of publication, rather than composition. On this issue, see the Introduction to this volume, particularly notes 2 and 17.

3. "This chapter ... materialism" in *Ji* only.

4. *Jieduan* in Ji; *jieji* in *Bujuan*, apparently a misprint.

5. "Indirectly" only in *Ji*.

6. "... the establishment of a completely new Chinese democratic republic ..." only in *Ji*.

7. "... through peaceful means..." only in *Ji*.

8. This last clause only in *Bujuan*.

9. This quote is an inverted and rather loose translation of a passage from Lenin's "On the Question of Dialectics", in V.I. Lenin, *Collected Works* (London: Lawrence & Wishart, 1961), Vol. 38, p. 363. In *Bujuan*, the inverted commas cease before "This is very true".

10. This last sentence in *Bujuan* only.

11. "... as a result of the practice of the proletariat..." in *Bujuan* only.

12. "... results..." in *Bujuan* only.

13. This sentence and the following list of headings appear in *Ji* only.

14. This sentence in *Ji* only.

15. This last clause in *Bujuan* only.

16. "... at present ..." in *Ji* only.

17. "... in order to arrive at socialism and communism..." in *Bujuan* only.

18. "adopt" in *Bujuan* only.

19. "... they will have gained..." in *Bujuan* only.

20. *Gaizao* in *Bujuan*; *Jianshe* (reconstruct) in *Ji*.

21. The last sentence in *Bujuan* only.

22. *Chenfu* in Ji; *fandong* (reactionary) in *Bujuan*.

23. Inverted commas in *Bujuan* only.

24. "One-sided" in *Bujuan* only.

25. "Fideism" is the doctrine that knowledge depends on faith or revelation.

26. "Formal logic" in *Bujuan* only.

27. "... natural world of logical concepts (*lunlilguannian de ziran*)..." in *Bujuan* only. The *Ji* text reads here as though part of the sentence has been inadvertently deleted.

28. *Lun fazhan de xueshuo* in *Bujuan*. The world "*lun*" has been left out of *Ji*, making the English translation, "this developing theory".

29. See Frederick Engels, *Anti-Dühring* (Peking: FLP, 1976), p. 180; also Frederick Engels, *Dialectics of Nature* (Moscow: FLPH, 1954), p. 353.

30. According to the editors of *Ji*, the direct quote from Lenin commences here. In *Bujuan*, it commences at "cut in two (*jiequ*)".

31. *Zhexuejia* in *Bujuan*. The *jia* has been omitted in *Ji*.

32. These quotes are from Lenin's "Conspectus of Hegel's *Science of Logic*", in *Collected Works* (Moscow: FLPH, 1963), Vol. 38, pp. 90, 190, 217.

33. "... firstly an understanding of..." in *Ji* only.

34. This last sentence in *Bujuan* only.

35. "The Chinese" in *Bujuan*.

36. "Idealists" in *Bujuan*.

37. *Bujuan* reads: "... and nicely demonstrated the correctness of the recognition by the materialist viewpoint of dialectical materialism of the materiality and objective existence of the world".

38. "history" in *Ji* only.

39. "only" in *Bujuan* only.

40. This last clause in *Bujuan* only.

41. *Yuanli* (principle, tenet) in *Ji*.

42. See *Dialectics of Nature*, pp. 92-93.

43. A quotation from Dong Zhongshu (179-104BC). Mao also uses this quotation in the official text of *On Contradiction*. See *Selected Works*, I, p. 313.

44. "... as the unity and motion of the limitless diversity of the world's matter", in *Bujuan* only.

45. This quote is drawn from Engels, *Dialectics of Nature*, p. 328. I have stayed as close to the official Soviet English translation as the Chinese permits.

46. See Lenin's "Conspectus of Hegel's book *Lectures on the History of Philosophy*", in Collected Works, Vol. 38, p. 256. Lenin states, "... the universal principle of development must be combined, linked, made to correspond with the universal principle of the *unity of the world,* nature, motion, matter, etc." (emphasis in original).

47. "molecules" in *Bujuan* only.

48. This quote is drawn from Engels, *Dialectics of Nature*, p. 330. Emphasis in original. The official Soviet English translation has been used.

49. Parentheses in *Bujuan* only.

50. Engels, *Dialectics of Nature*, p. 313. Emphasis in original. The official Soviet English translation has been used.

51. The paragraphing of the following four paragraphs is based on *Ji.* They are all incorporated in one paragraph in the *Bujuan* text.

52. *Renlei* in *Bujuan*; *Keguan* (objective) in *Ji.*

53. For a lengthy discussion on space and time, and the Kantian and Machian conceptions of them, see V.I. Lenin, *Materialism and Empirio-Criticism* (Peking: FLP, 1972), pp. 202-218.

54. "Note (*xianzhu*)" in *Bujuan* only.

55. "time" in *Bujuan* only.

56. Lenin, *Materialism and Empirio-Criticism*, p. 203. The translation used here is taken from this source.

57. *Lishizhuyi.* Mao also uses this term in his 1938 speech "On the New Stage". See *Ji*, Vol. 6, p. 260. Stuart Schram has translated the sentence "Women shi Makesizhuyi de lishizhuyizhe" as "We are Marxist historicists". See *The Political Thought of Mao Tse-tung* (Harmondsworth: Penguin, 1969, revised ed.), p. 172. For my reasons for rejecting this translation, see N.J. Knight, *Mao and History: An Interpretive Essay on Some Problems in Mao Zedong's Philosophy of History* (Unpublished Ph.D thesis, University of London, 1983), pp. 222-223.

58. "Development" in *Bujuan* only.

59. "Form (*xingtai*)" in *Ji* only.

60. This last clause in *Bujuan* only.

61. This last sentence in *Bujuan* only.

62. "All (*fan*)" in *Bujuan* only.

63. The negative *bu* omitted from *Ji.*

64. "Left-wing" in *Bujuan.*

65.   *Bujuan* reads: "They understand consciousness as a physico-chemical physiological process, and consider that the study of the behaviour of this advanced substance can be carried out through the study of objective physiology and biology. They do not understand the qualitatively particular characteristics of the essence of consciousness, and do not recognise that consciousness is a product of the social practice of humankind".

66.   "Relationship" in *Bujuan* only.

67.   "Principles" in *Ji* only.

68.   *Zonghe* in *Bujuan*; *liangmeng* (alliance, coalition) in *Ji*.

69.   "... and the 'mutual assistance' of these two methods" in *Bujuan* only.

70.   Identity (*yizhi*) in *Bujuan* only.

71.   "Stone" appears in *Bujuan* only.

72.   No paragraph break in *Ji*.

73.   *Wuli* in *Bujuan*; *wufa* in *Ji*.

74.   *Quanti* in *Ji*, possibly a typographical error.

75.   *zhuti* in *Bujuan*; *zhuguan* in *Ji*.

76.   *Zizaizhiwu* in *Bujuan*; *Zizailun* in *Ji*.

77.   *Sixiang*.

78.   Apparent typographical error in *Ji*; the negative *bu* appears before "approach" (*jiejin*). Replaced by *zhi* in *Bujuan*.

79.   Lenin, *Materialism and Empirio-Criticism*, pp. 152-153. Emphasis in original. The official Soviet English translation has been used. In *Ji*, the quotation is incorrectly extended for a further sentence.

80.   *Bu* in *Ji*, an apparent typographical error; replaced by *you* in *Bujuan*.

81.   Lenin, "Conspectus of Hegel's *Science of Logic*", *Collected Works*, Vol. 38, p. 195. The official Soviet English translation has been used. The Chinese version reads slightly differently. The quote is incorrectly broken in two in *Bujuan*.

82.   *Ganjuezhuyi*: the doctrine that sensation is the sole origin of knowledge.

83.   Lenin, "Conspectus of Hegel's *Science of Logic*", *Collected Works*, Vol. 38, p. 182. The Soviet English translation has been modified, as the quotation has been slightly altered in the Chinese texts.

84.   Given as a direct quote in *Ji*, but not in *Bujuan*.

85.   "Content" (*neirong*) in *Bujuan* only.

86.   This last clause in *Bujuan* only.

87.   "Guidance" (*zhidao*) in *Bujuan* only.

88.   This sentence in parentheses in *Ji* only. The last clause in *Ji* reads: "it is the truth of the objective world".

89.   *Puji* in *Bujuan*; *dongxi* in *Ji*.

90.   The following paragraph in *Bujuan* only.

91.   Engels, *Dialectics of Nature*, p. 310.

92.   This sentence in *Bujuan* only.

93.   Paragraph break in *Bujuan* only.

94.   *Chengren* in *Bujuan*; *fouren* in Ji.

95.   *zhuyi*, in *Bujuan* only.

96.   "Subjective" (*zhuguan*) in *Ji*.

97.   Paragraph break in *Bujuan* only.

98.   Paragraph break in *Bujuan* only.

99.   "Idealism" in *Ji*.

100.   "Idealism" in *Ji*.

101.   "Logic" in *Bujuan* only.

102.   "Think about and resolve the problems of the world" in *Bujuan* only.

103.   *Yilun* in *Bujuan*; *renshi* (to know) in *Ji*.

104.   "Marxism" in *Ji*.

105.   *Faze.*

106.   Paragraph break in *Ji*.

107.   "Revolution" in *Ji*.

108.   See Engels, *Dialectics of Nature,* pp. 83-91. In this source, the law on contradiction is referred to as "the law of the interpenetration of opposites".

109.   In *Bujuan* only.

110.   Engels, *Dialectics of Nature*, p. 83. Mao has left out a significant clause in Engels' quote, perhaps to make his attack on idealism more forceful. The quote is as follows, with the clause omitted by Mao shown in emphasis:

"It is, therefore, from the history of nature and human society that the laws of dialectics are abstracted. For they are nothing but the most general laws of these two aspects of historical development, *as well as of thought itself....*"

111.   "Practice" in *Bujuan* only.

112.   "Good at..." in *Bujuan* only.

3 | On Practice

(On the Relation between Knowledge and Practice, **between Theory and Reality**, between Knowing and Doing).

[p. 220] Before Marx, materialism examined the problem of knowledge apart from the social nature of man and apart from his historical development, and was therefore incapable of understanding the dependence of knowledge on social practice, that is, the dependence of knowledge on production and class struggle.

Above all, Marxists regard man's activity in production as the most fundamental practical activity, the determinant of all his other activities. Man's [p. 221] knowledge depends mainly on his activity in material production through which he comes gradually to understand the phenomena, the properties of nature (the laws of nature),[1] and the relations between himself and nature; and through his activity in production he also comes **at the same time** to understand the relations that exist between

Source: Takeuchi Minoru (ed.), *Mao Zedong Ji Bujuan* [supplements to the Collected Works of Mao Zedong] (Tokyo: Sososha, 1984), Vol. V, pp. 220-234. Page numbers in square brackets refer to this source. Bold type refers to sections *not* included in the official version contained in *Selected Works of Mao Tse-tung*. Translated and annotated by Nick Knight.

man and man.[2] None of this knowledge can be acquired apart from activity in production.

Every person,[3] as a member of society, joins in common effort with the other members,[4] and engages in production to meet man's material needs.[5] This is the primary source from which human knowledge develops.

Man's social practice is not confined to activity in production, but has taken many other forms - class struggle, political life, scientific pursuits;[6] in short, as a social being, man participates in all spheres of the practical life of society. Thus man[7] comes **to understand**[8] the different and **complex** relations between man and man, not only through his material life but also through his political and cultural life (both of which are intimately bound up with material life). Of these other types of social practice, class struggle in particular, in all its various forms, exerts a profound influence on the development of man's knowledge; **and this is because**, in class society,[9] every kind of thinking, without exception, is stamped with the brand of a class.[10]

Because of this, Marxists hold that man's social practice alone is the criterion of the truth of his knowledge of the external world. What actually happens is that man's knowledge **is strengthened**[11] only when he achieves the anticipated results in the process of social practice (material production, class struggle or scientific experiment). **Why is it that peasants are unable to harvest their crops, that workers are unable to use their tools, that there are strikes and struggle, that troops go to war, and that the national revolution has not achieved victory? It is because man's knowledge has not faithfully reflected the regularities** (*guilüxing*) **of the processes of the external world, and therefore cannot achieve the anticipated results in his practical activities.** If a man wants to succeed[12] (that is, to achieve the anticipated results),[13] he must bring his ideas into correspondence with the laws of the objective external world; if they do not correspond, he will fail in his practice. After he fails, he draws his lessons, corrects his ideas to make them correspond to the laws of the external world, and can thus turn failure into success; this is what is meant by "failure is the mother of success" and "a fall into the pit, a gain in your wit". The dialectical-materialist theory of knowledge [p. 222] places practice in the primary position, holding that human knowledge can in no way be separated from practice and repudiating all the erroneous theories which deny the importance of practice or separate knowledge from practice. Thus Lenin said, "Practice is higher than (theoretical) knowledge, for it has not only the dignity of universality, but also of immediate actuality".[14] The Marxist philosophy of dialectical materialism has two outstanding characteristics. One is its class nature: it openly avows that dialectical materialism is in the service of the proletariat. The other is its practicality: it emphasizes the dependence of theory on practice, emphasizes that theory **has its origin in** practice[15] and in turn serves practice. The truth of any knowledge or theory is determined not by subjective feelings, but by objective results in social practice. Only social practice can be the criterion of truth. The standpoint of practice is the primary and basic standpoint in the dialectical materialist theory of knowledge.

But how then does human knowledge arise from practice and in turn serve practice? This will become clear if we look at the process of development of knowledge.

In the process of practice, man at first sees only the phenomenal side, the separate aspects, the external relations of things. For instance, on the first day or two in Yan'an, **a Guomindang inspection team**[16] sees its topography, streets, and houses, they meet many people, attend banquets, evening parties, and mass meetings, hear talk of various kinds and read various documents, all these being the phenomena, the separate aspects and the external relations of things. That is called the perceptual stage of cognition, namely, the stage of sense perceptions and impressions. That is, these particular things in Yan'an act on the sense organs of the members of the observation group, evoke sense perceptions and give rise in their brains to many impressions together with a rough sketch of the external relations among these impressions: this is the first stage of cognition. At this stage, man cannot as yet form concepts, which are deeper, or draw **theoretical** conclusions.[17]

[p. 223] As social practice continues, things that give rise to man's sense perceptions and impressions in the course of his practice are repeated many times; then a sudden change[18] takes place in the brain in the process of cognition, and concepts are formed. Concepts are no longer the phenomena, the separate aspects and the external relations of things; they grasp the essence, the totality and the internal relations of things. Between concepts and sense perceptions there is not only a quantitative but also a qualitative difference. Proceeding further, by means of judgement and inference one is able to draw **theoretical** conclusions.[19] The expression in *San Guo Yan Yi*, "Knit the brows and a stratagem comes to mind", or in everyday language, "let me think it over", refers to man's use of concepts in the brain to form judgements and inferences. **This is the rational stage of knowledge, otherwise known as its logical stage.** This is the second stage of cognition. When the members of the observation group have collected various data, and what is more, have "thought them over", they are able to arrive at the judgement that the "Communist Party's policy of the National United Front Against Japan **and cooperation between the Guomindang and the Communist Party** is thorough, sincere and genuine". Having made this judgement, they can, if they too are genuine about uniting to save the nation, go a step further and draw the following conclusion, **"Cooperation between the Guomindang and the Communist Party can succeed"**.[20] This stage of conception, judgement, and inference is the **most**[21] important stage in the entire process of knowing a thing.[22] **The real task of knowing is not perceptual knowledge, but rational knowledge.** The real task of knowing is, through perception, to arrive at thought, to arrive[23] at the comprehension of the internal contradictions of objective things, of their laws and of the internal relations between one process and another, **of the internal relations between objective processes**, that is, to arrive at theoretical[24] knowledge. To repeat, logical knowledge differs from perceptual knowledge in that perceptual knowledge pertains to the separate aspects, the phenomena and the external relations of things, whereas logical knowledge takes a big stride forward to reach the totality, the essence and the internal relations of things and discloses the inner contradictions in the surrounding world. Therefore, logical knowledge is capable of grasping the development of the surrounding world in its totality, in the internal relations of all its aspects.

[p. 224] The dialectical-materialist theory of the process of development of knowledge, basing itself on practice and proceeding from the shallower to the deeper, was never worked out by anybody before the rise of Marxism. Marxist **dialectical** materialism solved this problem correctly for the first time, pointing out both materialistically and dialectically the deepening movement of cognition, the movement in which man in society progresses from perceptual knowledge to logical knowledge in his complex, constantly recurring practice of production and class struggle. Lenin said, "The abstraction of *matter*, of a *law* of nature, the abstraction of *value* etc., in short *all* scientific (correct, serious, not absurd) abstractions reflect nature more deeply, truly and completely".[25] **Lenin has also pointed out**[26]: each of the two stages in the process of cognition has its own characteristics, with the knowledge manifesting itself as perceptual at the lower stage and logical at the higher stage, but that both are stages in an integrated process of cognition. The perceptual and the rational are qualitatively different, but are not divorced from each other; they are unified on the basis of practice. Our practice proves that what is perceived cannot at once be comprehended and that only what is comprehended can be more deeply perceived. Perception only solves the problem of phenomena; **comprehension**[27] alone can solve the problem of essence. The solving of both these problems is not separable in the slightest degree from practice. Whoever wants to know a thing has no way of doing so except by coming into contact with it, that is, by living (practising) in its environment. In feudal society it was impossible to know the laws of capitalist society in advance because capitalism had not yet emerged, the relevant practice was lacking. Marxism could be the product only of capitalist society. In the era of laissez-faire capitalism, it[28] could not know [29] certain laws peculiar to the era of imperialism beforehand, because imperialism[30] had not yet emerged and the relevant practice was lacking; only

Leninism[31] could undertake this task. **Marxism-Leninism also could not have been produced in the economically backward colonies, because although they were contemporaneous with them, there was a difference in location.** Leaving aside their genius, the reason why Marx, Engels, and Lenin[32] could work out their theories was mainly that they personally took part in the practice of the class struggle and the scientific experimentation of their time; lacking this condition, no genius could have succeeded. The saying, "without stepping outside his gate the scholar knows all the wide world's affairs", was mere empty talk in past times when technology was undeveloped [p. 225]. Even though this saying can be valid in the present age of developed technology, the people with real personal knowledge are those engaged in practice the wide world over. And it is only when these people have come to "know" through their practice and when their knowledge has reached him through writing and technical media that the "scholar" can indirectly "know all the world's affairs". If you want to know a certain thing or a certain class of things directly, you must personally participate in practice[33] to change reality, to change that thing or class of things, for only thus can you come into contact with them as phenomena; only through personal participation in practice[34] to change reality can you uncover the essence of that thing or class of things and comprehend them. This is the path to knowledge which every man actually travels, though some people, deliberately distorting matters, argue to the contrary. The most ridiculous person in the world is the "knowall" who picks up a smattering of hearsay knowledge and proclaims himself "the world's Number One authority"; this merely shows that he has not taken a proper measure of himself. Knowledge is a matter of science, and no dishonesty or conceit whatsoever is permissable. What is required is definitely the reverse - honesty and modesty. If you want knowledge, you must take part in the practice of changing reality. If you want to know the taste of a pear, you must change the pear by eating it yourself. If you want to know the structure and properties of the atom, you must make the experiments of the chemist[35] to change the state of the atom. If you want to know the **concrete** theory and methods of revolution, you must take part in revolution. All genuine knowledge originates in direct experience. But one cannot have direct experience of everything; as a matter of fact, most of our knowledge comes from indirect experience, for example, all knowledge from past times and foreign lands. To our ancestors and to foreigners, such knowledge was - or is - a matter of direct experience, and this knowledge is reliable if in the course of their direct experience the requirement of "scientific **(correct, serious, not absurd)** abstraction", spoken of by Lenin, was - or is - fulfilled,[36] otherwise it is not reliable. Hence a man's knowledge consists only of two parts, that which comes from direct experience and that which comes from indirect experience. Moreover, what is indirect experience for me is direct experience for other people. Consequently, considered as a whole, knowledge of any kind is inseparable from direct experience. All knowledge originates in perception of the objective external world through man's physical sense organs. Anyone who denies such perception denies direct experience, or denies personal participation in the practice that changes reality, is not a materialist. That is why the "know all" is ridiculous. **Chinese merchants have a saying: "If one wants to profit [p. 226] from the household animals, one must live with them".** This holds true for the profit making of the merchant,[37] and also holds true for the theory of knowledge. There can be no knowledge apart from practice.

To make clear the dialectical-materialist movement of cognition arising on the basis of practice which changes reality - to make clear the gradually deepening movement of cognition - a few additional concrete examples are given below.

In its knowledge of **the process** of capitalism,[38] the proletariat was only in the perceptual stage of cognition in the first period of its practice, the period of machine-smashing and spontaneous struggle; the proletariat was still then a "class-in-itself". But when it reached the **later** period[39] of its practice, the period of conscious and organized economic and political struggles, the proletariat was able to comprehend the essence of capitalist society, the relations of exploitation between social classes,[40] and create the theory of Marxism; and it was able to do so because of its own practice and because of the **lessons taught it through** experience of prolonged struggle.[41] It was then that the proletariat became a "class-for-itself".

Similarly with the Chinese people's knowledge of imperialism. The first stage was one of superficial, perceptual knowledge, as shown in the indiscriminate anti-foreign struggles of the Movement of the Taiping Heavenly Kingdom, the Yi Ho Tuan Movement, and so on. It was only in the second stage that the Chinese people reached the stage of rational knowledge, saw the internal and external contradictions of imperialism and saw the essential truth that imperialism had aligned itself with China's[42] feudal classes to oppress and exploit the great masses of the Chinese people. This knowledge began about the time of the May 4th Movement.[43]

Next, let us consider war. If those who lead a war lack experience of war, then at the initial stage they will not understand the profound laws pertaining to the directing of a specific war (such as our **Soviet** War[44] of the past decade). At the initial stage they will merely experience a good deal of fighting and, what is more, suffer many defeats. But this experience (the experience of battles won and especially of battles lost) enables them to comprehend the inner thread of the whole war, namely the laws of that specific war, to understand its strategy and tactics, and consequently to direct [p. 227] the war with confidence. If, at such a moment, the command is turned over to an inexperienced person, then he too will have to suffer a number of defeats (gain experience) before he can comprehend the true laws of the war.

"I am not sure I can handle it". We often hear this remark when a comrade hesitates to accept an assignment. Why is he unsure of himself? Because he has no systematic[45] understanding of the content and circumstances of the assignment, or because he has had little or no contact with such work, and so the laws governing it are beyond him. After a detailed analysis of the nature and circumstances of the assignment, he will feel more sure of himself and do it willingly. If he spends some time at the job (and gains experience)[46] and if he is a person who is willing to look into **objective** matters with an open mind and not one who approaches problems subjectively, one-sidedly and superficially, then he can draw conclusions for himself as to how to go about the job and do it with much more courage. Only those who are subjective, one-sided, and superficial in their approach to problems will smugly issue orders or directives the moment they arrive on the scene, without considering the circumstances, without viewing things in their totality (their history and their present state as a whole) and without getting to the essence of things (their nature and the internal relations between one thing and another). Such people are bound to trip and fall.

Thus it can be seen that the first step in the process of cognition is contact with the objects of the external world; this belongs to the stage of perception. The second step is to synthesize the data of perception by arranging and reconstructing them; this belongs to the stage of conception, judgement, and inference. It is only when the data of perception are very rich (not fragmentary) and correspond to reality (are not illusory) that they can be the basis for forming correct concepts and theories.

Here two important points must be emphasized. The first, which has been stated before but should be repeated here, is the dependence of rational knowledge upon perceptual knowledge. Anyone who thinks that rational knowledge need not be derived from perceptual knowledge is an idealist. In the history of philosophy [p. 228] there is the "rationalist" school that admits the reality only of reason and not of experience, believing that reason alone is reliable while perceptual experience is not; this school errs by turning things upside down. The rational is reliable precisely because it has its source in sense perceptions, otherwise it would be like water without a source, a tree without roots, subjective, self-engendered, and unreliable. As to the sequence in the process of cognition, perceptual experience comes first; we stress the significance of social practice in the process of cognition precisely because social practice alone can give rise to human knowledge and it alone can start man on the acquisition of perceptual experience from the objective world. For a person who shuts his eyes, stops his ears and totally cuts himself off from the objective world there can be no such thing as knowledge. Knowledge begins[47] with experience - this is the materialism[48] of knowledge.

The second point is that knowledge needs to be deepened,[49] needs to be developed to the rational stage - this is the dialectics of the theory of knowledge. To think that knowledge can stop at the lower perceptual stage and that perceptual knowledge alone is reliable while rational knowledge is not would be to repeat the historical **theory**[50] of "empiricism". This theory errs in failing to understand that, although the data of perception reflect certain realities in the objective world (I am not speaking here of idealist empiricism which confines experience to[51] introspection), they are merely one-sided and superficial, reflecting things incompletely and not reflecting their essence. Fully to reflect a thing in its totality, to reflect its essence, to reflect its inherent laws, it is necessary through the exercise of thought to reconstruct the rich data of sense perception, discarding the dross and selecting the essential, eliminating the false and retaining the true, proceeding from the one to the other and from the outside to the inside, in order to form a system of concepts and theories - it is necessary to make a **change**[52] from perceptual to rational knowledge. Such reconstructed knowledge is not more empty or more unreliable; on the contrary, whatever has been scientifically reconstructed in the process of cognition, on the basis of practice, reflects objective reality, as Lenin said, more deeply, more truly, more fully. As against this, vulgar "practical men" respect experience but despise theory, and therefore cannot have a comprehensive view of an entire objective process, lack clear direction and long-range perspective, and are complacent over occasional successes and glimpses of the truth. If such persons [p. 229] direct a revolution, they will lead it up a blind alley.

Rational knowledge depends upon perceptual knowledge and perceptual knowledge remains to be developed into rational knowledge - this is the dialectical-materialist theory of knowledge.   In philosophy, neither rationalism nor empiricism[53] understands the historical or the dialectical nature of knowledge, and although each of these schools contains one aspect of the truth (here I am referring to materialist, not to idealist, rationalism and empiricism), both are wrong on the theory of knowledge as a whole. The dialectical-materialist movement of knowledge from the perceptual to the rational holds true for a minor process of cognition (for instance,[54] a single thing or task) as well as for a major process of cognition (for instance,[55] a whole society or a revolution).

But the movement of knowledge does not end here. If the dialectical-materialist movement of knowledge were to stop at rational knowledge, only half the problem would be dealt with. And as far as Marxist philosophy is concerned, only the less important half at that. Marxist philosophy holds that the most important problem does not lie in understanding the laws of the objective world and thus being able to explain it,[56] but in applying the knowledge of these laws actively to change the world.[57] From the Marxist viewpoint, theory is important, and its importance is fully expressed in Lenin's statement, "Without revolutionary theory there can be no revolutionary movement".[58] **Each of man's actions (practice) is guided by his thought (*sixiang*), so naturally without thought there can be no action whatsoever.** But Marxism emphasizes the importance of theory precisely and only because it can guide action. If we have a correct theory but merely prate about it, pigeonhole it, and do not put it into practice, then that theory, however good, is of no **use**.[59] Knowledge begins with practice and theoretical knowledge is acquired through practice and must then return to practice. The active function of knowledge manifests itself not only in the active leap from perceptual to rational knowledge, but - and this is more important - it must manifest itself in the leap from rational knowledge to revolutionary practice. The knowledge which grasps the laws **of the reality** of the world, must be directed to the practice of changing the world, must be applied anew in the practice of production, in the practice of revolutionary class struggle and revolutionary national struggle and in the [p. 230] practice of scientific experiment. This is the process of testing and developing theory, the continuation of the whole process of cognition. The problem of whether theory **or rational knowledge** corresponds to objective reality is not, and cannot be, completely solved in the movement of knowledge from the perceptual to the rational, mentioned above. The only way to solve this problem completely is to redirect rational knowledge to social practice, apply theory to practice and see whether it can achieve the objectives one has in mind. Many theories of natural science are held to be true not only because they were so considered when they were discovered,[60] but because they have been verified in subsequent scientific practice. Similarly, Marxism[61] is held to be true not only because it was so considered when it was scientifically formulated by Marx **and others**[62] but because it has been verified in the subsequent practice of revolutionary class struggle.[63] **Whether** dialectical materialism is the truth **or not depends on whether**[64] it is impossible for anyone to escape from its domain in his practice. **The practice of** the history of[65] knowledge tells us that the truth of many theories is incomplete and that this incompleteness is remedied through the test of practice. Many theories are erroneous and it is through the test of practice that their errors are corrected. That is why "practice is the criterion of truth"[66] and why "the standpoint of practice is first and fundamental in the theory of knowledge".[67] Stalin has well said, "Theory **which departs from practice is empty theory, practice which departs from theory** gropes in the dark".[68]

When we get to this point, is the movement of knowledge completed? Our answer is: it is and yet it is not. When men in society throw themselves into the practice of changing a certain **definite** objective process (whether natural or social) at a certain **definite** stage of its development, they can, as a result of the reflection of the objective process in their brains and the exercise of their subjective activity, advance ideas, theories, plans, or programmes which correspond in general to the laws of that objective process. They then apply these ideas, theories, plans, or programmes in practice in the same objective process. And if they can realize the aims they have in mind, that is, if in that same process of practice they can translate, or on the whole translate, those previously formulated ideas, theories, plans, or programmes into fact, then the movement of knowledge may be considered completed with regard to that particular process. In the [p. 231] process of changing nature, take for example the fulfillment of an engineering plan, the verification of a scientific hypothesis, the manufacture of an implement, or the reaping of a crop; or in the process of changing society, take for example the victory of a strike, victory in a war, the fulfillment of an educational plan, **the establishment of an organization to save the nation**. All these may be considered the realization of aims one has in mind. But generally, whether in the practice of changing nature or of changing society, men's original ideas, theories, plans, or programmes are seldom realized without any alteration. This is because people engaged in changing reality are usually subject to numerous limitations; they are limited not only by existing scientific and technological conditions but also by[69] the degree to which the objective process has become manifest (the aspect and the essence of the objective process have not yet been fully revealed). In such a situation, ideas, theories, plans, or programmes are usually altered partially and sometimes even wholly, because of the discovery of unforeseen circumstances in the course of practice. That is to say, it does happen that the original ideas, theories,[70] plans, or programmes fail to correspond with reality either in whole or in part and are wholly or partially incorrect. In many instances, failures have to be repeated many times before errors in knowledge can be corrected and correspondence with the laws of the objective process achieved, and consequently before the subjective can be transformed into **correct knowledge of** the objective (or in other words, before the anticipated results can be achieved in practice).[71] But when that point is reached, no matter how, the movement of human knowledge regarding a certain **definite** objective process at a certain **definite** stage of its development may be considered completed.

However, so far as the progression of the process is concerned, the movement of human knowledge is not completed. Every process, whether in the realm of nature or of society, progresses and develops by reasons of **society's**[72] contradiction and struggle, and the movement of human knowledge should also progress and develop along with it. As far as social movements are concerned, **valuable**[73] revolutionary leaders must not only be good at correcting their theories, ideas,[74] plans, or programmes when errors are discovered, as has already been indicated above; but when a certain **definite** objective process has already developed from one **definite** stage of development to another, they must also be good at making themselves and[75] their fellow revolutionaries progress in their subjective knowledge along with it, that is to say, [p. 232] they must ensure that the proposed new revolutionary tasks and new working methods[76] correspond to the new changes in the situation. In a revolutionary period the situation changes very rapidly; if the knowledge of revolutionaries does not change rapidly in accordance with the changed situation, they will be unable to lead the revolution to victory.[77] It often happens, however, that thinking lags behind reality; this is because man's cognition suffers from numerous limitations.[78] **Many humans are limited by class conditions (the reactionary exploiting class has no knowledge with the capacity for truth, and which as a result has no capacity for transforming the universe; on the contrary, they have become the enemy which obstructs knowledge of the truth and the transformation of the world). Some humans are limited by the division of labour (the division between mental and manual labour, and the division between the various industries), while some are limited by originally erroneous ideas (idealism and mechanism and so on; many are exploiting elements, but there are also exploited elements, and this is due to the education of the exploiting elements). However, a general reason is the limitation which results from the historical condition of the level of technology and science. The proletariat and its political party should utilise their own naturally superior class conditions (which no other class possesses), utilise the new technology and science, and employ Marxism's world view and methodology; and closely relying on revolutionary practice as its basis, ensure that their knowledge changes as does the objective situation change, ensure that the logical**

keeps abreast of the historical, so that they attain the goal of completely transforming the world.[79] We are opposed to diehards in the revolutionary ranks whose thinking fails to advance with changing objective circumstances and has manifested itself historically as Right opportunism. **In China, the Chen Duxiu-ism of 1927, and Bukharinism in the Soviet Union were of this type.** These people fail to see that the struggle of opposites has already pushed the objective process forward while their knowledge has stopped at the old stage. This is characteristic of the thinking of all diehards. Their thinking is divorced from social practice, and they cannot march ahead to guide the chariot of society; they simply trail behind, grumbling that it goes too fast and trying to drag it back or turn it in the opposite direction.

We are opposed to "Left" phrase-mongering. **China's Li Lisan-ism of 1930, Trotskyism in the Soviet Union when it could still be regarded as a Communist faction [p. 233] (but which has now become a most reactionary faction), and ultra-left thought in all countries of the world, are all of this sort.** The thinking of "Leftists" outstrips a given stage of development of the objective process; some regard their fantasies as truth, while others strain to realize in the present an ideal which can only be realized in the future. They alienate themselves from the current practice of the majority of the people and from the realities of the day, and show themselves adventurist in their actions.

Idealism and mechanistic thinking (*jixielun*),[80] opportunism and adventurism, **none of these is based on the epistemology of dialectical materialism**, and are all characterized by the breach between the subjective and the objective, by the separation of knowledge from practice. The Marxist[81] theory of knowledge, characterized as it is by scientific social practice, cannot but resolutely oppose these wrong ideologies. Marxists recognize that in the absolute and general process of development of the universe, the development of each particular process is relative, and that hence, in absolute truth,[82] man's knowledge of a particular process at any given stage of development is only relative truth.[83]   The development of an objective process is full of contradictions and struggles, and so is the development of the movement of human knowledge. All the dialectical movements of the objective world can sooner or later be reflected in knowledge.[84] In practice,[85] the process of[86] developing and passing away is infinite, and so is the process of coming into being, developing and passing away in human knowledge. As man's practice which changes objective reality in accordance with given theories, ideas,[87] plans, or programmes, advances further and further, his knowledge of objective reality likewise becomes deeper and deeper. The movement of change in the world of objective reality is never-ending and so is man's cognition of truth through practice.[88] Marxism[89] has in no way exhausted truth but ceaselessly opens up roads to the knowledge of truth in the course of practice. Our conclusion is the concrete, historical unity of the subjective and the objective, of theory and practice, of knowing and doing, and we are opposed to all erroneous ideologies, whether "Left" or "Right",[90] which depart from concrete history.

In the whole universe, in the present epoch of the development of nature and society, the responsibility of correctly knowing and changing the world[91] has been placed by history upon the shoulders of the proletariat and its party. This process, the practice of changing the world, which is determined in accordance with scientific knowledge, has already reached a historic moment in the world and in China, [p. 234] a great moment unprecedented in human history, that is, the moment for completely banishing darkness from the world and from China and for changing the world into a world of light such as never previously existed. The struggle of the proletariat and the revolutionary people to change the world comprises the fulfillment of the following tasks: to change the objective world, and at the same time, their own subjective world - to change their cognitive ability and change the relations between the subjective and the objective world. Such a change has already come about in one part of the globe, in the Soviet Union. There the people are pushing forward this process of change, for themselves and the world. The people of China and the rest of the world are either just beginning to go through, or will go through, such a process. And the objective world which is to be changed also includes all the opponents of change, who, in order to be changed, must go through a stage of compulsion before they can enter the stage of voluntary, conscious change. The epoch of world communism will be reached when all mankind voluntarily and consciously changes itself and the world.

Produce[92] the truth through practice, and again through practice verify and develop the truth. Start from perceptual knowledge and actively develop it into rational knowledge; then start from rational knowledge and actively guide revolutionary prctice to change both the subjective and the objective world. Practice, knowledge, again practice, and again knowledge. This form **develops**[93] in endless cycles, and with each cycle the content of practice and knowledge rises to a higher level. Such is the whole of the dialectical-materialist theory of knowledge, and such is the dialectical-materialist theory of the unity of knowing and doing.

Notes

1. No brackets in the official text, in which the clause 'the laws of nature' (*ziran de guilüxing*) appears independently of the previous clause.

2. Official text reads: "... he also gradually comes to understand, in varying degrees, certain relations that exist between man and man". *Selected Works of Mao Tse-tung* (Peking: FLP, 1965), Vol. I, p. 295 (hereafter SWI); also *Mao Zedong Xuanji* (Beijing: Renmin Chubanshe, 1966), Vol. I, p. 260 (hereafter XJI).

3. Official texts reads: "In a classless society every person ..."; SWI, p. 295; XJI, p. 260.

4. Addition in official text: "... enters into definite relations of production with them..."; SWI, p. 295; XJI, p. 260.

5. Addition in official text: "In all class societies, the members of the different social classes also enter, in different ways, into definite relations of production and engage in production to meet their material needs". SWI, pp. 295-296; XJI, p. 260.

6. Official text reads: "... scientific and artistic pursuits..."; SWI, p. 296; XJI, p. 260.

7. Addition in official text: "..., in varying degrees, ..."; SWI, p. 296; XJI, p. 260.

8. *liaojie; zhidao* in official text; SWI, p. 296; XJI, p. 260.

9. Addition in official text: "... everyone lives as a member of a particular class..."; SWI, p. 296; XJI, p. 260.

10. Major addition to official text:

"Marxists hold that in human society activity in production develops step by step from a lower to a higher level and that consequently man's knowledge, whether of nature or of society, also develops step by step from a lower to a higher level, that is, from the shallower to the deeper, from the one-sided to the many-sided. For a very long period in history, men were necessarily confined to a one-sided understanding of the history of society because, for one thing, the bias of the exploiting classes always distorted history and, for another, the small scale of production limited man's outlook. It was not until the modern proletariat emerged along with immense forces of production (large-scale industry) that man was able to acquire a comprehensive, historical understanding of the development of society and turn this knowledge into a science, the science of Marxism". SWI, p. 296; XJI, p. 260.

11. Official text reads: "... is verified ..."; SWI, p. 296; XJI, p. 261.

12. Addition to official text: "... in his work..."; SWI, p. 296; XJI, p. 261.

13. No brackets in official text.

14. This quote has been reproduced from the official text, although there are some minor differences between the two Chinese texts. The quote is from V.I. Lenin, "Conspectus of Hegel's *The Science of Logic*", *Collected Works* (Moscow: FLPH, 1958), Vol. 38, p. 205.

15. Official text reads: "... theory is based on practice..."; SWI, p. 297; XJI, p. 261.

16. Official text reads: "... some people from outside..."; SWI, p. 297; XJI, p. 261.

17. Official text reads: "... logical conclusions"; SWI, p. 297; XJI, p. 262.

18. Addition in official text: "... (leap) ..."; SWI, p. 298; XJI, p. 262.

19. Official text reads: "... logical conclusions"; SWI, p. 298; XJI, p. 262.

20. Official text reads: "The National United Front Against Japan can succeed"; SWI, p. 298; XJI, p. 262.

21. Official text reads: "... more ..."; SWI, p. 298; XJI, p. 262.

22.   Addition in official text: "...; it is the stage of rational knowledge"; SWI, p. 298; XJI, p. 262.

23.   Addition in official text: "... step by step ..."; SWI, p. 298; XJI, p. 262.

24.   Official text reads: "... logical..."; SWI, p. 298; XJI, p. 262.

25.   This quote has been reproduced from the official text, although there are some minor literary differences between the two Chinese texts. The quote is from V.I. Lenin, "Conspectus of Hegel's *The Science of Logic*", *Collected Works*, Vol. 38, p. 161. Emphases in the official Chinese English translation.

26.   Official text reads: "Marxism-Leninism holds that..."; SWI, p. 299; XJI, p. 263.

27.   *lijie*; "theory" (*lilun*) in official text; SWI, p. 299; XJI, p. 263.

28.   Official text reads: "Marx..."; SWI, p. 299; XJI, p. 264.

29.   Official text reads: "...concretely know..."; SWI, p. 299; XJI, p. 264.

30.   Addition in official text: "..., the last stage of capitalism,..."; SWI, p. 299; XJI, p. 264.

31.   Official text reads: "... Lenin and Stalin..."; SWI, p. 299; XJI, p. 264.

32.   Addition in official text: "... and Stalin..."; SWI, p. 299; XJI, p. 264.

33.   Official text reads: "... the practical struggle..."; SWI, p. 300; XJI, p. 264.

34.   Official text reads: "... the practical struggle..."; SWI, p. 300; XJI, p. 264.

35.   Official text reads: "... physical and chemical experiments..."; SWI, p. 300; XJI, p. 264.

36.   Addition in official text: "... and objective reality scientifically reflected..."; SWI, p. 300; XJI, p. 265.

37.   Official text reads: "There is an old Chinese saying, 'How can you catch tiger cubs without entering the tiger's lair?' This saying holds true for man's practice and..."; SWI, p. 300; XJI, p. 265.

38.   Official text reads: "... of capitalist society..."; SWI, p. 301; XJI, p. 265.

39.   Official text reads: "... the second period..."; SWI, p. 301; XJI, p. 265.

40.   Addition in official text: "... and its own historical task..."; SWI, p. 301; XJI, p. 265.

41. Addition in official text: "... which Marx and Engels scientifically summed up in all its variety to create the theory of Marxism for the education of the proletariat". SWI, p. 301; XJI, p. 265.

42. Addition in official text: "... comprador and..."; SWI, p. 301; XJI, p. 266.

43. Addition in official text: "... of 1919"; SWI, p. 301; XJI, p. 266.

44. Official text reads: "Agrarian Revolutionary War"; SWI, p. 301; XJI, p. 266.

45. *guilüxing de.*

46. No brackets in official text; SWI, p. 302; XJI, p. 266.

47. *Fayuan; Kaishi* in official text; SWI, p. 303; XJI, p. 267.

48. Addition in official text: "... of the theory..."; SWI, p. 303; XJI, p. 267.

49. Addition in official text: "... that the perceptual stage of knowledge..."; SWI, p. 303; XJI, p. 267.

50. Official text reads: "... error ..."; SWI, p. 303; XJI, p. 267.

51. Addition in official text: "... so-called ..."; SWI, p. 303; XJI, p. 267.

52. Official text reads: "... leap ..."; SWI, p. 303; XJI, p. 268.

53. Official text reads: "... 'rationalism' nor 'empiricism' ..."; SWI, p. 304; XJI, p. 268.

54. Addition in official text: "... knowing ..."; SWI, p. 304; XJI, p. 268.

55. Addition in official text: "... knowing ..."; SWI, p. 304; XJI, p. 268.

56. *Yuzhou; shijie* in official text; SWI, p. 304; XJI, p. 268.

57. *Yuzhou; shijie* in official text; SWI, p. 304; XJI, p. 268.

58. V.I. Lenin, "What is to be Done?", *Collected Works* (Moscow: FLPH, 1961), Vol. 5, p. 369.

59. Official text reads: "... significance"; SWI, p. 304; XJI, p. 269.

60. Official text reads: "... when natural scientists originated them ..."; SWI, p. 305; XJI, p. 269.

61. Official text reads: "... Marxism-Leninism..."; SWI, p. 305; XJI, p. 269.

62. Official text reads: "... Marx, Engels, Lenin and Stalin ..."; SWI, p. 305; XJI, p. 269.

63. The 1946 text adds: "... and revolutionary national struggle". This is the same as the official text; SWI, p. 305; XJI, p. 269. See *Bujuan* V, p. 280.

64.   Official text reads: "Dialectical materialism is universally true because..."; SWI, p. 305; XJI, p. 269.

65.   Addition in official text: "... human ..."; SWI, p. 305; XJI, p. 269.

66.   No quotation marks in official text; SWI, p. 305; XJI, p. 269.

67.   Official text reads: "... 'the standpoint of life, of practice, should be first and fundamental in the theory of knowledge'"; SWI, p. 305; XJI, p. 269. The quote is from V.I. Lenin, *Materialism and Empirio-Criticism* (Moscow: FLPH, 1952), p. 141.

68.   Official text reads: "Theory becomes purposeless if it is not connected with revolutionary practice, just as practice gropes in the dark if its path is not illumined by revolutionary theory"; SWI, p. 305; XJI, pp. 269-270. The quote is from J.V. Stalin, "The Foundations of Leninism", *Problems of Leninism* (Moscow: FLPH, 1954), p. 31.

69.   Addition in official text: "... by the development of the objective process itself and ..."; SWI, p. 306; XJI, p. 270.

70.   Throughout this paragraph, the sequence of "ideas, theories..." is reversed in the official text.

71.   No brackets in official text; SWI, p. 306; XJI, p. 271.

72.   This has changed in the 1946 text to read: "... its internal contradiction and struggle ...", which is the same as the official text. SWI, p. 306;   XJI, p. 271.

73.   Official text reads: "... true ..."; SWI, p. 306; XJI, p. 271.

74.   Order of "theories, ideas" reversed in official text; SWI, p. 306; XJI, p. 271.

75.   Addition in official text: "... all ..."; SWI, p. 306; XJI, p. 271.

76.   Official text reads: "... programmes ..."; SWI, p. 306; XJI, p. 271.

77.   Paragraph break in official text. SWI, p. 306; XJI, p. 271.

78.   Official text reads: "... man's cognition is limited by numerous social conditions"; SWI, p. 306; XJI, p. 207.

79.   No paragraph break in official text. SWI, p. 306; XJI, p. 271.

80.   Official text reads: "... mechanical materialism..."; SWI, p. 307; XJI, p. 272.

81.   Official text reads: "... Marxist-Leninist ..."; SWI, p. 307; XJI, p. 272.

82.   Official text reads: "... in the endless flow of absolute truth ..."; SWI, p. 307; XJI, p. 272.

83.   Addition in official text: "The sum total of innumerable relative truths constitutes absolute truth"; SWI, p. 307; XJI, p. 272.

84.   Official text reads: "... human knowledge";   SWI, p. 307;   XJI, p. 272.

85.   Official text reads: "In social practice...";   SWI, p. 307;   XJI, p. 272.

86.   Addition in official text: "... coming into being ...";   SWI, p. 307; XJI, p. 272. The 1946 text reads: "In practice, the process of coming into being and passing away...".

87.   Official text reads: "... ideas, theories ...";   SWI, p. 307;   XJI, p. 272.

88.   "... and so is man's cognition of truth through practice" does not appear in the 1946 text.

89.   Official text reads: "Marxism-Leninism...";   SWI, p. 307;   XJI, p. 272.

90.   No inverted commas in official text.   SWI, p. 308;   XJI, p. 272.

91.   *yuzhou*;   official text reads *shijie*;   SWI, p. 308;   XJI, p. 272.

92.   Official text reads: "Discover ...";   SWI, p. 308;   XJI, p. 273.

93.   Official text reads: "... repeats itself ...";   SWI, p. 308;   XJI, p. 273.

4 | The Law of the Unity of Contradictions [On Contradiction]

[p. 240] This law is the **basic law of dialectics. Lenin said: "Dialectics in the proper sense is the study of contradictions in the very essence of objects."** Therefore, **Lenin often called this law the essence of dialectics; he also called it the kernel of dialectics.** Because of this, in our study of dialectics, discussion should commence from this problem, and moreover should receive somewhat closer attention than other problems.

This question includes many problems, **and these are:** The two views of development;

the law of identity in formal logic and the law of contradiction in dialectics;

the universality of contradiction;

the particularity of contradiction;

the principal contradiction and the principal aspect of a contradiction;

the identity and struggle of a contradiction;[1]

the place of antagonism in contradiction.[2]

These problems will be explained in sequence below.

Source: Takeuchi Minoru (ed.), *Mao Zedong ji bujuan* [Supplements to Collected Writings of Mao Zedong] (Tokyo: Sososha, 1983-1986), Vol. 5, pp. 240-278. In this translation, words shown in bold type are those incorporated into the official text of *On Contradiction* in *Selected Works of Mao Tse-tung*, Vol. I, pp. 311-347. Translated and annotated by Nick Knight.

[p. 241] I. *The Two Views of Development*

Throughout the history of human thought
(*sixiang*),[3] there have been two conceptions concerning
the development of the world,[4] the metaphysical view[5]
of development, **and the dialectical** view of development.
What are the differences between these two views of
development?[6]

(1) *The Metaphysical View of Development*[7]

Another name for metaphysics is *xuan-xue,* and
this occupied a dominant position in the thought of former
times. The content of this philosophy was an explanation of
those things supposedly outside experience, that is, a theory
which discussed absolutes and essences, etc.   In   modern
philosophy, so-called metaphysics is a method of thought
which employs a static viewpoint to observe things, and which
holds that all the different things in the world and all their
characteristics have been forever unchanged.   This type of
thought prevailed in seventeenth and eighteenth century Europe.
With the arrival of the present era, namely the nineteenth
and twentieth centuries, because of the results of the class
struggle and the development of science, dialectical thought
rapidly strode onto the world stage.   But metaphysics, in the
form also of vulgar evolutionism (vulgar, that is superficial,
simple), stubbornly opposed dialectics.
In summary, the view of development of so-called
metaphysics and vulgar evolutionism is that development is a
quantitative increase or decrease, that the motive force is
external, involves a change in place in all things, and that the
reflection of these things in man's thought is eternally of this
nature.   The special characteristics of a thing are present in that
thing from its beginning, and remain thus from its state of
germination in inception right through to the zenith of its
development.   They ascribe social development to the growth
and repetition of certain special characteristics, the nature of
which remain forever unchanged.   For example, **capitalist
exploitation and competition, individualism** and so on,

can all be found in ancient slave society or even in primitive savage society. They ascribe the causes of social development to factors external to society, such as geography and climate. [p. 242] This view of development searches[8] outside a thing for the causes of its development, and opposes[9] the theory which holds that development arises from the contradictions inside a thing; it can thus explain neither the qualitative diversity of things, nor the phenomenon of one quality changing into another. In the seventeenth and eighteenth centuries, this mode of thinking existed as a theory of unchangeable natural absolutes[10] (mechanical materialism) - and in the twentieth century as vulgar evolutionism (the theory of equilibrium of Bukharin and others) and so on.[11]

(2) *The Dialectical View of Development*

This holds that in order to understand the development of a thing, we should study it internally and in its relationship with other things; in other words, the development of things should be seen as their internal, necessary and independent self-movement; that is, the automaticity of things.[12] The fundamental cause of the development of a thing is not external but internal; it lies in the contradictoriness within the thing. There is internal contradiction in every single thing, hence its motion and development.

Thus, the dialectical view of development combats the theory of external causes, or of an external motive force,[13] advanced by metaphysics and vulgar evolutionism. It is evident that purely external causes can only give rise to mechanical motion, that is, to changes in scale or quantity, but cannot explain why things differ qualitatively in thousands of ways.[14] As a matter of fact, even mechanical motion under external force occurs through the internal contradictoriness of things. Simple growth in plants

and animals is not only quantitative increase, it is at the same time the emergence of qualitative change; simple growth **is likewise**[15] **the result of development arising from contradictions. Similarly, social development is due chiefly not to external but to internal causes. Countries with almost the same geographical and climatic conditions display great diversity and unevenness in their development.** Moreover, great **social changes may take place in one and the same country although its geography and climate remain unchanged,** and this condition exists in many countries around the globe. Old Russian imperialism[16] **changed into the socialist Soviet Union, and** a purely **feudal Japan, which had locked its doors against the world, changed into imperialist Japan, although no change occurred in the geography and climate of either country.** Change was extremely limited in China with its several thousand year old feudal system, but recently there have been great changes, **and is just now changing into a new China, liberated and free.** Is it conceivable there are any differences between the geography and climate of China today and of several decades ago? It is quite evident, [p. 243] it is not due to external reasons but to internal reasons.[17] **Changes**[18] **in nature are due chiefly to the development of the contradictions** within things **in nature. Changes in society are due**[19] **to the development of the internal contradictions in society, the contradiction between the productive forces and the relations of production, and the contradiction between classes,**[20] **and it is these that push society forward.**[21] **Does dialectics**[22] **exclude external causes? Not at all. The external causes are the condition of change and internal causes are the basis of change, the external causes become operative through internal causes. In a suitable temperature an egg changes into a chicken, but no temperature can change a stone into a chicken,** because the basis of the internal causes is different. The pressure of imperialism accelerated change in Chinese society, and these changes were effected through the inner regularities (*guilüxing*) of China itself. **In battle, one army is victorious and the other is defeated; both the victory and the defeat are determined by internal causes. The one is victorious either because it is strong or because of its competent generalship, the other is vanquished either because it is weak or because of its incompetent generalship; it is through internal causes that external causes** bring about change.[23] **In 1927,**[24] **the defeat of the proletariat by the bourgeoisie came about through the opportunism then to be found within the Chinese proletariat itself (inside the Chinese Communist Party).**[25] **To lead a revolution to victory a class or a political party must rely on its own political line** having no mistakes,[26] **and on the solidity of its own political organization.** In China, the loss of Manchuria and the crisis in North China are due principally to China's weakness (because of the defeat of the 1927 revolution, the people lost political power, and this produced civil war and a dictatorial system). Japanese imperialism took advantage of this situation and invaded. In order to drive out the Japanese robbers, we must rely principally on the national united front to carry out a determined revolutionary war. "Only after something has first become rotten will worms breed in it; and only after a man first doubts will malicious talk make its entry." This is a saying by Su Dongpo.[27] "When internal examination discovers nothing wrong, what is there to be anxious about, what is there to fear?"[28] This is a Confucian truth. If a person strengthens himself in his youth, he doesn't easily catch cold; the Soviet Union to this day has not suffered attack by Japan, and this is due completely to its strength. "When Lei Gong beat the bean curd, he chose a weak object to bully."[29] Things under heaven depend solely on one's strength, so it is no use blaming heaven or other people; man is the master of his own fate, difficulties can be overcome, and external conditions can be changed; this is our philosophy.

We oppose the metaphysical view of development, and advocate the dialectical view of development. We are advocates of the theory of change, and oppose the theory of non-changeability;[30]   we are advocates of the theory of internal causation, and oppose the theory of external causation.

[p. 244]   II. *The Law of Identity in Formal Logic and the Law of Contradiction in Dialectics*

We have discussed above the metaphysical and dialectical views of development. The struggle between these two ways of looking at the world constitutes the struggle in methods of thought between formal logic and dialectical logic.

Bourgeois formal logic has three fundamental laws: the first is called the law of identity, the second the law of contradiction, and the third the law of excluded middle. What is the law of identity? The law of identity states: In the process of thought, a concept remains unchanged throughout, being forever equal to itself. For example, a chemical element is forever equal to that chemical element; China is forever equal to China, and a certain person is forever equal to that certain person. Its formula is A equals A; this law is metaphysical. Engels says that it is the fundamental law of the old view of the universe. Its mistake lies in not recognizing contradiction and change within a thing, and because of this, removing temporariness and relativity from a concept, attributing it with permanence and absoluteness. It doesn't understand that a thing and the concept that reflects a thing are both relative and changeable; a certain chemical element is certainly not forever equal to that certain element, and all forms of chemical element are changing. China also will not forever be equivalent to China, for China is changing; the age-old feudal China of the past and the free and liberated China of the future are two things. A certain person is also not forever equal to that certain person; a person's physique and thought change. Concepts in thought are reflections of objective things, and objective things are changing; the content of a concept is also changing. In fact, there is no such thing as a concept which is forever equivalent to itself.

What is the law of contradiction? The law of contradiction states: A concept itself cannot at the same time contain two or more mutually contradictory meanings, and if a certain concept contains two contradictory meanings, then that is regarded as a logical error. A contradictory concept cannot simultaneously have both sides correct or both sides incorrect, and the correct one is, and can only be, one of those two. Its formula is A is not equal to not-A. Kant has enumerated the four following antinomies (*maodun sixiang*):[31] The world's time has a [p. 245] beginning and an end, and is limited in space; the world has no beginning or end in time, and also is limitless in space. This is the first of them. In the world everything is constituted of simple matter (cannot be re-divided); in the world there are no simple things, everything is complex (can be re-divided). This is the second of them. In the world there exists free causation; in the world there is no freedom, everything is inevitable. This is the third of them. In the world there exists a certain inevitable essence (*biran de shizhi*); in the world nothing is inevitable, everything is accidental. This is the fourth of them. Kant gave these irreconcilable and mutually opposed principles the one title of "The Second Law of Contradiction". However, he stated that these were only contradictions in man's thought, in the real world they really did not exist. According to the law of contradiction in formal logic, these contradictions were thus a mistake, and had to be rejected. However, in reality, thought is a reflection of things. There is not one thing which does not contain contradiction, and because of this, there is no concept which does not contain contradiction. This is not an error in thought, but precisely where thought is correct, and the law of the unity of contradictions of dialectical logic is founded on this base. It is only with formal logic's rejection of the contradictory law of contradiction that it becomes really incorrect thought. The law of contradiction in formal logic is only a manifestation of the negative of the law of identity, and it functions as a supplement to the law of identity, the purpose of which is to consolidate the law of identity's so-called a concept is equal to itself, A is equal to A.

What is the law of excluded middle? The law of excluded middle states: Of the two opposite meanings of a concept, the correct one must be one or the other, for it is not possible for both to be incorrect, or to rush to a third as the correct meaning. Its formula is "A is equal to B, or not equal to B, but cannot be equal to C". They do not realize that things and concepts are developing, and in the process of development of things and concepts, not only are their internal contradictory elements made manifest, but these contradictory elements can be removed, negated, and resolved to become a third thing which is not-A and not-B, change to become a new and higher thing or concept. Correct thought should not exclude the third factor, should not exclude the law of the negation of the negation. According to the law of the excluded middle, in the contradiction between the proletariat and the bourgeoisie, the correct one is either the former or the latter. It cannot be a society without classes. However, it is a fine thing that the process of social evolution does not stop at class [p. 246] struggle, but progresses towards a proletarian society. China and Japanese imperialism are in a state of contradiction. We oppose the invasion of Japanese imperialism, but we do not agree that a post-independence China must remain forever in a state of hostility with Japan. We advocate that through national revolution and a revolution within Japan, the two nations will reach a stage of free association. The same applies to the opposition between bourgeois democracy and proletarian democracy; a higher stage to both of them will be the epoch in which there will be no states and no governments, and this will be arrived at through proletarian democracy. The law of excluded middle in formal logic also supplements its law of identity, which only recognizes the fixed condition of a concept, and which opposes its development, opposes revolutionary leaps, and opposes the principle of the negation of the negation.

It can, therefore, be seen that all the laws of formal logic oppose contradictoriness and advocate the characteristic of identity, oppose development and change of concepts and things, and advocate their solidification and immobility. This is in direct opposition to dialectics.

Why do formal logicians advocate these things? Because they observe things separate from their continual mutual function and interconnections; that is, they observe things at rest rather than in movement, and as separate rather than in connection. Therefore it is not possible for them to consider and acknowledge the importance of contradictoriness and the negation of the negation within things and concepts, and so they advocate the rigid and inflexible law of identity.

Dialectics on the other hand observes things in movement and in connection, and is in direct opposition to the law of identity of formal logic, advocating rather the revolutionary law of contradiction.

Dialectics considers that the contradictions in thought are none other than the reflection of objective external contradictions. Dialectics does not ritualistically adhere to two principles which appear externally to be in a state of mutual conflict (for example, the many antinomies raised by Kant in his four contradictory principles and to which I referred above), but sees through to a thing's internal essence. The task of dialecticians is to perform the task that those formal logicians have not carried out - study of an object - to concentrate attention on finding out the strength of its contradictions, the tendency of the contradictions, the aspects of the contradictions, and the fixity of the contradictions' internal relations. The external world and man's thought are both in motion and are dialectical; they are not static and metaphysical. For this reason, the revolutionary law of contradiction (namely the principle of the unity of contradictions) therefore occupies the principal [p. 247] position in dialectics.

The entirety of formal logic has only one nucleus, and that is the reactionary law of identity. The entirety of dialectics also has only one nucleus, and that is the revolutionary law of contradiction.

Does dialectics oppose the identity of things or concepts? It does not. Dialectics recognizes the relative identity of things or concepts. Why then does dialectics oppose the law of identity of formal logic? It is because the law of identity of formal logic is an absolute law which rejects contradictions. Dialectics acknowledges the identity of things or concepts, but asserts that they simultaneously contain contradictions and are interconnected; this kind of identity indicates the interconnection of contradictions, it is relative and temporary. Since the law of identity of formal logic is an absolute law which rejects contradictions, it cannot but advance the law of excluded middle which opposes one concept changing into another concept, or one thing changing into another thing. Dialectics on the other hand regards the identity of a thing or concept as temporary, relative and conditional; because the struggle of contradictions guides the regularities (*guilüxing*) of change and development of a thing or a concept, such struggle is forever absolute and unconditional. Because formal logic does not reflect a thing in its true condition, dialectics cannot allow its existence. There is only one scientific truth, and that truth is dialectics.

III. *The Universality of Contradiction*

This problem has two aspects, the first part of which is that contradiction exists in all processes; the second is that in every process the movement of contradiction exists from start to finish. This is called the universality or absoluteness of contradictions.[32]

Engels said "motion itself is a contradiction". Lenin defined the law of the unity of opposites (*maodun tongyi*) as "the recognition (discovery) [p. 248] of the mutually exclusive opposite tendencies in all natural phenomena and processes (including society and mind)". Are these ideas correct? Yes, they are. The interdependence of the contradictory aspects present in all things and the struggle between aspects determine the life of all things and push their development forward. Without contradiction nothing would exist.[33] As a result, this law is the most universal law, applicable to all phenomena of the objective world, and also applicable to the phenomenon of thought (*sixiang*). Within dialectics, it is the most fundamental law having decisive significance.

Why do we say that contradiction is motion? Haven't there been those who have disputed Engels' assertion? This is because the theory of contradiction discussed by Marx, Engels, and Lenin has become the most important theoretical base of the proletarian revolution. This has led to all-out attacks by bourgeois theorists who constantly hope to overturn Engel's law that "motion is contradiction". Raising aloft their obstreperous refutations they have moreover produced the following reasons: the motion of things in the real world is in different instances of time, and through different points in space; when a thing is positioned at a certain point, it occupies that point, and when it moves to another point it occupies that other point. In this way, the motion of things in time and space is divided into many sections;   there are no contradictions, for if there were contradictions there could be no movement.

Lenin has pointed out the absurdity of this reasoning, pointed out that this reasoning in fact, by observing continual motion as many sections in time and space and as many static conditions, results in denying motion. They do not know that when a thing occupies a new position, it is because the thing has moved in space from one point to another; namely, as a result of motion. Without the contradiction in so-called motion in which a thing occupies a point and at the same time does not occupy a point, and without this continuous and interrupted unity, the unity of motion and rest, inaction and action, motion would be fundamentally impossible. To deny contradiction is to deny motion. All motion in nature, society, and thought is this motion of the unity of contradictions.

Ceaseless **contradiction is the basis of the simple forms of motion (for instance, the mechanical motion** discussed above) and is moreover [p. 248] the basis of all **complex forms of motion.**

There is an indivisible relationship between the process of life and the opposing process of death, and this regardless of whether it is in the various forms of organic life, or within the life of cells within an organism. The supersession of the old by the new, the succession of life and death - this motion of the unity of opposites (*maodun tongyi*) is the necessary condition for all organic life and development. Without this contradiction, the phenomenon of life is unthinkable.[34]

Within mechanics, any "action" contains internal contradictoriness, and leads to "reaction"; without "reaction", there could be no discussion of action.[35]

In mathematics, any number contains internal contradictoriness, and can become a positive or negative number, a whole number, or a fraction. Positive and negative, whole number, and fraction, constitute the movement of contradictions within mathematics.

The law of the unity of opposites of dissociation and combination in chemistry, constitutes the countless motion of chemical change; without this contradiction, chemical phenomena could not exist.

In social life, any phenomenon contains class contradictions. The buying and selling of labour, the organization of the state, and the content of philosophy are like this. The fundamental law of class society is class struggle.

In war, offence and defence, advance and retreat, victory and defeat are all contradictory phenomena. One cannot exist without the other. The two aspects are at once in conflict and in interdependence, and this constitutes the totality of war, and pushes its development forward.[36]

Every difference in men's concepts should be regarded as reflecting an objective contradiction. Objective contradictions are reflected in subjective thinking, and this process constitutes the contradictory movement of concepts, and pushes forward the development of thought.[37]

[p. 250] Opposition and struggle between ideas of different kinds constantly occur within the Party; this is a reflection within the Party of contradictions between classes in society. If there were no contradictions in the Party and no ideological struggles to resolve them, the Party's life would come to an end.

Contradiction[38] exists universally and in all processes, whether in the simple or in the complex forms of motion, whether in objective phenomena or ideological phenomena.

At this point there are those who say although they can admit the principle of Engels and Lenin that contradiction is motion, and that contradiction exists in all processes, isn't it unnecessary for the movement of contradictions within all processes to exist from beginning to end?[39] Was it not Deborin and others who clearly asserted that there is no such thing as the so-called motion of contradictions from beginning to end in every process? According to Deborin, contradictions exist, but **not at the inception of a process but only when it has developed to a certain stage.**[40] According to Deborin, the development of a process follows on from this stage; at its inception there are simple differences. There subsequently emerge opposites which finally become contradictions. Is this formula correct or mistaken?

It is mistaken. The so-called universality of contradictions exists not only within all processes, but at each stage of development of every process. This is the revolutionary law of contradictions of Marxism. According to the Deborin school,[41] **contradiction appears not at the inception of a process, but only when it has developed to a certain stage: if this were the case, then the cause of the development of the process before that stage would be external and not internal. Deborin thus reverts to the metaphysical theories of external causality and of mechanism. Applying this view in the analysis of concrete problems, the Deborin school sees only differences but not contradictions between** the workers and the peasants[42] **under existing conditions in the Soviet Union, thus entirely agreeing with Bukharin. In analyzing the French Revolution, it holds that before the Revolution there were likewise only differences but not contradictions within the Third Estate, which was composed of the workers, the peasants, and the bourgeoisie (Gorev's explanation).[43] This school does not understand that each and every difference already contains contradictions and that difference itself is contradiction. Labour and capital have been in contradiction ever since the two classes came into being,** [p. 251] **only at first the contradiction had not become intense. Even under the conditions[44] existing in the Soviet Union, the difference between workers** and peasants is a contradiction, although, unlike the contradiction between labour and capital, it will not become intensified into antagonism or assume the form of class struggle.[45] The question is one of different kinds of contradiction, not of the presence or absence of contradiction. Contradiction is universal and absolute, it is present in the process of development of all things and permeates every process from beginning to end.[46] What is meant by the emergence of a new process? The old unity with its constituent opposites yields to a new unity with its constituent opposites; a new process emerges to replace the old.[47] The new process contains new contradictions and begins its own history of the development of contradictions.

As Lenin pointed out, Marx in his *Capital* made a model application[48] of this principle of the movement of opposites which runs through a process[49] from beginning to end. He pointed out that this is the method which must be employed in studying any process.[50]

> In his *Capital*, Marx first analyses the simplest, most ordinary and fundamental, most common and everyday *relation* of bourgeois (commodity) society, a relation encountered billions of times, viz. the exchange of commodities. In this very simple phenomenon (in this "cell" of bourgeois society) analysis reveals *all* the contradictions (or the germs of *all* the contradictions) of modern society. The subsequent exposition shows us the development (*both* growth *and* movement) of these contradictions and of this society in the $\sum$ (summation) of its individual parts, from its beginning to its end.[51]

Lenin added, "Such must be the method of exposition (or study) of dialectics in general".

Fine, we don't need to study the ancient literary method (*yifa*) of the *Tong Cheng* school,[52] for Lenin has informed us of an even better method (*yifa*), and that is the Marxist scientific method of study.[53]

IV. The Particularity of Contradiction

[p. 252] Contradiction is present in all processes;[54] it permeates each and every process from beginning to end.[55] This is the universality and absoluteness of contradiction which we have discussed above. Now let us discuss the particularity and relativity of contradiction.[56] This problem should be studied on several levels.

First, the contradiction in each form of motion of matter has its particularity. Man's knowledge of matter is knowledge of its forms of motion, because there is nothing in this world except matter in motion.[57] In considering each form of motion, we must observe the points which it has in common with other forms of motion. But what is especially important, constituting as it does the foundation of our knowledge of a thing, is to observe what is particular to this form of motion of matter, namely, to observe the qualitative difference between this form of motion and other forms. Only when we have done so can we distinguish between things. Materialist dialectics indicates clearly: Every form of motion contains within itself its own particular contradiction. This particular contradiction constitutes the particular essence which distinguishes one thing from another.[58] There are many forms of motion in nature, mechanical motion, sound, light, heat, electricity, dissociation, combination, and so on. All these forms are interdependent, but in its essence each is different from the others. The particular essence of each form of motion is determined by its own particular contradiction. This holds true not only for nature but also for social and ideological phenomena.

Every form of society, every form of ideology, has its own particular contradiction and particular essence.

The sciences are differentiated precisely on the basis of the particular contradictions inherent in their respective objects of study. Thus the contradiction peculiar to a certain field of phenomena constitutes the object of study for a specific branch of science. For example, positive and negative numbers in mathematics; action and reaction in mechanics; positive and negative electricity in physics; dissociation and combination in chemistry; forces of production and relations of production, and class struggle, in social science;[59] offence and defence in military science; idealism and materialism, the metaphysical outlook and the dialectical outlook, in philosophy; and so on - all these are the objects of study of different branches of science precisely because each branch has its own particular contradiction and particular essence. Of course, unless we study[60] the universality of contradiction, we have no way of discovering the universal cause[61] for the movement or development of things; however, unless we study the particularity of contradiction, we have no way of determining the particular essence of a thing which differentiates it from other things, no way of discovering the particular cause[62] for the movement or development of a thing, [p. 253] and no way of distinguishing one thing from another or of demarcating the fields of science.[63]

It is necessary not only to study the particular contradiction and the essence determined thereby of every great system of the forms of motion of matter, but also to study the particular contradiction and the essence of each process in the long course of development of each form of motion of matter. In every form of motion, each process of development[64] is qualitatively different; in the entire world (*tianxia*) there are no identical contradictions, and **our study must emphasize**[65] **this point.**

Qualitatively different contradictions can only be resolved by qualitatively different methods. For instance, the contradiction between the proletariat and the bourgeoisie is resolved by the method of socialist revolution; the contradiction between the colonies and imperialism is resolved by national[66] **war; the contradiction between the great masses of the people and the feudal system is resolved by the method of democratic revolution;**[67] **the contradiction between the** proletariat[68] **and the peasantry**[69] **is resolved by** the socialization **of agriculture; contradiction within the Communist Party, is resolved by the method of** ideological struggle;[70] **the contradiction between society and nature is resolved by the method of developing the productive forces. Processes change, old processes and old contradictions disappear, new processes and new contradictions emerge, and the methods of resolving contradictions differ accordingly. In Russia, there was a fundamental difference between the method used for resolving the contradiction resolved by the February Revolution and the contradiction resolved by the October Revolution.**[71] It is a principle to use different methods to cope with different contradictions.

In order to reveal the particularity of the contradiction in any process,[72] **in their totality or interconnections, that is in order to reveal the essence of the process, it is necessary to reveal the particularity of the two aspects of each of the contradictions in that process; otherwise it will be impossible to discover the essence of the process. This requires the utmost attention in** the study of problems.[73]

A major process contains many contradictions.[74] **For instance, in the course of China's bourgeois-democratic revolution, where the contradictions are exceedingly complex, there exist the contradiction** between imperialism and the entire Chinese society, the contradiction within Chinese society between the feudal system and the great masses of the people, the contradiction between the proletariat and the bourgeoisie, the contradiction between the peasantry and the petty bourgeoisie[75] on the one hand and the bourgeoisie on the other, the contradiction between the various ruling groups,[76] and so on. These contradictions cannot be treated in the same way since each has its own particularity; moreover, the two aspects of each contradiction cannot be treated in the same way since each aspect has its own characteristics. We who are engaged in the Chinese revolution [p. 254] should not only understand the particularity of these contradictions in their totality, that is, in their interconnections, but should also study the two aspects of each contradiction as the only means of understanding the totality. When we speak of understanding each aspect of a contradiction, we mean understanding what specific position each aspect occupies, what concrete forms it assumes in its interdependence[77] with its opposite, and what concrete methods are employed in the struggle with its opposite, when the two are both interdependent,[78] and also after the interdependence breaks down. It is of great importance to study these problems. The principal feature of Leninism is that it is the science which studies the various forms of struggle between the proletariat and the bourgeoisie.[79]

In studying a problem we must shun subjectivity, one-sidedness and superficiality. To be subjective means not to look at problems objectively, that is, not to use the materialist viewpoint in looking at problems. This has already been discussed in Chapter Two, and I will return to it at the end of this section. Now I come to a discussion of one-sidedness and superficiality.[80] To be one-sided means not to look at problems all-sidedly, for example, to understand only China but not Japan, only the Communist Party but not the Guomindang, only the proletariat but not the bourgeoisie, only the peasants but not the landlords, only the favourable conditions but not the difficult ones, only the gentleman but not the scroundrel, only the present **but not the future,**[81] only oneself but not others, only pride but not modesty,[82] **only the defects but not the achievements, only the plaintiff's case but not the defendant's, only underground**[83] **work but not open**[84] **work, and so on.** In a word, it means not to understand the characteristics of both aspects of a contradiction. That is what we mean by looking at a problem one-sidedly. Or it may be called seeing the part but not the whole.[85] That way it is impossible to find the method for resolving a contradiction, it is impossible to accomplish the tasks of the revolution, to carry out assignments or to develop inner-Party ideological struggle correctly. When Sun Wu Zi said in discussing military science, "Know the enemy and know yourself, and you can fight a hundred battles with no danger of defeat", he was referring to the two sides in a battle. Tang Taizong[86] also understands the error of one-sidedness when he said, "Listen to both sides and you will be enlightened, heed only one side and you will be benighted". But our comrades often look at problems one-sidedly, and so they often run into snags. [p. 255] In the countryside, if two families or clans are engaged in conflict, the mediator must recognize the reasons for the conflict on both sides, the bone of contention, the present situation, demands, and so on; only then will he be able to think out a method of resolving the dispute. There are such people in the countryside who are good at mediation, and they are constantly invited to mediate when a dispute arises; these people actually understand the dialectic of which we speak, the need to understand the particular characteristics of the various aspects of a contradiction. **In the novel** *Shui Hu Zhuan*, **Song** Gongming[87] **thrice attacked the Zhu village. Twice he was defeated because he was ignorant of the local conditions and used the wrong method. Later he changed his**

method; first he investigated the situation, and he
familiarized himself with the maze of roads, then he
broke up the alliance between the Li, Hu, and Zhu
villages and sent his men in disguise into the enemy
camp to lie in wait.[88] And on the third occasion he
won. There are many examples of materialistic
dialectics in *Shui Hu Zhuan*, of which the episode of
the three attacks on Zhu village is one of the best. On
several occasions Lenin spoke of the need to observe a problem
from all sides, resolutely opposing one-sidedness.[89] We
should remember his words. To be superficial means
to consider neither the characteristics of a
contradiction in its totality nor the characteristics of
each of its aspects; it means to deny the necessity
for probing deeply into a thing and minutely studying
the characteristics of its contradiction, but instead
merely to look from afar and, after glimpsing the
rough outline, immediately to try to resolve the
contradiction (to answer a question, settle a dispute,
handle work, or direct a military operation). This
way of doing things is bound to lead to trouble.[90]

Not only does the whole process of the
movement of opposites,[91] both in their
interconnections and in each of the aspects, have
particular features to which we should give attention,
but each stage in the process has its particular
features to which we must give attention too.[92] The
fundamental contradiction in a process[93] and the
essence of the process determined by this
fundamental contradiction will not disappear until the
process is completed; but the conditions usually
differ at each stage of development of a process.[94]
The reason is that, although the nature of the
fundamental contradiction in a process[95] and the
essence of the process remain unchanged, the
fundamental contradiction becomes more and more
intensified as it passes from one stage to another.[96]
In addition, among the numerous major and minor
contradictions which are determined[97] by the

fundamental contradiction, some become intensified, some are temporarily or partially resolved or mitigated, and some new ones emerge; hence the process is marked by stages.[98]
For instance, when imperialism differed from non-monopoly capitalism,[99] there was no change in the[100] nature of the two classes in fundamental contradiction, namely, the proletariat and the bourgeoisie, [p.256] or in the capitalist essence of society; however, the contradiction between these two classes became intensified, the contradiction between monopoly and non-monopoly capital emerged, the contradiction between the various monopoly cliques emerged, the contradiction between the export of capital and the export of commodities emerged, the contradiction between the colonial powers and the colonies became intensified, the contradiction among the capitalist countries resulting from their uneven development intensified,[101] and thus arose the special stage of imperialism.[102]
Take the process of China's democratic revolution,[103] which began with the Revolution of 1911; it, too, has several distinct stages.[104] Perhaps there are still several stages through which it must pass before this revolution will be completed. Although no change has taken place in the nature of the fundamental contradiction in the process as a whole, i.e., in the anti-imperialist, anti-feudal, democratic-revolutionary nature of the process (the opposite of which is its semi-colonial and semi-feudal nature), China has nonetheless[105] passed through four or five[106] stages of development in the course of more than twenty years; during this time many great events have taken place - the failure of the Revolution of 1911 and the establishment of the regime of the Northern Warlords, the formation of the first national united front and the great revolution,[107] the break-up of the united front and the desertion of the bourgeoisie to the side of the counter-revolution, the

wars among the warlords,[108] the war of the Soviets,[109] the loss of Manchuria, the ending of the war of the Soviets, the transformation of the Guomindang policy, **the establishment of the second united front,**[110] and so on. **These stages are marked by particular features such as the intensification of certain contradictions** (e.g., the contradiction between China and Japan),[111] **the partial or temporary resolution of other contradictions** (e.g., **the destruction of the Northern Warlords and the confiscation of the lands of the landlords** in the Soviet areas), **and the emergence of yet another contradiction** (e.g., **the conflicts among the new warlords, and the landlords' recapture of the land after the loss** of the Soviet areas).[112]

In studying the particularities of the contradictions at each stage in a process,[113] we not only observe[114] them in their interconnections or their totality, but also observe the two aspects.[115]

For instance, consider the Guomindang and the Communist Party. In the period of the first united front, the Guomindang[116] was revolutionary and vigorous, and it was an alliance of various classes for the democratic revolution. After 1927, it changed into its opposite.[117] After the Xian Incident, it began to change in the direction of a new phase.[118] Such have been the particular features of the Guomindang in the three stages. Of course, these features have arisen from a variety of causes. Now take the other aspect, the Communist Party.[119] In the period of the first united front, the Chinese Communist Party was in its infancy; it led the first Great Revolution[120] but revealed its immaturity in its understanding of the character, the tasks and the methods, etc. of the revolution. Because of this Chen Duxiuism emerged.[121] After 1927, [p. 257] the Communist Party led the war of the Soviets, steeling itself in this struggle with its international and internal enemies, and established the Soviets and the Red Army;[122] however, it committed political and military errors.[123] Since 1935, the Party has[124] again been leading a new united front,[125] and has raised the slogan of anti-Japanese national war and a democratic republic. These have been the particular features of the Communist Party during one stage. These features, too, have arisen from a variety of causes. Without studying both these sets of features we cannot understand the particular relation between the two parties during the various stages of their development, namely, the united front,[126] the break-up of the united front, and a further united front.[127] What is even more fundamental[128] than the relations between the two parties is the resultant contradictions which have arisen between each party and other forces.[129] For instance,[130] the Guomindang stood in contradiction to foreign imperialism[131] (sometimes adopting compromise), and in contradiction to the great masses of the people within the country.[132] The Communist Party has stood in contradiction to foreign imperialism,[133] and in contradiction to internal exploiting classes.[134] Because of these contradictions, there has been created both struggle and alliance between the two parties.[135] If we do not understand the particular features of both aspects of the contradiction, we shall fail to understand not only the relations of each party with other forces, but also the relations between the two parties; why is there the possibility of new co-operation between the Guomindang and the Communist Party? It is because of internal changes within the Guomindang which have emerged as a result of the people's dissatisfaction over Japanese oppression.

It can thus be seen that in studying the particularity of any kind of contradiction - the contradiction in each form of motion of matter, the contradiction in each of its processes of development, the two aspects of the contradiction in each process, the contradiction at each stage of a process, and the two aspects of the contradiction at each stage - in studying the particularity of all of these contradictions, we must not be subjective and arbitrary but must analyse it concretely. Without concrete analysis there can be no knowledge of the particularity of any contradiction.[136]

Marx and Engels[137] have provided us with excellent models of such concrete analysis.

When Marx and Engels applied the law of the unity of contradictions[138] to the study of the socio-historical process, they discovered the basic causes of social development to be the contradiction between the productive forces and the relations of production, the contradiction of class struggle,[139] and also the resultant contradiction between the economic base and its [p. 258] superstructure (politics, ideology).[140]

When Marx applied this law to the study of the economic structure of capitalist society, he discovered that the basic contradiction of this society is the contradiction between the social character of production and the private character of ownership. This contradiction manifests itself in the contradiction between the organized character of production in individual enterprises and the anarchic character of production in society as a whole. In terms of class relations, it manifests itself in the contradiction between the bourgeoisie and the proletariat.[141]

On the question of using dialectics in the study of objective phenomena, Marx and Engels[142] were not in any way subjective and arbitrary but, from the concrete conditions in the actual objective movement of these phenomena, discovered their concrete contradictions, the concrete position of each aspect of every contradiction and the concrete inter-relations of the contradiction, and so on.[143] We must study this attitude, which is the only correct one in study.

The relationship between the universality and the particularity of contradiction is the relationship between the general character and the individual character of contradiction. By the former we mean that contradiction exists in and runs through all processes from beginning to end; motion, things,

processes, the world, **and thinking - all are contradictions. To deny contradiction is to deny everything. This is a universal truth for all times and all countries, which admits of no exception. Hence the general character, the absoluteness of contradiction. But this general character is contained in the**[144] **individual character,** the general character is made manifest in each individual character; **without individual character there can be no general character. If all individual character were removed, what general character would remain? It is because each contradiction is particular that** not one thing in the whole universe is the same, that change is limitless, and that its existence is temporary, and therefore relative.[145] Su Dongpo stated "If things are observed as they change, then heaven and earth can't even remain for a moment". In modern terms, it could be said that what he was speaking of was the particularity of contradiction, its relativity. "If things are observed unchanging, all the things and myself will last forever".[146] This speaks of the universality of contradiction, its absoluteness. **This truth concerning general and individual character, concerning absoluteness and relativity, is the quintessence of the** theory of contradiction.[147] If this is understood, then anything can be mastered (*yi tong bai tong*); what the ancients called "to be familiar with the *Dao*" (*wen Dao*), viewed from today's perspective is to be familiar with the *Dao* of contradiction.

[p. 259] V. *The Principal Contradiction and the Principal Aspect of a Contradiction*

There are still two points in the problem of the particularity of contradiction which must be singled out for analysis, namely, the principal contradiction and the principal aspect of a contradiction.

There are many contradictions in a complex process,[148] and one of them is necessarily the principal contradiction whose existence and development

determines or influences the existence and development of the other contradictions.
For instance, in capitalist society the[149] contradiction between the proletariat and the bourgeoisie forms the principal contradiction. The others[150] such as those between the remnant feudal forces[151] and the bourgeoisie, between the peasant petty bourgeoisie and the bourgeoisie, between the proletariat and the peasant petty bourgeoisie, between non-monopoly capitalists and finance[152] capitalists, between bourgeois democracy and[153] fascism, among the capitalist countries and between imperialism and the colonies, are all determined or influenced by this principal contradiction.

In a semi-colonial country such as China, the relationship between the principal contradiction and the non-principal contradictions presents a complicated picture. Before a semi-colony suffered from imperialist oppression, its principal contradiction was the contradiction between the feudal or semi-feudal system and the broad masses of the people. All other contradictions are determined by this principal contradiction. However, when such a society suffers under imperialist oppression, the internal principal contradiction temporarily changes into a non-principal contradiction, and the contradiction between imperialism and the entire, or almost entire, semi-colonial society becomes the principal one, determining the development of all other contradictions. The status of the principal or non-principal contradiction changes at this time according to the extent of imperialist oppression and the extent of the people's revolution of the semi-colony.

For instance, when imperialism launches a war of aggression against such a country, all its various classes[154] can temporarily unite in a national war against imperialism. At such a time, the contradiction between imperialism and the country concerned becomes the principal contradiction, while all the contradictions among the various classes within the country [p. 260] (including what was the principal contradiction, between the feudal system and the great masses of the people) are temporarily relegated to a secondary and subordinate position. So it was in China in the Opium War,[155] the Yi He Tuan War, the Sino-Japanese War of 1894, and so it is now in the present Sino-Japanese War. Externally, the American War of Independence, the war between England and South Africa, the war between Spain and the Philippines, and so on, have all been like this.

But in another situation, the contradictions change position. When imperialism carries on its oppression not by war, but by milder means - political, economic, and cultural - the ruling classes in semi-colonial countries capitulate to imperialism, and the two form an alliance; opposition changes to unity between the two for the joint oppression of the masses of the people. At such a time, the masses often resort to civil war against the alliance of imperialism and the feudal classes, while imperialism often gives secret assistance to the internal ruling strata to oppress the internal revolutionary war, and so avoids direct action.[156] Thus the internal contradictions become particularly sharp. For instance, in China, the Taiping War, the revolutionary war of 1911, the great Revolution of 1925-27, the war of the Soviets after 1927;[157] externally, there were the February and October revolutions in Russia (Russia too had had many semi-colonial characteristics), the revolutionary characteristics of the numerous civil wars in Central and South America, and so on. Wars among the various ruling groups in the semi-colonies also manifest the intensification of internal contradictions; there have been many of these in China, and Central and South America, which fall into this category.[158]

When a[159] civil war develops to the point of threatening the very existence of imperialism and its running dogs, the domestic rulers,[160] imperialism often adopts other methods in order to maintain its rule; it either tries to split the revolutionary front from within, for example, the treachery of the Chinese bourgeoisie in 1927, **or sends armed forces to help the domestic rulers**[161] **directly,** for example, the latter period of the civil war in the Soviet Union, and the present war in Spain (editor's note: the Spanish civil war lasted from 1936-39). **At such a time,**[162] imperialism and the domestic feudal classes and even the bourgeoisie **stand completely at one pole while the masses of the people stand at the other pole.**[163] It is clearly evident at such a time that the principal external contradiction between imperialism and the semi-colony, and the principal internal contradiction between the feudal forces and broad masses of people, [p. 261] almost merge to form a principal contradiction which determines the development and status of the other contradictions.

But whatever happens, there is no doubt at all that at every stage in the development of a process, there is only one principal contradiction which plays the leading role.

Hence, if in any process there are a number of contradictions, one of them must be the principal contradiction playing the leading and decisive role, while the rest occupy a secondary and subordinate position. Therefore, in studying any process,[164] we must firstly ascertain clearly whether it is a simple or a complex process. If it is a **complex process in which there are two or more contradictions, we must devote every effort to finding its principal contradiction. Once this principal contradiction is grasped, all problems can be readily solved. This is the method Marx taught us in his study of capitalist society.** Likewise Lenin in his study of imperialism,[165] and **Lenin and Stalin in** their study of the economics of the transitional period in the Soviet Union, have **taught us this method. There are thousands of scholars and men of action who do not understand it, and the result is that, lost in a fog, they are unable to get to the heart of a problem and naturally cannot find a way to resolve its contradictions.**

As we have said, one must not treat all the contradictions in a process as being equal but must

distinguish between the principal and the secondary contradictions, and pay special attention to grasping the principal one. But, within a contradiction, whether principal or secondary, should the two contradictory aspects or profiles (*cemian*) be treated as equal? Again, no. In any contradiction, and at whatever time, the development of the contradictory aspects or profiles is uneven. Sometimes they seem to be in equilibrium, which is however only temporary and relative, while unevenness is basic; that is, when they seem to be in equilibrium, there is in fact no absolute equilibrium. Of the two contradictory aspects, one must be principal and the other secondary. The principal aspect is the one playing the leading role in the contradiction.[166]

But this situation is not static; the principal and the non-principal aspects of a contradiction transform themselves into each other.[167] In a given process or at a given stage in the development of a contradiction, A is the principal aspect and B is the non-principal aspect; at another stage or in another process the roles are reversed - [p. 262] a change determined by the strength of the struggle between the two sides.[168]

For instance, for a long period the bourgeoisie has occupied the principal position in capitalist society, playing the leading role, while the proletariat remained subordinate to it. However, prior to and after the revolution, the proletariat changes into the principal position and plays the leading role, while the bourgeoisie changes in the opposite direction. The Soviet Union on the eve of the October Revolution was like this.[169]

In capitalist society, capitalism has changed its position from being a subordinate force in the feudal society of the past to being the principal force,[170] while the feudal forces changed from their principal position to a subordinate one; but how do we explain Japan and pre-revolutionary Russia? In these cases, the feudal forces still enjoyed superiority, and capitalism was still not performing the function of deciding everything. This was due to their contradictory aspects not yet having completed their decisive change. Because of the era, this change could not travel the old historical road, but was change which came into being under other historical circumstances; that is, in which the landlord class and the bourgeoisie changed entirely to a position of being dominated, and in which the proletariat and the peasantry rose to occupy the leading position. At present, all countries which have still not yet completed a capitalist transformation (including China) will follow this new road, although they do not leap over the stage of the democratic revolution; however, this revolution will be led and carried out by the proletariat.[171]

In the contradiction between imperialism and the entire Chinese society, the former occupies the principal aspect, and it enjoys superiority in the struggle between the two sides. But in this situation of mutual opposition, this state of affairs is in the process of changing; China on the one hand is changing from being oppressed to being free and independent; imperialism, however, is moving toward a position at which it will be overthrown.

In China, the antagonistic situation existing internally between the feudal forces and the broad masses of the people is also changing. The people will rely on revolutionary struggle to transform themselves into the leading and dominant force. There has already been illustration of this in the past; the Southern revolutionary forces changed from a secondary to the principal position, and the Northern warlords changed in the opposite direction; and there was a similar situation in the Soviet areas, in which the peasants changed from the ruled to the rulers, and the landlords changed in the opposite direction.

[p. 263] In the relationship in China between the proletariat and the bourgeoisie, because the bourgeoisie has retained the means of production and sovereignty, to the present it still occupies the leading position. However, in terms of leadership of the anti-imperialist, anti-feudal revolution, the proletariat occupies the leading position because of its level of consciousness and revolutionary thoroughness as compared to the vacillation of the bourgeoisie. This point will influence the future of the revolution in China. Only if the proletariat allies itself with the peasantry and the petty bourgeoisie will it be able to occupy politically and materially the leading position. If it can do this, the proletariat will assume the decisive leading function of the revolution.

With regards the contradiction between the peasantry and the workers, the workers have changed from their former subordinate position to their present leading position, and the peasantry have changed in the opposite direction. In the contradictions between the industrial workers and the handicraft workers, skilled and unskilled workers, town and countryside, mental and manual labour, materialism and idealism, all have made the same sort of change.

At certain times in the revolutionary struggle, the difficulties outweigh the favourable conditions and so constitute the principal aspect of the contradiction and the favourable conditions constitute the secondary aspect. But through their efforts the revolutionaries, by utilizing their favourable conditions as a base, **can overcome the difficulties step by step and open up a favourable new situation;** the difficulties which made up the principal position will change so that favourable conditions become principal.[172] **This is what happened after the failure of the revolution**[173] **in 1927 and during the Long March of the**[174] **Red Army. In the present Sino-Japanese War, China is again in a very difficult position, but we** should and can exert ourselves to change that situation.[175] **Conversely, favourable conditions can be transformed into difficulty if the revolutionaries make mistakes. Thus the victory of the revolution of 1925-27**[176] **turned into defeat.** The victory of the Central Soviet in smashing the first, second, third, and fourth encirclement campaigns changed into the defeat of the fifth encirclement campaign.[177]

When we engage in study, the same holds good for the contradiction in the passage from ignorance to knowledge. For those who have not studied Marxism, **ignorance or scanty acquaintance is the** principal aspect of the contradiction, while the depth and extensiveness of Marxism is the other aspect of the contradiction.[178] But by assiduous study, ignorance can be transformed into knowledge, and scanty knowledge into substantial knowledge.[179] Many of our comrades are moving in that direction. The opposite situation is the same; if one refuses to progress when only half the distance has been covered, [p. 264] or lets one's thoughts become confused, or takes the wrong path, then one's knowledge can change to ignorance and correctness change to error. Kautsky, Plekhanov, Chen Duxiu, and others have taken this road. Some conceited types within our ranks are also in a similar danger if they don't change.

I regard all principal and non-principal positions of the aspects of a contradiction as involved in this mutual change. Some people think that this is not true of certain contradictions. For instance, in the contradiction between the productive forces and the relations of production, the productive forces are the principal aspect; in the contradiction between theory and practice, practice is the principal aspect; in the contradiction between the economic base and the superstructure, the economic base is the principal aspect; and there is no change in their respective positions.[180] It should be realized that under normal conditions, and viewed from a materialist point of view, they really are unchanging and absolute things; however, there are historically many particular situations in which they do change. The productive forces, practice, and the economic base generally play the principal and decisive role; whoever denies this is not a materialist. But it must also be admitted that sometimes[181] such aspects as the relations of production, theory, and the superstructure in turn manifest themselves in the principal and decisive role. When it is impossible for the productive forces to develop without a change in the relations of production, then the change in the relations of production plays the principal and decisive role. The creation and advocacy of revolutionary theory plays the principal and decisive role in those times of which Lenin said, "Without revolutionary theory there can be no revolutionary movement". When a task, no matter which, has to be performed, but there is as yet no guiding line, method, plan, or policy, the principal and decisive thing is to decide on a guiding line, method, plan, or policy. When the superstructure (politics, culture, etc.) obstructs the development of the economic base, political and cultural changes become principal and decisive. Are we going against materialism when we say this? No. The reason is that we recognize that in the general development of history the material determines the mental.[182] We also - and indeed must - recognize the reaction of mental on material things.[183] This does not go against materialism; on the contrary, it avoids mechanical materialism and firmly upholds dialectical materialism.

In studying the particularity of contradiction, unless we examine these two facets - the principal and the non-principal contradictions in a process, and the principal and the non-principal aspects of a contradiction - that is, [p. 265] unless we examine the distinctive character of these two facets of contradiction, we shall get bogged down in abstractions, be unable to understand contradiction concretely and consequently be unable to find the correct method of resolving it. The distinctive character or particularity of these two facets[184] represents the unevenness[185] that is in contradiction. Nothing in this world develops absolutely evenly, hence the world as it is; we must oppose the theory of even development (or the theory of equilibrium).[186] The study of the various states of unevenness in contradictions, of the principal and non-principal contradictions and of the principal and the non-principal aspects of a contradiction constitutes an essential method by which a revolutionary political party correctly determines its strategic and tactical policies both in political (and in military affairs). Therefore this question cannot be overemphasized.[187]

VI. The Identity and Struggle of a Contradiction[188]

When we have resolved the problem of[189] t h e universality and the particularity of contradiction, we must proceed to study the problem of the identity and struggle of[190] a contradiction; only by doing so can the study of the law of the unity of contradiction be completely resolved.

Identity, unity, coincidence, interpenetration, interpermeation, interdependence (or mutual dependence for existence), interconnection, or mutual co-operation - all these different terms mean the same thing and refer to the following two points: first, the existence of each of the two aspects of a contradiction in a process[191] presupposes the existence of the other aspect, and both aspects coexist in a single entity; second, in given conditions, each of the two contradictory aspects transforms itself into its opposite. This is the meaning of identity.

Lenin said:

Dialectics is the teaching which shows how *opposites* can be and how they happen to be (how they become) *identical* - under what conditions they are identical, transforming themselves into one another, - why the human mind should take these opposites not as dead, rigid, but as living, conditional, mobile, transforming themselves into one another.

[p. 266] What does this passage mean? The contradictory aspects in every process[192] are in opposition to each other, are in mutual disharmony, unequal in strength, at odds with one another, and in dispute;

all are replete with such hostile phenomena. Without exception they are contained in all processes, phenomena, things, and thought.[193] **A simple process contains only a single pair of opposites (***yuanjia***),[194] while a complex process contains two or more. And in turn, the pairs of opposites are in contradiction to one another. That is how all** processes, phenomena, and **things**[195] **are constituted and set in motion.**

This being so, there is an utter lack of identity or unity. How then can one speak of identity or unity? In this do the strangeness and wonder of the world find themselves.

The fact is that no contradictory aspect can exist in isolation. Without its opposite aspect, each loses the condition for its existence. Just think, can any one contradictory aspect of a thing or of a concept in the human mind exist independently? It cannot. **Without life, there would be no death; without death, there would be no life. Without "above", there would be no "below"; without "below", there would be no "above". Without misfortune, there would be no good fortune; without good fortune, there would be no misfortune. Without facility, there would be no difficulty; without difficulty, there would be no facility.[196] Without the bourgeoisie, there would be no proletariat; without the proletariat, there would be no bourgeoisie. Without colonies, there would be no imperialist oppression; without imperialist oppression, there would be no colonies.[197] It is so** with the opposition of both sides in all processes, phenomena, and things; **in given conditions, on the one hand they are opposed to each other, and on the other they are interconnected, interpenetrating, interpermeating, interdependent,** and in alliance - both in contradiction and in union - **and this character is described as identity. In given conditions, all contradictions[198] possess the character of non-identity and hence are described as being in contradiction. But they also possess the**

character of identity and hence are interconnected. This is what Lenin means when he says that dialectics studies how there can be identity.[199] This is the first meaning of identity.

[p. 267] But is it enough to say merely that each of the contradictory aspects is the condition for the other's existence, that there is identity between them and that consequently they can coexist in a single entity? No, it is not. The matter does not end with their dependence on each other for their existence;   what is more important is their transformation into each other.   In given conditions[200] each of the contradictory aspects within a thing transforms itself into its opposite.   This is the second meaning of the identity of contradiction.

Why is there identity here, too?   You see, in the relationship between life and death, whether within an organism or in cellular life within an organism, life is transformed into death;   life can never last indefinitely, and under certain conditions it moves towards its opposite, and changes into death. Death? Under certain conditions, death too can produce new life, and death is transformed into life; it is not something which comes to an end with death. One could ask: if there is between life and death no connection, no involvement or relationship, that is to say, no identity, why is it that the two opposed entities of life and death are capable of changing into one another?

The oppressed and deprived proletariat moves towards a dictatorship of the proletariat, that is, it changes to no longer being oppressed or deprived;   the bourgeoisie, however, through the collapse of its class, changes to the point where it comes under the rule of the proletarian state.[201] This has already taken place in the Soviet Union, as it will take place throughout the world.   If there were no interconnections and identity of opposites in given conditions, how could such a change take place?

Neither imperialist oppression of the colonies nor the fate of the colonies to suffer under that oppression can last forever.   The imperialists will be overthrown by the revolutionary efforts of their own peoples and the peoples of the colonies, and will come under the rule of the people. How about the peoples of the colonies and the imperialist countries? The day will come when oppression will be discarded and freedom and liberation (the opposite aspect to oppression) will be achieved; because of certain conditions, there are identity and common characteristics between the two aspects.

The regular warfare of the Great Revolution of 1927 changed into Soviet guerilla war, which commenced the period of Soviet guerilla war which again changed subsequently into regular warfare. From now on, it will change again from Soviet war into anti-Japanese national war. There emerged an identity in these periods because of certain conditions, an interpenetration, an interpermeation and alliance between the two opposite things.

[p. 268] **Because of its class character and imperialist blandishments (these being the conditions),** the Guomindang's revolutionary Three People's Principles changed after 1927 into a reactionary policy;[202] **but it has been compelled to** change to one of resistance to Japan and saving the nation[203] **because of the sharpening of the contradiction between China and Japan and because of the Communist Party's policy of the united front (these being the conditions). Things in contradiction change into one another, and herein lies that kind of identity.**[204]

The agrarian revolution of the Soviet areas has been a process in which the landlord class owning the land is transformed into a class that has lost its land, while the peasants who once lost their land are transformed into small holders who have acquired land, and it will be such a process once again. In given conditions, having and not having, acquiring and losing, are interconnected to give identity.[205] **Under socialism, private peasant ownership is transformed into the public ownership of socialist agriculture; this has already taken place in the Soviet Union,** and we will be able to do the same.[206] **There is a bridge leading from private property to public**

property, which in philosophy is called identity,[207] or interpenetration.

Bourgeois democracy and proletarian democracy are in opposition, but the former inevitably changes into the latter; under certain conditions there are complementary elements produced between things in opposition.

To raise the national culture is in fact to prepare the conditions for changing to an international culture; to strive for a democratic republic is in fact to prepare the conditions for abolishing the democratic republic and changing to a new state system; **to consolidate the dictatorship of the proletariat**[208] **is in fact to prepare the conditions for abolishing this dictatorship and advancing to**[209] **the elimination of all state systems.** To establish and **build the Communist Party is in fact to prepare the conditions for the elimination of the Communist Party and all political parties.** To build a **revolutionary army**[210] **and to carry on revolutionary war is in fact to prepare the conditions for the permanent elimination of war.** These opposites are at the same time complementary.

There are those who say that the Communist Party is internationalist, and is therefore incapable of being at the same time patriotic. However, we make a declaration that we are internationalists but at the same time, because we are a political party of a colony (the condition), we struggle for the protection of the motherland, and in opposition to imperialist oppression. Only when we have firstly escaped from imperialist oppression, can we participate in a world communist society; it is this that allows the two to constitute an identity. Under certain conditions, patriotism [p. 269] and internationalism are both in opposition and complementary. Why is it that the Communist Parties of imperialist countries resolutely oppose patriotism? It is because patriotism in that context has identity only with the interests of the bourgeoisie, and is fundamentally opposed to the interests of the proletariat.

There are those who say that the Communist Party cannot also believe in the Three People's Principles at the same time. However, we declare that, prior to the stage of the

Communist movement, while remaining adherents to the Party's communist programme, we can do no other than resolutely lead the anti-imperialist, anti-feudal national democratic revolution (this is the condition). Therefore, not only do we not oppose them, we previously implemented the true programme of the Three People's Principles (anti-imperialist nationalism, the democratic principle of soviets of workers and peasants, and the principle of people's livelihood through agrarian revolution). Moreover, in the past decade, the tradition of the true Three People's Principles has remained only with the Communist Party. Besides a few elements like Song Qingling, He Xiangning, Li Yangjiu, etc., the Guomindang has discarded this tradition. The political programme of the Communist Party for the democratic revolution is not in conflict with the true Three People's Principles, the thorough-going and progressive Three People's Principles. When we have passed through the democratic stage, we will change to communism. The Three People's Principles and communism are not a single entity, and the two are in contradiction; in the present and future stages they are not a single entity, and they are in contradiction. However, they are both in opposition and complementary; a certain condition can create identity.

We can also speak of something that is happening at this very moment. War and peace are in contradiction, but they are also connected;[211] **war is transformed into peace (for instance, the First World War was transformed into** the Treaty of Versailles;[212] China's **civil war** was transformed into **internal peace** following the Xian Incident).[213] **Peace is transformed into war** (the present world peace is temporary, and will be **transformed into the second world war;**[214] the peace following Japan's invasion of the four eastern provinces was temporary, and has now begun to change into a continental war). **Why is this so? Because**[215] **they have an identity in given conditions.** The Chinese proletariat and bourgeoisie have agreed upon an anti-Japanese united front; this is one aspect of the contradiction. The proletariat must raise its political consciousness and pay close attention to the bourgeoisie's political vacillations, and its corrupting and destructive effect on the Communist Party, in order to guarantee the independence of Party and class; this is the other aspect of the contradiction. A united front of the various political parties [p. 270] with independence for those parties, are the two aspects of the contradiction constituting the present political movement. There would be no united front if one of these two aspects, the party's right to determine its own policies, was removed. We give the people freedom; this is one aspect. We also suppress the Chinese traitors and wreckers; this is the other aspect. Because of certain conditions, these two, freedom and unfreedom, are connected, and it won't do to be without either of them; this is the unity or identity of opposites. The organizational form of the Communist Party and the Soviets, as well as the anti-Japanese government which we advocate, is democratic centralist; they are democratic but also centralist, and the two are in contradiction and unity because, under certain conditions, they have identity. The proletarian democratic dictatorship in the Soviet Union, and our democratic dictatorship of workers and peasants of the last decade, are democratic toward the revolutionary classes; they are also dictatorial (or despotic) toward counter-revolutionary classes. There is identity between the two extremes of these opposites.

The resting and training of troops is at the same time a condition for victory in battle; "to train troops for a thousand days" in order to "use them for one morning". To separate and advance is at the same time a condition for a combined attack (develop to attack jointly); retreat and defence, are at the same time in order to counter-attack and take the offensive (retreat to advance, and defend to attack). There is no other reason for being devious than it is the most effective method of wiping out the enemy (be devious to be direct); in order to succeed in the west, make a thrust towards the east (cause an uproar in the east, and strike in the west). Divide the soldiers to win over the masses, in order to facilitate centralization to wipe out the enemy; centralize to wipe out the enemy in order to facilitate the division of the soldiers to win over the masses. In order to carry out orders decisively, flexible freedoms need be allowed under a unified scheme; the strict implementation of discipline requires the development of conscious initiative; the statement of individual interest is permissable, but in the end these must be subordinated to the group decision; work at the front is important, but work at the rear cannot be discarded or ignored; if one's health is poor one must think of convalescence, but in times of urgency, one also must think of sacrifice; everybody wants life to be easy, but when economic difficulties arise, one has to suffer; military training is important, and without it we could not smash the enemy, but political work is also of importance for without it we would be defeated; the abundant experience of the old soldiers and cadres is worthwhile and valuable, but if there are no new soldiers and cadres, the war and our work cannot be continued; courage is important, but there must be a strategem; although Zhang Fei was alright, he was after all not as good as Zhao Zilong;[216] [p. 271] the part of the work which we lead is important, but that part led by others and the entire work is also important if not more important; small group mentality is incorrect, and when one's own opinion and that of the group or higher authorities is in contradiction, one's opinion can and should be explained; it is, however, impermissable to freely express that opinion to any other member at a time when the group or higher authorities have not yet given approval, still less to instigate the subordinate members to oppose the higher authorities; the discipline of the minority subordinating itself to the majority, and the lower level subordinating itself to the higher level, is the minimum discipline of the Communist Party and the Red Army. "Good medicine is bitter to the taste but beneficial for the sickness". "Sincere advice is not pleasant to hear but it is beneficial for one's conduct".[217] "It is on disaster that good fortune perches, it is beneath good fortune that disaster crouches".[218] "To love yet know their bad qualities, to hate and yet know their excellences".[219] "To glance ahead but not behind is called being a boorish oaf; to know one but not two is he who is not yet a wise man".[220]

All contradictory things are interconnected; not only do they coexist in a single entity in given conditions, but in other given conditions, they also transform themselves into each other. This is the full meaning of the unity of opposites.[221] **This is what Lenin meant when he talked of how they happen to**

be identical, under what kind of conditions they become identical, transforming themselves into one another.[222] Why is it that the human mind should take these opposites not as dead, rigid, but as living, conditional, mobile, transforming themselves into each other? Because this is just how things are in objective reality. The fact is that the unity or identity of opposites in objective things is not dead or rigid; but is living, conditional, mobile, temporary, and relative; in given conditions, every contradictory aspect transforms itself into its opposite.[223] Why can an egg but not a stone be transformed into a chicken? Why is there identity between war and peace and none between war and a stone? Why can human beings give birth only to human beings and not to anything else? The sole reason is that the identity of opposites exists only in[224] given conditions. Without these necessary given conditions there can be no identity whatsoever.

[p. 272]   Why is it that in Russia[225] the democratic[226] revolution was directly linked with the[227] socialist revolution, while in France the democratic[228] revolution was not directly linked with a socialist revolution and the Paris Commune[229] ended in failure? Why is it, on the other hand, that the nomadic system of Mongolia and Central Asia has been directly linked with socialism? Why is it that the Chinese revolution can avoid a capitalist future and be directly linked with socialism and avoid[230] the old historical road of England, America, France, etc?[231] Why is it that the Russian Revolution of 1905 and the Chinese Revolutions of 1911 and 1927 were not linked with revolutionary victory, but to failure? Why is it that in his entire life, most of Napolean's wars were linked to victory, while at the one battle of Waterloo, he was roundly defeated, his army beaten and himself taken prisoner? Why is it possible to build a railroad to Xinjiang and not to the moon? Why have the cordial relations between Germany and the Soviet Union turned into enmity, while the enmity between France and the Soviet Union turned temporarily into cordial relations? In all of these questions, **the sole reason is the concrete conditions of the time. When certain necessary conditions are present,[232] contradictions arise in processes[233] and, moreover, the opposites contained in them are interdependent and become transformed into one another; otherwise none of this would be possible.** It is for this reason that none of the following can become an identity of opposites, or a concrete contradiction, and merely add to the material for annoyance and amusement amongst men: Don Quixote's mighty battle with the windmill, Sun Wukong's somersault of one hundred and eight thousand *li* over the clouds, Alice's journey through Wonderland, Robinson's wanderings on his lone island, Ah Q's spiritual victory, Hitler's world domination, Hegel's absolute spirit, Bukharin's theory of equilibrium, Trotsky's permanent revolution, the ideological unity of the emperor's scholars, Chen Duxiu's opportunism, the pro-Japanese faction's theory that weapons decide everything, and including from among Ancient China's legends, "the man of Qi's concern that the sky might fall", "Gua Fu's race with the moon",[234] and so on.[235]

Such is the problem of identity. What then is struggle? And what is the relation between identity and struggle?

Lenin said:

The unity (coincidence, identity, equal action) of opposites is conditional, temporary, transitory, relative. The struggle of mutually exclusive opposites is absolute, just as development and motion are absolute.

What does this passage mean?

All processes have a beginning and an end, all processes transform themselves into their opposites. The constancy of all processes is relative, but[236] the [p. 273] **transformation of one process into another is absolute.** The unity, identity, consistency, constancy, and union of contradictions are contained within the struggle of contradictions, and become an element in the struggle of contradictions. That is the meaning of Lenin's statement.[237]

That is to say, it is insufficient to simply acknowledge that contradiction leads to movement; it must also be understood under which conditions contradiction gives rise to movement.

The first condition of unity (identity) in which contradiction gives rise to movement is the particular condition of movement. In daily life it is called rest, constantly unchanging, immobile, death, at a standstill, deadlock, stalemate, peaceful, equilibrium, balance, harmony, compromise, union, and so on; all of these are relative, temporary, and conditional. The second condition of unity in which contradiction gives rise to movement also must be recognized, that is the general condition of movement. This is the splitting of unity, its struggle, life, movement, impermanence, liveliness, change, intranquility (*bu heping*), disequilibrium, disharmony, intransigence, and even conflict, antagonism, or war; this is absolute. The relative condition of contradiction of identity, unity, rest, death, etc., is contained in the condition of contradiction which is absolute and in struggle. Because struggle permeates a process from beginning to end, permeates all processes, it becomes that which is absolute in them. Not to understand this principle is metaphysical and mechanistic, and to actually reject dialectics.

International peace treaties are relative, while international struggle is absolute. A united front between classes is relative, while class struggle is absolute. Unanimity in intra-party ideology is relative, while struggle in intra-party ideology is absolute. Equilibrium, solidity, attraction, and association, etc. in natural phenomena are relative, while disequilibrium, insolidity, rejection, dissociation, etc. are absolute. When a process is in a condition of peace treaty, united front, in unity and solidarity, equilibrium, solidity, attraction, association, etc., contradiction and struggle still exist, but they have not adopted an acute form; it is certainly not a case of there being no contradictions, or of a cessation of struggle. Struggle ceaselessly destroys one relative condition and transforms it into another relative condition, destroys one process and transforms it into another process, and this ubiquitous characteristic of struggle is the absoluteness of contradiction.

[p. 274] **When we said above that two opposite things can coexist in a single entity and can transform themselves into each other because there is identity between them, we were speaking of conditionality, that is to say, in given conditions two contradictory things can be united and can transform themselves into each other, but in the absence of these conditions, they cannot constitute a contradiction, cannot coexist in the same entity and cannot transform themselves into one another. It is because the identity of opposites obtains only in given conditions that we have said identity is conditional and relative. We may add that struggle[238] permeates a process from beginning to end and makes one process transform itself into another, that it is ubiquitous, and that struggle is therefore unconditional and absolute.**

The combination of conditional, relative identity and unconditional, absolute struggle constitutes the movement of opposites in all things.

So that this point may be clearly understood, we again utilize as examples the relationship between life and death, and the relationship between labour and capital: within an organism, the death of old cells is the precondition for the production of new cells, and is the precondition for the process of life. The two contradictory aspects of life and death are united within an organism, and also change into each other; live cells change into dead cells, and dead cells change into live cells (live cells are regenerated (*tuotai*) from dead cells). But this unity of life and death, their coexistence within an oganism, are conditional, temporary, and relative. However, from start to finish, the incompatibility of life and death, their mutual rejection, struggle, negation, and transformation, are unconditional, eternal, and absolute. The absoluteness of struggle is indicated by live elements within an organism ceaselessly triumphing over dead elements and moreover controlling the dead elements. Under given conditions life changes into death and death into life; such conditions allow an identity between life and death, and enable them to change into each other. Due to the mutual struggle of these two contradictory entities, life and death, life is inevitably transformed into death and death is inevitably transformed into life. This inevitability is unconditional and absolute. From this it can be seen that there must at a certain stage in development be a certain condition of temperature and environment, etc., for life and death to change from one to another, and for there to be an identity between them. This is one problem. The reasons for the so-called temporariness and relativity of life and death, that is, where the conditions do not change and are unable to lengthen life or death, are to be found in the struggle, negation, and mutual rejection between the two. [p. 275] This situation is eternal and absolute. This is the other problem.

The proletariat produces surplus value for the bourgeoisie, and the bourgeoisie exploits the proletariat's labour power. This is a unified process which determines the survival of capitalism. Labour and capital are each a condition for the other's existence. However, this condition has a given limit, and capitalist development must remain within this given limit; if it is exceeded, ruptures emerge in the unified process, and a socialist revolution appears. These ruptures emerge abruptly, but also emerge gradually in that preparations for their emergence commence from the day the two classes come into existence; the struggle of both sides is continual, and it is this which lays the ground for a sudden change. From this it can be seen that the coexistence of the two classes is preserved as a result of given conditions; this coexistence under given conditions produces a unity or identity between the two classes. Under given conditions the two classes also change from one to the other, such that the exploiters change into the exploited and the exploited change into the exploiters, and capitalist society is transformed into a socialist society. The two contradictory entities have an identity under given conditions. This is one problem. The two sides are in constant struggle. There is struggle within an entity, and especially the struggle of revolution. This unavoidable condition is unconditional, absolute, and inevitable. This is the other problem.[239]

In identity there is struggle.[240] **To quote Lenin, "...there is an absolute in the relative".** Because of this, the unity of opposites is itself a manifestation or an element of the struggle of contradictions. This is our conclusion with regard to this problem.

According to this conclusion, it is perfectly evident whether or not the so-called theories of class harmony and the unity of ideology still have any standing. The theory of international class harmony becomes the opportunism of the workers' movements in every country, and they have no other function than to simply serve as the running dogs of the bourgeoisie. China too has a so-called theory of class harmony, but this is a tune sung by bourgeois reformism. It has no other purpose than specifically to swindle the proletariat so that it will remain forever the slave of the bourgeoisie. The meaningless clichés of the so-called theory of the unity of ideology, directly or indirectly depend on the nonsense spewed out by officialdom that it is "the learned opinion of the scholars". Its purpose is nothing but the suppression of the truth, and the obstruction of the progress of the revolution. True scientific theory is the law of the unity of opposites of materialist dialectics, and not these other melodies.

[p. 276] VII. *The Place of Antagonism in Contradiction*

The question of the struggle of opposites includes the question of what is antagonism. Our answer is that contradiction exists in all processes from beginning to end, and that there is a struggle between the two sides of a contradiction from start to finish. **Antagonism is one form of struggle,** but not all contradictions have it;[241] when certain contradictions in a certain process of development adopt a form in which force becomes overt and there is mutual conflict, the struggle of contradictions manifests itself as

antagonism. **Antagonism is**[242] **a particular manifestation of the struggle of opposites.**
For instance, consider the contradiction between the exploiting and the exploited classes. Such contradictory classes coexist for a long time in the same society, be it slave society, feudal society, or capitalist society, and they struggle with each other, but it is not until the contradiction between the two classes develops to a certain stage that it assumes the form of open antagonism, and it is then that society ruptures and revolution and war are engendered.[243]

The explosion of a bomb, the hatching of a chicken from its egg, and animal regeneration (*tuotai*), are all contradictory things coexistent in a single entity, and which at a certain moment, adopt the form of conflict, disruption (*poju*), and rupture.[244]

In the peaceful coexistence between countries, included in which is that between socialist and capitalist states, contradiction and struggle exist without ceasing; only at a certain stage in development does war emerge.[245]

In the Soviet Union, the New Economic Policy permitted a considerable development of capitalist elements. Lenin considered that at that time there was a possibility of utilizing state capitalism under the dictatorship of the proletariat; that is to say, the utilization of certain bourgeois elements to develop the forces of production, simultaneous with their control by Soviet laws, following which they could be limited [p. 277] and prohibited. At this time the two contradictions of socialism and capitalism coexisted within socialist society in mutual struggle and interconnection; it was only after the task of eliminating the rich peasantry and capitalist remnants had been raised that the existence of both elements became an impossibility, and a life and death struggle of overtly antagonistic form emerged.

The first united front between the Guomindang and the Communist Party was also like this.

However, the contradictions in many processes, phenomena, and things do not develop into antagonistic ones.

For instance, the contradictions between correct and incorrect ideas in the Communist Party, between the advanced and the backward in culture, between town and country in economics, between the forces and relations of production, between production and consumption, between exchange value and use value, between the various technical divisions of labour, between workers and peasants in class relations, between life and death in nature, between heredity and mutation, between cold and hot, between day and night; none has an antagonistic condition of existence.[246]

Bukharin regarded contradiction and antagonism as one and the same thing. He therefore considered that in a society in which socialism had been accomplished there were neither antagonisms nor contradiction. **Lenin said:** "This is extremely incorrect, **antagonism and contradiction are not at all one and the same. Under socialism, the first will disappear, the second will remain**".[247] Bukharin is an advocate of the theory of equilibrium which refuses to recognize that the development of a thing is due to the movement of internal contradictions, and which considers that society will continue to develop even though there are no contradictions under socialism.

Trotsky sets out from a different extreme, but also regards contradiction and antagonism as one and the same thing. As a result, he considers that under socialism there not only exists a contradiction between workers and peasants, but that this will develop into an antagonism like the contradiction between labour and capital, which can only be resolved by employing revolutionary methods. The Soviet Union however has used the method of the socialization of agriculture to resolve it, and moreover has resolved it under the conditions of socialism in one country, without having to wait for the international revolution alleged as necessary by the Trotskyites.

Bukharin has reduced contradiction to the point of elimination, while the Trotskyites have elevated contradiction into antagonism; neither of the two extremes of the right or left wing understands the problem of contradiction.

[p. 278] The method for resolving a general contradiction is fundamentally different from the method of resolving antagonism; this is the particularity of contradiction and the particularity of the method of resolving contradiction. This is a problem which should be given specific recognition. Whatever is antagonistic contains contradictoriness, but not all contradictions necessarily adopt an antagonistic form, and here we have a general distinction.[248]

The law of the unity of contradictions is the fundamental law of the universe, **and the fundamental law** of ideological method (*sixiang fangfa*).[249] Lenin called it the kernel of dialectics, and it stands opposed to the metaphysical view of development. It is opposed to the absolute law of identity of formal logic. Contradiction exists in all objective and subjective processes of things, and throughout all processes **from beginning to end;**[250] **this is the universality and absoluteness of contradiction.** The **aspects of contradiction** and the universe each **have their respective characteristics;**[251] people's minds are all different just like their faces, and contradictions likewise all differ in the form they take. **This is the particularity and relativity of contradiction. In given conditions, opposites possess identity and consequently can coexist in a single entity and can transform themselves into each other; this again is the particularity and relativity of contradiction. But the struggle of opposites is ceaseless, it goes on both when the opposites are coexisting and when they are transforming themselves into each other, and becomes especially conspicuous when they are transforming themselves into one another; this again is the universality and absoluteness of contradiction. In studying the particularity and relativity of contradiction, we must give attention to the distinction between the principal**[252] **aspect and the non-principal aspect of the contradiction.** When studying the struggle of contradictions we must give attention to the general and the particular forms of the struggle of contradiction — that is, the distinction in which contradiction develops into antagonism. This is what we know of the law of the unity of contradictions.[253]

Notes

1. Official text reads: "the identity and struggle of the aspects of a contradiction". *Selected Works of Mao Tse-tung* (Peking: FLP, 1967), Vol. 1, p. 311 (hereafter SW); *Mao Zedong xuanji* [Selected Works of Mao Zedong] (Beijing: Renmin chubanshe, 1968), Vol. I, p. 274 (hereafter XJ).

2. Addition in official text: "The criticism to which the idealism of the Deborin school has been subjected in Soviet philosophical circles in recent years has aroused great interest among us. Deborin's idealism has exerted a very bad influence in the Chinese Communist Party, and it cannot be said that the dogmatist thinking in our Party is unrelated to the approach of that school. Our present study of philosophy should therefore have the eradication of dogmatist thinking as its main objective". SW I, p. 311; XJ I, p. 274.

3. Official text reads: "knowledge"; SW I, p. 311; XJ I, p. 275.

4. Official text reads: "universe"; SW I, p. 311; XJ I, p. 275.

5. Official text reads: "conception"; SW I, p. 312; XJ I, p. 275.

6. Addition in official text:

"Lenin said:

The two basic (or two possible ? or two historically observable ?) conceptions of development (evolution) are: development as decrease and increase, as repetition, *and* development as a unity of opposites (the division of a unity into mutually exclusive opposites and their reciprocal relation).

"Here Lenin was referring to these two different world outlooks." SW I, p. 312; XJ I, p. 275.

7. Official text reads: "In China another name for metaphysics is *xuanxue*. For a long period in history whether in China or in Europe, this way of thinking, which is part and parcel of the idealist world outlook, occupied a dominant position in human thought. In Europe, the materialism of the bourgeoisie in its early days was also metaphysical. As the social economy of many European countries advanced to the stage of highly developed capitalism, as the forces of production, the class struggle, and the sciences developed to a level unprecedented in history, and as the industrial proletariat became the greatest motive force in historical development, there arose the Marxist world outlook of materialist dialectics. Then, in addition to open and bare-faced reactionary idealism, vulgar evolutionism emerged among the bourgeoisie to oppose materialist dialectics.

"The metaphysical or vulgar evolutionist world outlook sees things as isolated, static and one-sided. It regards all things in the universe, their forms and their species, as eternally isolated from one another and immutable. Such change as there is can only be an increase or decrease in quantity or a change of place. Moreover, the cause of such an increase or decrease or change of place is not inside things but outside them, that is, the motive force is external. Metaphysicians hold that all the different kinds of things in the universe and all their characteristics have been the same ever since they first came into being. All subsequent changes have simply been increases or decreases in quantity. They contend that a thing can only keep on repeating itself as the same kind of thing and cannot change into anything different. In their opinion, capitalist exploitation...". SW I, p. 312; XJ I, p. 275-276.

8.   Official text reads: "...searches in an over-simplified way..."; SW I, p. 312; XJ I, p. 276.

9.   Official text reads: "deny"; SW I, p. 313; XJ I, p. 276.

10.   *Ziran juedui bubianlun.*

11.   Official text reads: "In Europe, this mode of thinking existed as mechanical materialism in the 17th and 18th centuries and as vulgar evolutionism at the end of the 19th and the beginning of the 20th centuries. In China, there was the metaphysical thinking exemplified in the saying 'Heaven changeth not, likewise the Dao changeth not', and it was supported by the decadent feudal ruling classes for a long time. Mechanical materialism and vulgar evolutionism, which were imported from Europe in the last hundred years, are supported by the bourgeoisie". SW I, p. 313; XJ I, p. 276.

12.   *Shiwu de zidong;* this has been replaced in the official text by "while each thing in its movement is interrelated with and interacts on the things around it". SW I, p. 313; XJ I, p. 276.

13.   *Beidonglun;* SW I, p. 313; XJ I, p. 277.

14.   Addition in official text: "...and why one thing changes into another". SW I, p. 313; XJ I, p. 277.

15.   Official text reads: "...chiefly (*zhuyao*) the result of..."; SW I, p. 313; XJ I, p. 277.

16.   Official text reads: "Imperialist Russia..."; SW I, p. 313; XJ I, p. 277.

17.   Official text reads: "Long dominated by feudalism, China has undergone great changes in the last hundred years and is now changing in the direction of a new China, liberated and free, and yet no change has occurred in her geography and climate. Changes do take place in the geography and climate of the earth as a whole and in every part of it, but they are insignificant when compared with changes in society; geographical and climatic changes manifest themselves in terms of tens of thousands of years, while social changes manifest

themselves in thousands, hundreds or tens of years, and even in a few months in times of revolution". SW I, p. 314; XJ I, p. 277.

18.   Official text reads: "According to materialist dialectics, changes in nature are due chiefly to the development of the internal contradictions in nature"; SW I, p. 314; XJ I, p. 277.

19.   Addition in official text: "chiefly" (*zhuyao*); SW I, p. 314; XJ I, p. 277.

20.   Addition in official text: "...and the contradiction between the old and the new..."; SW I, p. 314; XJ I, p. 277.

21.   Official text reads: "it is the development of these contradictions that pushes society forward and gives the impetus for the supersession of the old society by the new". SW I, p. 314; XJ I, p. 277.

22.   Official text reads: "...materialist dialectics..."; SW I, p. 314; XJ I, p. 277.

23.   Official text reads: "...become operative (*zuoyong*)". SW I, p. 314; XJ I, p. 278.

24.   Official text reads: "In China in 1927..."; SW I, p. 314; XJ I, p. 278.

25.   Addition in official text: "When we liquidated this opportunism, the Chinese revolution resumed its advance. Later, the Chinese revolution again suffered severe setbacks at the hands of the enemy, because adventurism had arisen within our party. When we liquidated this adventurism, our cause advanced once again. Thus it can be seen that to lead..."; SW I, p. 315; XJ I, p. 278.

26.   Official version reads: "...a political party must depend on the correctness of its own political line..."; SW I, p. 315; XJ I, p. 278.

27.   This quote from Su Dongpo (1036-1101 A.D.) comes from *Fan Zeng Lun* (On Fan Zeng).

28.   *Analects*, Book XII, Chapter IV. I have used Legge's translation; see *The Four Books* (Hong Kong: Wei Tung Book Store, 1973), p. 95.

29.   Mao also uses this quote in the original text of *On Protracted War* (1938); see *Mao Zedong Ji*, Vol. VI, p. 138.

30.   There appears to be a typographical error here; the negative *bu* has been replaced by a comma.

31.   Mao is referring here to the conflicts of the transcendental ideas from the *Critique of Pure Reason*; see Theodore Meyer Greene (ed.), *Kant: Selections* (New York: Charles Scribner's Sons, 1957), pp. 189-200.

32.   Addition in official text: "For convenience of exposition, I shall deal first with the universality of contradiction and then proceed to the particularity of contradiction. The reason is that the universality of

contradiction can be explained more briefly, for it has been widely recognized ever since the materialist-dialectical world outlook was discovered and materialist dialectics applied with outstanding success to analysing many aspects of human history and natural history and to changing many aspects of society and nature (as in the Soviet Union) by the great creators and continuers of Marxism - Marx, Engels, Lenin, and Stalin; whereas the particularity of contradiction is still not clearly understood by many comrades, and especially by the dogmatists. They do not understand that it is precisely in the particularity of contradiction that the universality of contradiction resides. Nor do they understand how important is the study of the particularity of contradiction in the concrete things confronting us for guiding the course of revolutionary practice. Therefore, it is necessary to stress the study of the particularity of contradiction and to explain it at adequate length. For this reason, in our analysis of the law of contradiction in things, we shall first analyse the universality of contradiction, then place special stress on analysing the particularity of contradiction, and finally return to the universality of contradiction.

"The universality or absoluteness of contradiction has a twofold meaning. One is that contradiction exists in the process of development of all things, and the other is that in the process of development of each thing a movement of opposites exists from beginning to end". SW I, pp. 315-316; XJ I, pp. 279-280.

33. Official text reads: "There is nothing that does not contain contradiction; without contradiction nothing would exist". SW I, p. 316; XJ I, p. 280.

34. Addition in official text: "Engels explained the universality of contradiction as follows:

If simple mechanical change of place contains a contradiction, this is even more true of the higher forms of motion of matter, and especially of organic life and its development. ...life consists precisely and primarily in this - that a being is at each moment itself and yet something else. Life is therefore also a contradiction which is present in things and processes themselves, and which constantly originates and resolves itself; and as soon as the contradiction ceases, life, too, comes to an end, and death steps in. We likewise saw that also in the sphere of thought we could not escape contradictions, and that for example the contradiction between man's inherently unlimited capacity for knowledge and its actual presence only in men who are externally limited and possess limited cognition finds its solution in what is - at least practically, for us - an endless succession of generations, in infinite progress.

...one of the basic principles of higher mathematics is the contradiction that in certain circumstances straight lines and curves may be the same....

But even lower mathematics teems with contradictions". SW I, pp. 316-317; XJ I, pp. 280-281.

35.   This and the next three paragraphs have been replaced in the official text with a direct quote from Lenin which reads:

"Lenin illustrated the universality of contradiction as follows:

In mathematics: + and -. Differential and integral.

In mechanics: action and reaction.

In physics: positive and negative electricity.

In chemistry: the combination and dissociation of atoms.

In social science the class struggle." SW I, p. 317; XJ I, p. 281.

36.   Official text reads: "...pushes its development forward and solves its problems." SW I, p. 317; XJ I, p. 281.

37.   Official text reads: "...pushes forward the development of thought, and ceaselessly solves problems in man's thinking". SW I, p. 317; XJ I, p. 281.

38.   Official text reads: "Thus it is already clear that contradiction..."; SW I, p. 317; XJ I, p. 281.

39.   Official text reads: "But does contradiction also exist at the initial stage of each process? Is there a movement of opposites from beginning to end in the process of development of every single thing?"; SW I, pp. 317-318; XJ I, p. 281.

40.   Mao repeats this sentence in the next paragraph, but one has been deleted from the official text; SW I, p. 318; XJ I, pp. 281-282.

41.   Official text reads: "As can be seen from the articles written by Soviet philosophers criticizing it, the Deborin school maintains that contradiction..."; SW I, p. 318; XJ I, p. 281. Compare footnote (2) above.

42.   Official text reads: "...between the kulaks and the peasants..."; SW I, p. 318; XJ I, p. 282.

43.   The Chinese rendering of this name is *Guoliefu*. It is difficult to be certain whether this is actually referring to Gorev, who was a Russian Marxist under Stalin.

44.   Official text reads: "...social conditions..."; SW I, p. 318; XJ I, p. 282.

45.   A clause has been added to the official text here which reads; "...the workers and the peasants have established a firm alliance in the course of socialist construction and are gradually resolving this contradiction in the course of the advance from socialism to communism." SW I, p. 318; XJ I, p. 282.

46.   There is no paragraph break here as there is in the official text.

47.   Addition in official text; "The old process ends and the new one begins". SW I, p. 318; XJ I, p. 282.

48.   *Yingyong*; official text uses the word "analysis" (*fenxi*); SW I, p. 318; XJ I, p. 282.

49.   Official text reads: "...process of development of things..."; SW I, p. 318-319; XJ I, p. 282.

50.   Same addition as footnote (49).

51.   In this and the following quote, I have reproduced the official translation, although the Chinese in the original text does differ in some minor respects from that shown in the original text.

52.   *Yifa* was a method of writing advocated by the *Tong Cheng* school in the Qing dynasty. It was characterized by austere simplicity, and an emphasis on utilizing ancient styles. There is something of a play on words in Mao's use of this Chinese term; he compares the *yifa* of the *Tong Cheng* school with the *yanjiu fa* (method of study) of Marxism.

53.   Addition in official text; "Chinese Communists must learn this method; only then will they be able correctly to analyse history and the present state of the Chinese revolution and infer its future". SW I, p. 319; XJ I, p. 283.

54.   Same addition as footnote (49).

55.   Same addition as footnote (49).

56.   No paragraph break here as in official text; SW I, p. 319; XJ I, p. 283.

57.   Addition in official text: "...and this motion must assume certain forms". SW I, p. 319; XJ I, p. 283.

58.   Addition in official text: "It is the internal cause or, as it may be called, the basis for the immense variety of things in the world". SW I, p. 320; XJ I, p. 284.

59.   Official text reads: "...classes and class struggle..."; SW I, p. 320; XJ I, p. 284.

60.   *Yanjiu*; official text has "understand" (*renshi*); SW I, p. 320; XJ I, p. 284.

61.   Addition in official text: "or universal basis..."; SW I, p. 320; XJ I, p. 284.

62.   Addition in official text: "...or particular basis..."; SW I, p. 320; XJ I, p. 284.

63.   There is an important addition here in the official text dealing with Mao's epistemology. It reads:

"As regards the sequence in the movement of man's knowledge there is always a gradual growth from the knowledge of individual and particular things to the knowledge of things in general. Only after man knows the particular essence of many different things can he proceed to generalization and know the common essence of things. When man attains the knowledge of this common essence, he uses it as a guide and proceeds to study various concrete things which have not yet been studied, or studied thoroughly, and to discover the particular essence of each; only thus is he able to supplement, enrich, and develop this knowledge of their common essence and prevent such knowledge from withering or petrifying. These are the two processes of cognition; one, from the particular to the general, and the other from the general to the particular. Thus cognition always moves in cycles and (so long as scientific method is strictly adhered to) each cycle advances human knowledge a step higher and so makes it more and more profound. Where our dogmatists err on this question is that, on the one hand, they do not understand that we have to study the particularity of contradiction and know the particular essence of individual things before we can adequately know the universality of contradiction and the common essence of things, and that, on the other hand, they do not understand that after knowing the common essence of things, we must go further and study the concrete things that have not yet been thoroughly studied or have only just emerged. Our dogmatists are lazy-bones. They refuse to undertake any painstaking study of concrete things, they regard general truths as emerging out of the void, they turn them into purely abstract unfathomable formulas, and thereby completely deny and reverse the normal sequence by which man comes to know truth. Nor do they understand the interconnection of the two processes in cognition - from the particular to the general and then from the general to the particular. They understand nothing of the Marxist theory of knowledge." SW I, pp. 320-321; XJ I, pp. 284-285.

64.   Addition in official text: "...which is real (and not imaginary)..."; SW I, p. 321; XJ I, p. 285.

65.   Addition in official text: "...and start from..."; SW I, p. 321; XJ I, p. 285.

66.   Addition in official text: "...revolutionary..."; SW I, p. 322; XJ I, p. 286.

67.   The last two clauses are in reverse order in the official text; SW I, pp. 321-322; XJ I, p. 286.

68.   Official text reads: "...working class...";   SW I, p. 322;   XJ I, p. 286.

69.   Official text reads: "...and the peasant class in socialist society is resolved by the method of collectivization and mechanization in agriculture". SW I, p. 322; XJ I, p. 286.

70.   Official text reads: "...criticism and self-criticism";   SW I, p. 322; XJ I, p. 286.

71.   Addition in official text: "...as well as between the methods used to resolve them.   The principle of using different methods to resolve different contradictions is one which Marxist-Leninists must strictly observe.   The dogmatists do not observe this principle;   they do not understand that conditions differ in different kinds of revolution and so do not understand that different methods should be used to resolve different contradictions;   on the contrary, they invariably adopt what they imagine to be an unalterable formula and arbitrarily apply it everywhere, which only causes setbacks to the revolution or makes a sorry mess of what was originally well done".   SW I, p. 322; XJ I, p. 286.

72.   Addition in official text: "...in the development of a thing...";   SW I, p. 322; XJ I, p. 286.

73.   Official text reads: "This likewise requires the utmost attention in our study". SW I, p. 322; XJ I, p. 286.

74.   Official text reads: "There are many contradictions in the course of development of any major thing". SW I, p. 322; XJ I, p. 286.

75.   Official text reads: "...urban petty bourgeoisie...";   SW I, p. 322; XJ I, p. 286.

76.   Official text reads: "...reactionary ruling groups...";   SW I, p. 322; XJ I, p. 286.

77.   Addition in official text: "...and in its contradiction..."; SW I, p. 323; XJ I, p. 287.

78.   Addition in official text: "...and in contradiction...";   SW I, p. 323; XJ I, p. 287.

79.   Addition in official text: "Lenin meant just this when he said that the most essential thing in Marxism, the living soul of Marxism, is the concrete analysis of concrete conditions.   Our dogmatists have violated Lenin's teachings;   they never use their brains to analyse anything concretely, and in their writings and speeches they always use stereotypes devoid of content,

thereby creating a very bad style of work in our Party". SW I, p. 323; XJ I, p. 287.

80.   Official text reads: "I have discussed this in my essay 'On Practice'". SW I, p. 323; XJ I, p. 287.

81.   Official text reads: "...only the past but not the future..." SW I, p. 323; XJ I, p. 287.

82.   Addition in official text: "...only individual parts but not the whole..."; SW I, p. 323; XJ I, p. 287.

83.   Addition in official text: "revolutionary"; SW I, p. 323; XJ I, p. 287.

84.   Same addition as footnote 83.

85.   Addition in official text: "...seeing the trees but not the forest". SW I, p. 323; XJ I, p. 288.

86.   Mao uses the name Wei Zheng in the official text; SW I, p. 323; XJ I, p. 288.

87.   Mao uses the name Song Jiang in the official text; SW I, p. 324; XJ I, p. 288.

88.   Addition in official text: "...using a strategem similar to that of the Trojan Horse in the foreign story". SW I, p. 324; XJ I, p. 288.

89.   Addition in official text: "Lenin said:
...in order really to know an object we must embrace, study, all its sides, all connections and 'mediations'. We shall never achieve this completely, but the demand for all-sidedness is a safeguard against mistakes and rigidity". SW I, p. 324; XJ I, p. 288.

90.   Addition in official text: "The reason the dogmatist and empiricist comrades in China have made mistakes lies precisely in their subjectivist, one-sided and superficial way of looking at things. To be one-sided and superficial is at the same time to be subjective. For all objective things are actually interconnected and are governed by inner laws, but instead of undertaking the task of reflecting things as they really are some people only look at things one-sidedly or superficially and who know neither their interconnections nor their inner laws, and so their method is subjectivist". SW I, p. 324; XJ I, pp. 288-289.

91.   Addition in official text: "...in the development of a thing..."; SW I, p. 324; XJ I, p. 289.

92.   No paragraph break here as in official text; SW I, p. 325; XJ I, p. 289.

93.   Same addition as footnote 91.

94.   Official text reads: "...but in a lengthy process the conditions usually differ at each stage". SW I, p. 325; XJ I, p. 289.

95.   Same addition as footnote 91.

96.   Addition in official text: "...in a lengthy process". SW I, p. 325; XJ I, p. 289.

97.   Addition in official text: "...or influenced by..."; SW I, p. 325; XJ I, p. 289.

98.   Addition in official text: "If people do not pay attention to the stages in the process of development of a thing, they cannot deal with its contradictions properly". SW I, p. 325; XJ I, p. 289.

99.   Official text reads: "...when the capitalism of the era of free competition developed into imperialism..."; SW I, p. 325; XJ I, p. 289.

100.   Addition in official text: "...class..."; SW I, p. 325; XJ I, p. 289.

101.   Official text reads: "...manifested itself with particular sharpness..."; SW I, p. 325; XJ I, p. 289.

102.   Addition in official text: "Leninism is the Marxism of the era of imperialism and proletarian revolution precisely because Lenin and Stalin have correctly explained these contradictions and correctly formulated the theory and tactics of the proletarian revolution for their resolution". SW I, p. 325; XJ I, p. 289.

103.   Official text reads: "...bourgeois-democratic revolution..."; SW I, p. 325; XJ I, p. 289.

104.   Addition in official text: "In particular, the revolution in its period of bourgeois leadership and the revolution in its period of proletarian leadership represent two vastly different historical stages. In other words, proletarian leadership has fundamentally changed the whole face of the revolution, has brought about a new alignment of classes, given rise to a tremendous upsurge in the peasant revolution, imparted thoroughness to the revolution against imperialism and feudalism, created the possibility of the transition from the democratic revolution to the socialist revolution, and so on. None of these was possible in the period when the revolution was under bourgeois leadership". SW I, pp. 325-326; XJ I, p. 290.

105.   Official text reads: "...nonetheless this process has..."; SW I, p. 326; XJ I, p. 290.

106.   Official text reads: "...several..."; SW I, p. 326; XJ I, p. 290.

107.   Official text reads: "...the revolution of 1924-27,..."; SW I, p. 326; XJ I, p. 290.

108.   Official text reads: "...new warlords..."; SW I, p. 326; XJ I, p. 290.

109. Official text reads: "...the Agrarian Revolutionary War..."; SW I, p. 326; XJ I, p. 290.

110. Official text reads: "...the second national united front and the War of Resistance Against Japan". SW I, p. 326; XJ I, p. 290.

111. Official text reads: "...(e.g., the Agrarian Revolutionary War and the Japanese invasion of the four northeastern provinces)..."; SW I, p. 326; XJ I, p. 290.

112. Official text reads: "...the loss of our revolutionary base areas in the South)." SW I, p. 326; XJ I, p. 290.

113. Official text reads: "...in the process of development of a thing..."; SW I, p. 326; XJ I, p. 290.

114. Official text reads: "...we must not only observe..."; SW I, p. 326; XJ I, p. 290.

115. Addition in official text: "...of each contradiction". SW I, p. 326; XJ I, p. 290.

116. Addition in official text: "...carried out Sun Yat-sen's Three Great Policies of alliance with Russia, co-operation with the Communist Party, and assistance to the peasants and workers; hence it was..."; SW I, p. 326; XJ I, p. 290.

117. Addition in official text: "...and become a reactionary bloc of the landlords and big bourgeoisie". SW I, pp. 326-327; XJ I, pp. 290-291.

118. Official text reads: "After the Xian Incident in December 1936, it began another change in the direction of ending the civil war and co-operating with the Communist Party for joint opposition to Japanese imperialism". SW I, p. 327; XJ I, p. 291.

119. Official text reads: "...Chinese Communist Party". SW I, p. 327; XJ I, p. 291.

120. Official text reads: "it courageously led the revolution of 1924-27 but..."; SW I, p. 327; XJ I, p. 291.

121. Official text reads: "...and consequently it became possible for Chen Duxiuism, which appeared during the latter part of this revolution, to assert itself and bring about the defeat of the revolution". SW I, p. 327; XJ I, p. 291.

122. Official text reads: "After 1927, the Communist Party courageously led the Agrarian Revolutionary War and created the revolutionary army and revolutionary base areas". SW I, p. 327; XJ I, p. 291.

123. Official text reads: "...it committed adventurist errors which brought about very great losses both to the army and to the base areas". SW I, p. 327; XJ I, p. 291.

124.   Addition in official text: "...has corrected these errors and has been..."; SW I, p. 327; XJ I, p. 291.

125.   Addition in official text: "...for resistance to Japan;   this great struggle is now developing.   At the present stage, the Communist Party is a Party that has gone through the test of two revolutions and acquired a wealth of experience.   Such have been the particular features of the Chinese Communist Party in the three stages".   SW I, p. 327; XJ I, p. 291.

126.   Official text reads: "...the establishment of a united front..."; SW I, p. 327; XJ I, p. 291.

127.   Official text reads: "...the establishment of another united front". SW I, p. 327; XJ I, p. 291.

128.   Addition in official text: "...for the study of the particular features of the two parties is the examination of the class basis of the two parties and the..."; SW I, p. 327; XJ I, p. 291.

129.   Addition in official text: "...at different periods."   SW I, p. 327; XJ I, p. 291.

130.   Addition in official text: "...in the period of its first co-operation with the Communist Party..."; SW I, p. 327; XJ I, p. 291.

131.   Addition in official text: "...and was therefore anti-imperialist..."; SW I, p. 327; XJ I, p. 291.

132.   Addition in official text: "... - although in words it promised many benefits to the working people, in fact it gave them little or nothing.   In the period when it carried on the anti-Communist War, the Guomindang collaborated with imperialism and feudalism against the great masses of the people and wiped out all the gains they had won in the revolution, and thereby intensified its contradictions with them.   In the present period of the anti-Japanese war, the Guomindang stands in contradiction to Japanese imperialism and wants co-operation with the Communist Party, without however relaxing its struggle against the Communist Party, and the people or its oppression of them.   As for the Communist Party..."; SW I, pp. 327-328; XJ I, pp. 291-292.

133.   Official text reads: "As for the Communist Party, it has always, in every period, stood with the great masses of the people against imperialism and feudalism..."; SW I, p. 328; XJ I, p. 292.

134.   Addition in official text: "...but in the present period of the anti-Japanese war, it has adopted a moderate policy towards the Guomindang and the domestic feudal forces because the Guomindang has expressed itself in favour of resisting Japan."   SW I, p. 328; XJ I, p. 292.

135.   Official text reads: "The above circumstances have resulted now in alliance between the two parties and now in struggle between them, and even

during the periods of alliance there has been a complicated state of simultaneous alliance and struggle". SW I, p. 328; XJ I, p. 292.

136.   Addition in official text: "We must always remember Lenin's words, the concrete analysis of concrete conditions". SW I, p. 328; XJ I, p. 292.

137.   Addition in official text: "...were the first to..."; SW I, p. 328; XJ I, p. 292.

138.   Addition in official text: "...in things..."; SW I, p. 328; XJ I, p. 292.

139.   Official text reads: "...they discovered the contradictions between the exploiting and exploited classes and also the ..."; SW I, p. 328; XJ I, p. 292.

140.   Addition in official text: "...and they discovered how these contradictions inevitably lead to different kinds of social revolution in different kinds of class society". SW I, p. 328; XJ I, p. 292.

141.   A major addition in the official text here, which reads as follows:

"Because the range of things is vast and there is no limit to their development, what is universal in one context becomes particular in another. Conversely, what is particular in one context becomes universal in another. The contradiction in the capitalist system between the social character of production and the private ownership of the means of production is common to all countries where capitalism exists and develops; as far as capitalism is concerned, this constitutes the universality of contradiction. But this contradiction of capitalism belongs only to a certain historical stage in the general development of class society; as far as the contradiction between the productive forces and the relations of production in class society as a whole is concerned, it constitutes the particularity of contradiction. However, in the course of dissecting the particularity of all these contradictions in capitalist society, Marx gave a still more profound, more adequate and more complete elucidation of the universality of the contradiction between the productive forces and the relations of production in class society in general.

"Since the particular is united with the universal and since the universality as well as the particularity of contradiction is inherent in everything, universality residing in particularity, we should, when studying an object, try to discover both the particular and the universal and their interconnection, to discover both particularity and universality and also their interconnections within the object itself, and to discover the interconnections of this object with the many objects outside it. When Stalin explained the historical roots of Leninism in his famous work, *The Foundations of Leninism,* he analysed the international situation in which Leninism arose, analysed those contradictions of capitalism which reached their culmination under imperialism, and showed how these contradictions made proletarian revolution a matter for immediate action and created favourable conditions for a direct onslaught on capitalism. What is more, he analysed the reasons why Russia became the cradle of Leninism, why tsarist Russia became the focus of all the contradictions of imperialism, and why it was possible for the Russian proletariat to become the vanguard of the international revolutionary proletariat. Thus, Stalin analysed the universality of contradiction in imperialism, showing why Leninism is the Marxism of the era of imperialism and proletarian revolution, and at the same time analysed the particularity of tsarist Russian imperialism within this general contradiction, showing why Russia became the birthplace of the theory and tactics of proletarian revolution and how the universality of contradiction is contained in this particularity. Stalin's analysis provides us with a model for understanding the particularity and the universality of contradiction and their interconnection". SW I, pp. 329-330; XJ I, pp. 293-294.

142. Addition in official text: "...and likewise Lenin and Stalin always enjoin people not to be ..."; SW I, p. 330; XJ I, p. 294.

143. Addition in official text: "Our dogmatists do not have this attitude in study and therefore can never get anything right". SW I, p. 330; XJ I, p. 294.

144. Addition in official text: "...each..."; SW I, p. 330; XJ I, p. 294.

145. Official text reads: "It is because each contradiction is particular that individual character arises. All individual character exists conditionally and temporarily, and hence is relative". SW I, p. 330; XJ I, pp. 294-295.

146. This quotation from Su Dongpo is taken from the first of two prose poems entitled *Chi bi fu* (The Red Cliff). For the context in which Su Dongpo wrote these beautiful poems and an alternative translation of the quotation, see Lin Yutang, *The Gay Genius: The Life and Times Of Su Tungpo* (Melbourne, London, and Toronto: William Heinemman Ltd., 1948), pp. 197-204, esp. p. 202; for two alternate translations, see C.D. Le Gros Clark, *Selections from the Works of Su Tung-p'o* (London: Jonathon Cape, 1931), pp. 48-51; and Burton Watson, *Su Tung-p'o: Selections from a Sung Dynasty Poet* (New York and London: Columbia University Press, 1965), p. 89.

147. Official text reads: "...of the problem of contradiction in things; failure to understand it is tantamount to abandoning dialectics". SW I, p. 330; XJ I, p. 295.

148. Official text reads: "...in the process of development of a complex thing..."; SW I, p. 331; XJ I, p. 295.

149.   Addition in official text: "...two forces in..."; SW I, p. 331; XJ I, p. 295.

150.   Official text reads: "The other contradictions..."; SW I, p. 331; XJ I, p. 295.

151.   Official text reads: "...remnant feudal classes..." ; SW I, p. 331; XJ I, p. 295.

152.   Official text reads: "...monopoly..."; SW I, p. 331; XJ I, p. 295.

153.   Official text reads: "...bourgeois..."; SW I, p. 331; XJ I, p. 295.

154.   Addition in official text: "...except for some traitors..."; SW I, p. 331; XJ I, p. 295.

155.   Official text reads: "...of 1840, the Sino-Japanese War of 1894, and the Yi He Tuan War of 1900..."; SW I, p. 331; XJ I, p. 296.

156.   Official text reads: "...while imperialism often employs indirect methods rather than direct action in helping the reactionaries in the semi-colonial countries to oppress the people,..."; SW I, p. 332; XJ I, p. 296.

157.   Official text reads: "This is what happened in China in the Revolutionary War of 1924-27, and the ten years of Agrarian Revolutionary War after 1927". SW I, p. 332; XJ I, p. 296.

158.   Official text reads: "Wars among the various reactionary ruling groups in the semi-colonial countries, e.g., the war among the warlords in China, fall into the same category". SW I, p. 332; XJ I, p. 296.

159.   Addition in official text: "...revolutionary..."; SW I, p. 332; XJ I, p. 296.

160.   Official text reads: "...reactionaries..."; SW I, p. 332; XJ I, p. 296.

161.   Same alteration as footnote 160.

162.   Official text reads: "At such a time, foreign imperialism and domestic reaction stand quite openly at one pole while the masses of the people stand at the other pole..."; SW I, p. 332; XJ I, p. 296.

163.   Addition in official text: "...thus forming the principal contradiction which determines or influences the development of the other contradictions. The assistance given by various capitalist countries to the Russian reactionaries after the October Revolution is an example of armed intervention. Chiang Kai-shek's betrayal in 1927 is an example of splitting the revolutionary front". SW I, p. 332; XJ I, p. 297.

164.   Addition in official text: "...complex process..."; SW I, p. 332; XJ I, p. 297.

165.   Official text reads: "Likewise Lenin and Stalin taught us this method when they studied imperialism and the general crisis of capitalism and when they studied the Soviet economy". SW I, p. 332, XJ I, p. 297.

166.   Addition in official text: "The nature of a thing is determined mainly by the principal aspect of a contradiction, the aspect which has gained the dominant position". SW I, p. 333; XJ I, p. 297.

167.   Addition in official text: "...and the nature of the thing changes accordingly". SW I, p. 333; XJ I, p. 297.

168.   Official text reads: "- a change determined by the extent of the increase or decrease in the force of each aspect in its struggle against the other in the course of the development of a thing". SW I, p. 333; XJ I, p. 297.

169.   This paragraph has been deleted from the official text, and the following one inserted in its place:

"We often speak of 'the new superseding the old '. The supersession of the old by the new is a general, eternal, and inviolable law of the universe. The transformation of one thing into another, through leaps of different forms in accordance with its essence and external conditions - this is the process of the new superseding the old. In each thing there is contradiction between its new and its old aspects, and this gives rise to a series of struggles with many twists and turns. As a result of these struggles, the new aspect changes from being minor to being major and rises to predominance, while the old aspect changes from being major to being minor and gradually dies out. And the moment the new aspect gains dominance over the old, the old thing changes qualitatively into a new thing. It can thus be seen that the nature of a thing is mainly determined by the principal aspect of the contradiction, the aspect which has gained predominance. When the principal aspect which has gained predominance changes, the nature of a thing changes accordingly". SW I, p. 333; XJ I, pp. 297-298.

170.   Official text reads: "...in the old feudal era to being the dominant force, and the nature of society has accordingly changed from feudal to capitalist. In the new, capitalist era, the feudal forces changed from their former dominant position to a subordinate one, gradually dying out". SW I, pp. 333-334; XJ I, p. 298.

171.   This, and the next four paragraphs, have been deleted from the official text, and replaced by the following passage:

"Such was the case, for example, in Britain and France. With the development of the productive forces, the bourgeoisie changes from being a new class playing a progressive role to being an old class playing a reactionary role, until it is finally overthrown by the proletariat and becomes a class deprived of privately owned means of production and stripped of power, when it, too, gradually dies out. The proletariat, which is much more numerous than the bourgeoisie and grows simultaneously with it but under its rule, is a new force which, initially subordinate to the bourgeoisie, gradually gains strength, becomes an independent class playing the leading role in history, and finally seizes political power and becomes the ruling class. Thereupon the nature of society changes and the old capitalist society becomes the new socialist society. This is the path already taken by the Soviet Union, a path that all other countries will inevitably take.

"Look at China, for instance. Imperialism occupies the principal position in the contradiction in which China has been reduced to a semi-colony, it oppresses the Chinese people, and China has been changed from an independent country into a semi-colonial one. But this state of affairs will inevitably change; in the struggle between the two sides, the power of the Chinese people which is growing under the leadership of the proletariat will inevitably change China from a semi-colony into an independent country, whereas imperialism will be overthrown and old China will inevitably change into New China.

"The change of old China into New China also involves a change in the relation between the old feudal forces and the new popular forces within the country. The old feudal landlord class will be overthrown, and from being the ruler it will change into being the ruled; and this class, too, will gradually die out. From being the ruled the people, led by the proletariat, will become the rulers. Thereupon, the nature of Chinese society will change and the old, semi-colonial and semi-feudal society will change into a new democratic society.

"Instances of such reciprocal transformation are found in our past experience. The Qing Dynasty which ruled China for nearly three hundred years was overthrown in the Revolution of 1911, and the revolutionary *Tong Meng Hui* under Sun Yat-sen's leadership was victorious for a time. In the Revolutionary War of 1924-27, the revolutionary forces of the Communist-Guomindang alliance in the south changed from being weak to being strong and won victory in the Northern Expedition, while the Northern warlords who once ruled the roost were overthrown. In 1927, the people's forces led by the Communist Party were greatly reduced numerically under the attack of Guomindang reaction, but with the elimination of opportunism within their ranks they gradually grew again. In the revolutionary base areas under Communist leadership, the peasants have been transformed from being the ruled to being the rulers, while the landlords have undergone a reverse transformation. It is always so in the world, the new displacing the old, the old being superseded by the new, the old being eliminated to make way for the new, and the new emerging out of the old". SW I, pp. 334-335; XJ I, pp. 298-299.

172.   Official text reads: "...thus a difficult situation yields place to a favourable one". SW I, p. 335; XJ I, p. 299.

173.   Addition in official text: "...in China..."; SW I, p. 335; XJ I, p. 299.

174.   Addition in official text: "...Chinese..."; SW I, p. 335; XJ I, p. 299.

175.   Official text reads: "...but we can change this and fundamentally transform the situation as between China and Japan". SW I, p. 335; XJ I, p. 299.

176.   Official text reads: "...1924-27..."; SW I, p. 335; XJ I, p. 299.

177.   Official text reads: "The revolutionary base areas which grew up in the southern provinces after 1927 had all suffered defeat by 1934". SW I, p. 335; XJ I, pp. 299-300.

178.   Official text reads: "At the very beginning of our study of Marxism, our ignorance of or scanty acquaintance with Marxism stands in contradiction to knowledge of Marxism". SW I, p. 335; XJ I, p. 300.

179.   Addition in official text: "...and blindness in the application of Marxism into mastery of its application". SW I, p. 335; XJ I, p. 300.

180.   Addition in official text: "This is the mechanical materialist conception, not the dialectical materialist conception. True..."; SW I, p. 336; XJ I, p. 300.

181.   Official text reads: "...in certain conditions..."; SW I, p. 336; XJ I, p. 300.

182.   Addition in official text: "...and social being determines social consciousness,..."; SW I, p. 336; XJ I, p. 300.

183.   Addition in official text: "...of social consciousness on social being and of the superstructure on the economic base". SW I, p. 336; XJ I, p. 301.

184.   Addition in official text: "...of contradiction..."; SW I, p. 336; XJ I, p. 301.

185.   Addition in official text: "...of the forces..."; SW I, p. 336; XJ I, p. 301.

186.   Addition in official text: "Moreover, it is these concrete features of a contradiction and the changes in the principal and non-principal aspects of a contradiction in the course of its development that manifest the force of the new superseding the old". SW I, pp. 336-337; XJ I, p. 301.

187.   Official text reads: "All Communists must give it attention"; SW I, p. 337; XJ I, p. 301.

188.   Official text reads: "The Identity and Struggle of the Aspects of a Contradiction". SW I, p. 337; XJ I, p. 301.

189.   Official text reads: "When we understand the..."; SW I, p. 337; XJ I, p. 301.

190.   Addition in official text: "...the aspects of..."; SW I, p. 337; XJ I, p. 301.

191.   Official text reads: "...the process of the development of a thing..."; SW I, p. 337; XJ I, p. 301.

192.   Addition in official text: "...exclude each other, struggle with each other and..."; SW I, p. 337; XJ I, p. 302.

193.   Official text reads: "Without exception, they are contained in the process of development of all things and in all human thought". SW I, p. 337; XJ I, p. 302.

194.   In this and subsequent passages, Mao frequently utilizes the expression *yuanjia* (enemy, antagonist, adversary) to indicate opposites. This has been replaced by *maodun* in the official text. I have followed the official translation, as the discrepancy is literary rather than substantive.

195.   Addition in official text: "...in the objective world and all human thought are..."; SW I, p. 338; XJ I, p. 302.

196.   Addition in official text: "Without landlords there would be no tenant-peasants; without tenant-peasants, there would be no landlords". SW I, p. 338; XJ I, p. 302.

197.   Official text reads: "Without imperialist oppression of nations, there would be no colonies or semi-colonies; without colonies or semi-colonies, there would be no imperialist oppression of nations". SW I, p. 338; XJ I, p. 302.

198.   Official text reads: "...all contradictory aspects..."; SW I, p. 338; XJ I, p. 303.

199.   Official text reads: "...dialectics studies 'how *opposites* can be ...*identical*'." SW I, p. 338; XJ I, p. 303.

200.   Official text reads: "That is to say, in given conditions..."; SW I, p. 338; XJ I, p. 303.

201.   Official text reads: "You see, by means of revolution the proletariat, at one time the ruled, is transformed into the ruler, while the bourgeoisie, the erstwhile ruler, is transformed into the ruled and changes its position to that originally occupied by its opposite". SW I, pp. 338-339; XJ I, p. 303.

202.   Official text reads: "The Guomindang, which played a certain positive role at a certain stage in modern Chinese history, became a counter-revolutionary party after 1927 because of its inherent class nature and

because of imperialist blandishments (these being the conditions)"; SW I, p. 339; XJ I, p. 303.

203.   Official text reads: "...to agree to resist Japan..."; SW I, p. 339; XJ I, p. 303.

204.   Official text reads: "...a definite identity". SW I, p. 339; XJ I, p. 303.

205.   Official text reads: "there is identity of the two sides". SW I, p. 339; XJ I, p. 304.

206.   Official text reads: "...as it will take place everywhere else". SW I, p. 339; XJ I, p. 304.

207.   Addition in official text: "...or transformation into each other..."; SW I, p. 339; XJ I, p. 304.

208.   Addition in official text: "...or the dictatorship of the people..."; SW I, p. 339; XJ I, p. 304.

209.   Official text reads: "...the higher stage when all state systems are eliminated". SW I, p. 339; XJ I, p. 304.

210.   Addition in official text: "...under the leadership of the Communist Party..."; SW I, p. 339; XJ I, p. 304.

211.   Official text reads: "War and peace, as everybody knows, transform themselves into each other". SW I, p. 339; XJ I, p. 304.

212.   Official text reads: "...the post-war peace..."; SW I, p. 339; XJ I, p. 304.

213.   Official text reads: "...and the civil war in China has now stopped, giving place to internal peace". SW I, p. 339; XJ I, p. 304.

214.   Official text reads: "...for instance, the Guomindang-Communist co-operation was transformed into war in 1927, and today's situation of world peace may be transformed into a second world war". SW I, p. 340; XJ I, p. 304.

215.   Addition in official text: "...in class society such contradictory things as war and peace have an..."; SW I, p. 340; XJ I, p. 304.

216.   Characters from the *Romance of the Three Kingdoms*.

217.   Although Mao has separated these two sentences with quotation marks, they are part of the same quotation from the *Kong zi jia yu*, Book VI.

218.   This quotation is from Lao Zi, Chapter 58. I have followed Lau's translation; See Lao Tzu, *Tao Te Ching*, trans. D.C. Lau (Harmondsworth: Penguin Books, 1963), p. 119.

219.   This quote comes from the *Da xue* (The Great Learning), commentary of the philosopher Zeng, Chapter VIII. I have adapted Legge's translation. Mao uses the quote out of context and the full passage runs:

"What is meant by 'The regulation of one's family depends on the cultivation of his person', is this: - Men are partial where they feel affection and love; partial where they despise and dislike, partial where they stand in awe and reverence; partial where they feel sorrow and compassion; partial where they are arrogant and rude. Thus it is that there are few men in the world who love (*hao*; Mao uses *ai*) and at the same time know the bad qualities of *the object of their love*, or who hate and yet know the excellence of *the object of their hatred*". (*The Four Books. Op.cit.*, pp. 10-11).

However, the exact meaning of this saying is not clear even in context. An alternative translation might be: "To love so as to know hatred; to hate so as to appreciate excellence".

220.   This is a popular Chinese saying and is not from a classical source.

221.   Official text reads: "...identity of opposites". SW I, p. 340; XJ I, p. 304.

222.   Here, as in the following paragraph, there are no quotation marks for this reference from Lenin. These have been added to the official text. There are also some differences in the Chinese rendering of this reference, but I have remained as close as possible to the official English translation. SW I, p. 340; XJ I, p. 304.

223.   Addition in official text: "Reflected in man's thinking, this becomes the Marxist world outlook of materialist dialectics. It is only the reactionary ruling class of the past and present and the metaphysicians in their service who regard opposites not as living, conditional, mobile and transforming themselves into one another, but as dead and rigid, and they propagate this fallacy everywhere to delude the masses of the people, thus seeking to perpetuate their rule. The task of Communists is to expose the fallacies of the reactionaries and metaphysicians, to propagate the dialectics inherent in things, and so accelerate the transformation of things and achieve the goal of revolution". SW I, p. 340; XJ I, p. 305.

224.   Addition in official text: "...necessary...";   SW I, p. 341; XJ I, p. 306.

225.   Addition in official text: "...in 1917...";   SW I, p. 341;   XJ I, p. 306.

226.   Official text reads: "...bourgeois-democratic...";   SW I, p. 341; XJ I, p. 306.

227.   Addition in official text: "...proletarian...";   SW I, p. 341; XJ I, p. 306.

228.   Official text reads: "...bourgeois...";   SW I, p. 341;   XJ I, p. 306.

229.   Addition in official text: "...of 1871..."; SW I, p. 341; XJ I, p. 306.

230.   Official text reads: "...without..."; SW I, p. 341; XJ I, p. 306.

231.   Official text reads: "...of the Western countries, without passing through a period of bourgeois dictatorship?" SW I, p. 341; XJ I, p. 306.

232.   Addition in official text: "...certain..."; SW I, p. 341; XJ I, p. 306.

233.   Official text reads: "...in the process of development of things and ..."; SW I, p. 341; XJ I, p. 306.

234.   The correct title of this legend is "Gua Fu's race with the Sun".

235.   Official text reads: "In speaking of the identity of opposites in given conditions, what we are referring to is real and concrete opposites and the real and concrete transformations of opposites into one another. There are innumerable transformations in mythology, for instance, Gua Fu's race with the sun in *Shan Hai Jing*, Yi's shooting down of nine suns in *Huai Nan Zi*, the Monkey King's seventy-two metamorphoses in *Xi You Ji*, the numerous episodes of ghosts and foxes metamorphosed into human beings in the *Strange Tales of Liao Zhai*, etc. But these legendary transformations of opposites are not concrete changes reflecting concrete contradictions. They are naive, imaginery, subjectively conceived transformations conjured up in men's minds by innumerable real and complex transformations of opposites into one another. Marx said, 'All mythology masters and dominates and shapes the forces of nature in and through the imagination; hence it disappears as soon as man gains mastery over the forces of nature'. The myriads of changes in mythology (and also in nursery tales) delight people because they imaginatively picture man's conquest of the forces of nature, and the best myths possess 'eternal charm', as Marx put it; but myths are not built out of the concrete contradictions existing in given conditions and therefore are not a scientific reflection of reality. That is to say, in myths or nursery tales the aspects constituting a contradiction have only an imaginery identity, not a concrete identity. The scientific reflection of the identity in real transformations is Marxist dialectics". SW I, pp. 340-341; XJ I, p. 305.

236.   Addition in official text: "...the mutability manifested in the..."; SW I, p. 342; XJ I, p. 306.

237.   Official text reads: "There are two states of motion in all things, that of relative rest and that of conspicuous change. Both are caused by the struggle between the two contradictory elements contained in a thing. When the thing is in the first state of motion, it is undergoing only quantitative and not qualitative change and consequently presents the outward appearance of being at rest. When the thing is in the second state of motion, the quantitative change of

the first state has already reached a culminating point and gives rise to the dissolution of the thing as an entity and thereupon a qualitative change ensues, hence the appearance of conspicuous change. Such unity, solidarity, combination, harmony, balance, stalemate, deadlock, rest, constancy, equilibrium, solidity, attraction, etc., as we see in daily life, are all the appearances of things in the state of quantitative change. On the other hand, the dissolution of unity, that is, the destruction of this solidarity, combination, harmony, balance, stalemate, deadlock, rest, constancy, equilibrium, solidity, and attraction, and the change of each into its opposite are all the appearances of things in the state of qualitative change, the transformation of one process into another. Things are constantly transforming themselves from the first into the second state of motion; the struggle of opposites goes on in both states but the contradiction is resolved through the second state. That is why we say that the unity of opposites is conditional, temporary, and relative, while the struggle of mutually exclusive opposites is absolute". SW I, p. 342; XJ I, pp. 306-307.

238. Official text reads: "...the struggle between opposites..."; SW I, p. 343; XJ I, p. 307.

239. This whole section has been replaced in the official text by the following paragraph: "We Chinese often say, 'Things that oppose each other also complement each other'. That is, things opposed to each other have identity. This saying is dialectical and contrary to metaphysics. 'Oppose each other' refers to the mutual exclusion or the struggle of two contradictory aspects. 'Complement each other' means that in given conditions the two contradictory aspects unite and achieve identity. Yet struggle is inherent in identity and without struggle there can be no identity". SW I, p. 343; XJ I, pp. 307-308.

240. Addition in official text: "...in particularity there is universality, and in individuality there is generality". SW I, p. 343; XJ I, p. 308.

241. Official text reads: "Our answer is that antagonism is one form, but not the only form, of the struggle of opposites". SW I, p. 343; XJ I, p. 308.

242. Official text reads: "In human history, antagonism between classes exists as a..."; SW I, p. 343; XJ I, p. 308.

243. Official text reads: "...and develops into revolution. The same holds for the transformation of peace into war in class society". SW I, p. 343; XJ I, p. 308.

244. Official text reads: "Before it explodes, a bomb is a single entity in which opposites coexist in given conditions. The explosion takes place only when a new condition, ignition, is present. An analogous situation arises in all those natural phenomena which finally assume the form of open conflict to resolve contradictions and produce new things". SW I, p. 343; XJ I, p. 308.

245. Addition in official text: "It is highly important to grasp this fact. It enables us to understand that revolutions and revolutionary wars are inevitable in class society and that without them, it is impossible to accomplish any leap in social development and to overthrow the reactionary ruling classes and therefore impossible for the people to win political power. Communists must expose the deceitful propaganda of the reactionaries, such as the assertion that social revolution is unnecessary and impossible. They must firmly uphold the Marxist-Leninist theory of social revolution and enable the people to understand that social revolution is not only entirely necessary but also entirely practicable, and that the whole history of mankind and the triumph of the Soviet Union have confirmed this scientific truth.

"However, we must make a concrete study of the circumstances of each specific struggle of opposites and should not arbitrarily apply the formula discussed above to everything. Contradiction and struggle are universal and absolute, but the methods of resolving contradictions, that is, the forms of struggle, differ according to the differences in the nature of the contradictions. Some contradictions are characterized by open antagonism, others are not. In accordance with the concrete development of things, some contradictions which were originally non-antagonistic develop into antagonistic ones, while others which were originally antagonistic develop into non-antagonistic ones". SW I, p. 344; XJ I, pp. 308-309.

246. The Chinese reads: *dou mei you duikang xingtai de cunzai.* This is a most unusual statement for Mao to have made, and it is little wonder that it has been dropped from the official text. Some of the contradictions raised by Mao obviously have an antagonistic form or condition of existence at a certain stage in their development. Perhaps what Mao meant here was that all of the contradictions he cites have a non-antagonistic (*fei duikang*) form as well as an antagonistic form of existence. This section has been almost completely rewritten in the official text, and reads as follows:

"As already mentioned, so long as classes exist, contradiction between correct and incorrect ideas in the Communist Party are reflections within the party of class contradictions. At first, with regard to certain issues, such contradictions may not manifest themselves as antagonistic. But with the development of the class struggle, they may grow and become antagonistic. The history of the Communist Party of the Soviet Union shows us that the contradictions between the correct thinking of Lenin and Stalin and the fallacious thinking of Trotsky, Bukharin, and others did not at first manifest themselves in an antagonistic form, but that later they did develop into antagonism. There are similar cases in the history of the Chinese Communist

Party. At first the contradictions between the correct thinking of many of our Party comrades and the fallacious thinking of Chen Duxiu, Zhang Guodao, and others also did not manifest themselves in an antagonistic form, but later they did develop into antagonism. At present the contradiction between correct and incorrect thinking in our Party does not manifest itself in an antagonistic form, and if comrades who have committed mistakes can correct them, it will not develop into antagonism. Therefore, the Party must on the one hand wage a serious struggle against erroneous thinking, and on the other give the comrades who have committed errors ample opportunity to wake up. This being the case, excessive struggle is obviously inappropriate. But if the people who have committed errors persist in them and aggravate them, there is the possibility that this contradiction will develop into antagonism.

"Economically, the contradiction between town and country is an extremely antagonistic one both in capitalist society, where under the rule of the bourgeoisie the towns ruthlessly plunder the countryside, and in the Guomindang areas in China, where under the rule of foreign imperialism and the Chinese big comprador bourgeoisie the towns most rapaciously plunder the countryside. But in a socialist country and in our revolutionary base areas, this antagonistic contradiction has changed into one that is non-antagonistic; and when communist society is reached it will be abolished". SW I, pp. 344-345; XJ I, pp. 309-310.

247.   Addition in official text: "That is to say, antagonism is one form, but not the only form, of the struggle of opposites; the formula of antagonism cannot be arbitrarily applied everywhere". SW I, p. 345; XJ I, p. 310.

248.   In the official text, there is a new section here with the heading "VII, Conclusion"; SW I, p. 345; XJ I, p. 310.

249.   Official text reads: "We may now say a few words to sum up. The law of the contradiction in things, that is, the law of the unity of opposites, is the fundamental law of nature and society and therefore also the fundamental law of thought. It represents a great revolution in the history of human knowledge". SW I, p. 345; XJ I, p. 310.

250.   Official text reads: "According to dialectical materialism, contradiction is present in all processes of objectively existing things and of subjective thought and permeates all these processes from beginning to end"; SW I, p. 345; XJ I, p. 310.

251.   Official text reads: "Each contradiction and each of its aspects have their respective characteristics"; SW I, p. 345; XJ I, p. 310.

252.   Addition in official text: "...contradiction and the non-principal contradiction and to the distinction between the..."; SW I, p. 346; XJ I, p. 311.

253.   Official text reads: "in studying the universality of contradiction and the struggle of opposites in contradiction, we must give attention to the distinction between the different forms of struggle. Otherwise we shall make mistakes. If, through study, we achieve a real understanding of the essentials explained above, we shall be able to demolish dogmatist ideas which are contrary to the basic principles of Marxism-Leninism and detrimental to our revolutionary cause, and our comrades with practical experience will be able to organize their experience into principles and avoid repeating empiricist errors. These are a few simple conclusions from our study of the law of contradiction". SW I, p. 346; XJ I, p. 311.

5 | Extracts from Ai Siqi's *Philosophy and Life*

(SEPTEMBER 1937)

Relativism and Absolutism

Mao	*Ai Siqi*
(a1) All the terms (or concepts, categories) we use, like "absolute" or "relative" etc., are all the reflection of real things. The term horse exists only because there are real horses in the world. The two terms relative and absolute are also not divorced from actual things.	(b1) All the terms (or concepts, categories) that we use are the reflections of real things. The term horse exists only because there are real horses in the world, the term capitalism exists only because there is a capitalist system. The two terms relative and absolute are also not divorced from actual things....
(a2) In everyday life absolutism often causes trouble.	(b2) In our lives we are often haunted and plagued by absolutism.

Source: Ai Siqi, *Zhexue yu shenghuo* (Yunan People's Publishing House, 1980). See also *Zhongguo zhexue* (Chinese Philosophy) Vol. 1 (April 1979), pp. 5-30. Translated by John Hanafin.

Mao

Ai Siqi

(a3) Like believing in fate and holding that things cannot change. Also, like considering that the circumstances of life of a certain place do not suit one, demanding a move, and thinking that circumstances cannot change. Also, like considering the people around one are not aware; not knowing that people are also able to change.

(b3) Today we can still come across a great many other people who still believe in the will of God, and consider that everything in the world has been arranged by a Supreme Director; that it is impossible ever to alter it; and that suffering in life also can only be blamed on fate....

Even though aware youth are progressive, we often see this kind of shortcoming: they often write letters saying: "My circumstances are odious and I cannot tolerate them, I must get away from them and go and live in a better place; perhaps you can recommend me to someone in the Save the Nation Organization so I can enter it and work happily". This kind of view is unintentionally governed by absolutist thinking. Although the originators of this sort of view are progressive youths who embrace new thinking and understand that the world changes, who understand that the duty of a Chinese at the present stage is national salvation and resistance, nevertheless, they have not taken their own progressive thinking, and without regret,

Mao

Ai Siqi

applied it to the approach towards their own life. *In looking at their own life they use a fixed, unchanging, and absolute viewpoint:* their circumstances are really gloomy, yet they forget that gloom also can be smashed; and that the effort of progressive youth can make circumstances change. The people around them are not aware; yet they forget people who are not aware, under certain conditions, will one day walk the path of awareness. They take gloom and the state of not being aware and render them absolute, holding that these are completely without the potential for change for the better. Consequently, they despairingly cry, "There's no way, the circumstances of my life already can't accommodate me, let me go to another more promising field of activity!"

(a4) Darkness is not absolute, neither is brightness absolute.

(b4) When we receive this kind of youth's letter, we can only reply: "Your ideas are wrong: you think your circumstances are bad and you want to flee this gloomy captivity; this is wrong.

Mao	Ai Siqi

Escape *is not an appropriate means in life*, because in current society there is basically not one place that is completely bright; you flee from your own circumstances, yet you will walk into a new gloomy captivity; escape is of no avail. But there is no need for you to be pessimistic, because brightness strikes out from within darkness; if darkness is not smashed then there can be no brightness; therefore you should remain in your own surroundings and to the best of your ability carry out your daily duty as a progressive - smash darkness. You do not want to regard darkness as too absolute!"

From this example we know that absolutism needs to be opposed; it makes us unwilling to proceed from the reality facing us, to work, and to struggle; we only dream of another promising place, or think of escaping from reality. Absolutism does not accord with the true condition of things, because all things are able to change; dark society can also develop into bright society; it is not an absolute darkness. Bright things are

Mao

Ai Siqi

also hatched from darkness; it is not an absolute brightness that has fallen from heaven.

(a5) Exceeding reality and seeking to realize the ideal, and avoiding reality, are both conceptualist (*guannianlun*). The majority of con- ceptualisms subscribe to absolutism.

(b5) One needs to grasp the significance of the new philosophy and new social science; one also needs to oppose this absolutism, otherwise, although this new philosophy is discussed in words, in reality one turns into a conceptualist. The emergence of this philosophy and social science requires that in actual dark society we use a variety of methods to promote the realization of the future society and goals. There are a few people who misunderstand this science; they regard the future society as an ideal; very impatiently they think of starting to establish it in the world immediately; but they do not know it is promoted from within actual society. Although their imagined ideal appears identical with the new philosophy and new science, in fact, they set too much store on ideals and forget reality; therefore this is still a conceptualism (the majority of conceptualisms subscribe to absolutism).

Mao

Ai Siqi

(a6) Infantile Leftism is a kind of absolutism because it renders ideals absolute; it is unaware that ideals can only be realized in accordance with prevailing conditions.

(b6) The term "Infantile Leftism" that we often hear can be blamed on this absolutism because it regards the ideals of the new social science in too absolute a fashion (i.e., forgets it is hatched from within the old society).

(a7) The changing of darkness and the obtaining of brightness is in proportion to one's efforts; strive and it is so, do not strive and it is not so; the relativity of these things is in terms of whether one strives or not; it is in terms of the duration of time.

(b7) First, we need to say: we must acknowledge that all things are relative because all things are changing. Since we acknowledge that finally one day the circumstances of our gloomy life will change for the better, we must also, at the same time, acknowledge that gloom only exists today; as long as we clearly see the path of the development of society, and in accordance with this path go on struggling, then, tomorrow or the day after tomorrow, there will always come a time when brightness will be discovered. This is to say that gloom is relative; it is relative to the duration of today's time; or it is relative to our making an effort; if we do not strive for one day the influence of gloom will be prolonged for one day. At the same time brightness is also relative;

Mao	*Ai Siqi*
	although the prospects for the development of society are bright, this cannot by itself suddenly come about; it needs us to promote it; it cannot be established by us in an easy way out of a void; it requires that we struggle and strive for it in actual society; its emergence and our efforts are relative.
(a8) Relativism considers that there is no definite truth; one person one truth; ten people ten truths; "isn't that all the same!" This is scepticism; doubt everything; nothing can be grasped.	(b8) To speak thus, in no way means we need to subscribe to relativism. The relativity of things must be acknowledged because things are continuously changing; they do not have an absolute, permanent existence. But acknowledging the relativity of things in no way means one needs to subscribe to relativism. Why can one not believe in relativism? Because it overstates the relativity of things. It makes us think as follows: "Everything is the same whether it be gloom or brightness; all is relative; all lacks a defining criterion; in the world there is no such thing as truth, because all truth is relative; I say it is true and another person may think it is false. Life is the same; why strive and struggle? Perhaps the promise of the

Mao	*Ai Siqi*
	future is only my idle dream; why suffer hardship for no purpose? Drift aimlessly through life; this is the way to pass one's days".
(a9) Doubting is correct; doubting everything is not.	**(b9)** Relativism overstates relativity. Its overstatement makes us unable to believe in anything, making us doubt everything; *relativism is a scepticism.* Doubt is necessary in observing things; doubting everything, not being able to grasp the least thing in life and thought, only intending to muddle through life at the present, this is a mess.
(a10) Old people tend more to relativism; young people tend more to absolutism.	**(b10)** This relativism and scepticism are noxious, but those amongst the youth who accept this poison are comparatively few; because the enthusiasm of youth is very great it is easy for absolutism to exercise a bad influence on them, but very few are affected by the poison of relativism. This poison mostly affects old people, although lethargic youth can also suffer from this tendency. Generally speaking, they are attacked and cannot withstand the attacker; they lack the courage to struggle forward; it is easy

Mao

Ai Siqi

for them to come to terms with the adverse influences immediately confronting them. Therefore a part of the shortcomings of Right deviationism comes from relativism. If one says absolutism is a defect of the youth, then, relativism is a defect of the old or adult.

(a11) Relativism overstates the relativity of things. The relative and absolute nature of change in things should be acknowledged; overstating that nothing can be grasped becomes relativism.

　　When acknowledging the nature of change in, and relativity of, things, at the same time also acknowledge fixed things amidst change and relativity, and the definite laws of the development of things; acknowledge absolute things amidst relativity. The absolute is embodied in the relative. Relativism does not acknowledge this regularity.

(b11) Relativism unduly overstates relativity and this becomes an abnormal, distorted thinking; this is what we need to oppose, and this has already been explained above. But we do not need to completely oppose the relativity of things. Since we acknowledge the change-ability of things, we must acknowledge their relativity. But this relativity and the relativity that doubts everything are not the same; this relativity only indicates change in things, it does not deny that in this change there are fixed, regular patterns and laws, as well as definite origins and prospects; there-fore, although we have not regarded present things as absolutely permanent, we also have not denied order and melody in the development of the world. This is to say that

Mao

Ai Siqi

it is not that relativity that doubts everything and does not believe in any regular patterns. Although it acknowledges relativity and changeability, at the same time it has not forgotten that in change there are fixed things, things with regular patterns. This is also to say that in relativity it still sees absolute things. Absolute things are embodied in the relative; relativism cannot see this point; this then is the difference between it and relativism.

(a12) Relative things embody definite absolute things; absolute things are manifested in each necessary stage in relative things; this is the relation between the two.

(b12) For example, at the present moment the Chinese people are demanding that the nation rise together in resistance against the enemy, and this, obviously, is relative, because it is only in recent years that this has been felt as a pressing need. Seven or eight years ago, we naturally wanted to oppose imperialist invaders, but at that time we did not concentrate the fury of the nation on an Asian imperialism. What about the future? One day this kind of thing may be no more, because the demand for national liberation stems from

Mao   *Ai Siqi*

the intensifying oppression of
the invader, and is relative to
this oppression. If, one day
the imperialist enemy are
defeated, or because of a
change in their own country,
they cease their assault on us,
we will not be able without
any reason to again kindle the
flames of resistance against
them. The demands of resisting the enemy and national
salvation can change; therefore, it is also relative.

But if we overstate this
relativity and say: good, this
kind of demand is only a
transient thing, perhaps
tomorrow it will not be the
same, and the day after
tomorrow it will again
change. We do not even have
to strive for this kind of
demand. It does not matter
because how will the affairs
of today turn out tomorrow;
we are completely ignorant of
this; why waste our energy?-
this, then becomes scepticism.

This kind of over-
statement, obviously, is incorrect. Although we ack-
nowledge that the unanimous
national resistance against the
enemy is only the present
stage of the movement for
national liberation, and that

Mao

Ai Siqi

its relativity is in respect to the "present stage", at the same time, we must also say that *at the present stage, making use of unanimous national resistance against the enemy to carry out national liberation is an absolutely necessary thing*; at the present stage, besides this path *there is absolutely no second path that can be taken.* In short, with regards to the viewpoint of development each thing is relative, but at each stage of development there must be a fixed regular pattern and the emergence of a definite thing; this is absolute. Relative things always embody definite absolute things; absolute things are manifested as each necessary stage in relative things. This is the relation between the two.

Dialectical and Formal Logic

(a13) Sublation is: on the one hand, the rejection and negation of the negative element, and, on the other hand, the subjection of the positive element to criticism and transformation, as well as its preservation; but, it is not simple rejection. Ye Qing

(b13) First, Ye Qing says again and again that he himself has not put formal logic and dialectical logic on an equal footing. He acknowledges that, "the latter assimilates the former, replaces the former". He also says the latter sublates the

Mao

says: "In the past formal logic governed all spheres of research, at present, however, it is limited to states of relative rest". This way, our negation of formal logic can only be of its scope of application and not its character. If this is not simple preservation - what is it? If this is not the essential acknowledgement that formal logic and dialectics are of equal significance - what is it? (Zhang Youren)

Ai Siqi

former, negates it. However, what is his understanding of sublation and negation? He says sublation is not simple rejection and that negation is not simple negation. It would seem this point is correct because sublation, on the one hand, rejects the negative element and negates it, on the other hand, it must subject the positive element to criticism and transformation and preserves it. This obviously is not simple rejection. However, what we should take note of is that Ye Qing, in speaking this sentence does not indicate he has this proper understanding. He wants to lead us to the other extreme. He regards preservation in sublation as simple and uncritical preservation. He considers that the dialectical sublation of formal logic is merely the preservation of formal logic within narrowly drawn limits and not the critical assimilation of dialectics into its content. He says, "In the past formal logic governed all spheres of research, at present, however, it is confined to states of relative rest". This way, our negation of formal logic can

Mao

Ai Siqi

only be the negation of its scope of application and not the negation of its character. If this is not simple preservation - what is it? Is not this the essential acknowledgement that formal logic and dialectics are of equal significance?

(a14) At any point in space, things in motion, at the same time, are at rest and not at rest. This is the unity of contradiction. Ye Qing says: "Motion is the accumulation of rest, rest is the cessation of motion, they engender each other and are mutually supportive as well as mutually determining". Rest is only a specific form of motion; it is certainly not the cessation of motion, and motion is certainly not the accumulation of rest; if it is only the accumulation of rest it would mean that motion is eliminated in rest. (Zhang Youren)

(b14) Secondly, although Ye Qing acknowledges in words that motion is absolute and that rest is relative, and it seems he has not so far put motion and rest on an equal footing, nevertheless, these are only words, in reality he has already put these two on an equal footing. He says, "Motion is the accumulation of rest, rest is the cessation of motion; they engender each other and are mutually supportive as well as mutually determining". This, then, is Ye Qing's understanding of the relation between motion and rest. Motion is merely the accumulation of rest! Motion in the world is able to cease. The two are mutually determining! According to what I know, rest is only a specific form of motion. It is certainly not the cessation of motion; and motion is certainly not the accumulation

Mao

Ai Siqi

of rest. If it is simply a case of the accumulation of rest then it is basically "not able to become motion", and it basically eliminates motion in rest. He says, "In its progress through time, motion must come to rest in space". This makes it clear that he does not basically know how to use dialectics to comprehend motion. At any point in space, things in motion, at the same time, are at rest and not at rest. This is the unity of contradiction of motion. If there is not this unity of contradiction and there is simply only rest, no matter how it accumulates it cannot become motion. Here, Ye Qing clearly forgets to use the law of the unity of contradiction to understand motion. Here, can one make out what his true colours are?

(a15) Formal and dialectical logic are most fundamental questions.

(b15) A great many readers have sent in letters asking about the criticism of *Zhexue jianghua* (Talks on philosophy). This criticism came from various quarters and there were sundry opinions. Some were sympathetic and some were not; some were well-meaning and some were

Mao

Ai Siqi

malicious. I thought that in addition I would write an article giving a general reply and at the same time take the opportunity to make a self-criticism, and regard this as the preface of the fourth edition of this book. Here, I only want to discuss Mr Zhang's and Mr Qu's request to explain the question of formal and dialectical logic. This, on the one hand, is because, just like Mr Zhang says, this question is a most fundamental one, on the other hand, it is because Ye Qing has used a special essay to dispute with me. Therefore, I am also using a special essay to reply to him.

(a16) Dialectical logic: A is A and at the same time it is not A; a thing is at the same time identical and not identical with itself. Formal logic only sees the aspect of identity. Dialectics, however, not only sees this aspect, it also sees the other aspect (not identical), therefore, it is able to embody, assimilate, and sublate formal logic. What formal logic cannot see, dialectics can see, what formal

(b16) According to Ye Qing the dialectical formula is "besides A is A, at the same time it maintains A is not A". We may make a simple point, and that is: A is A, and at the same time it is not A. This is contrary to the law of identity of formal logic. Its meaning is: "a thing is at the same time identical and not identical with itself".

In these two formulae we can already see the relation

Mao	*Ai Siqi*
logic has seen, dialectics not only sees but transforms and deepens.	between formal logic and dialectics. That is, at any one time, dialectics needs to see the identity and non-identity within a thing itself. Formal logic, however, only sees the aspect of "identity". Dialectics does not just see this aspect, and consequently can embody, assimilate, and sublate formal logic. What formal logic cannot see, dialectics can see. What formal logic has seen, dialectics can not only see, but transforms and deepens.
(a17) One cannot say: "on the one hand, acknowledge A is A, and, on the other hand, acknowledge A is not A" and then consider this to be dialectics. The relation between these two propositions is not a case of on the one hand and on the other hand; but is one where at the same time they permeate each other and are bound together. They are a unified whole and are not mechanically combined; neither can they be mechanically broken up. If they are broken up and understood in this way, then the result is eclecticism. The	**(b17)** All that has been said above is apparently not any different to Ye Qing. It seems to be what he has said. But, let us look into this in a more concrete fashion and then we may find out how much, in fact, Ye Qing, who proclaims that other people "basically do not understand dialectics", himself understands?

First, we need to pay attention to how dialectics "assimilates" formal logic. Dialectics, in order to assimilate formal logic needs to digest, transform, and dissolve it so it becomes its own flesh and blood. It does not simply invite it to enter its |

Mao

Ai Siqi

dialectics of Ye Qing, then, is this eclectic distortion.

house and assign to it its own domain, then think that in doing this it has elevated it. People who distort dialectics mechanically break up "A is A, at the same time A is not A" into two propositions of formal logic. They hold that as long as, on the one hand, one acknowledges A is A, and, on the other hand, acknowledges A is not A, then it is considered dialectics. They do not know that the relation between these two propositions is not "on the one hand" and "on the other hand" but "at the same time"; it is their mutual permeation. The two propositions are a unified whole and not a mechanical combination. Therefore, one cannot mechanically break these up in this way. Thus, when they do break them up in this way the result is an eclectic understanding of dialectics. Superficially, they can confuse what is said of dialectics. They acknowledge that one needs to "take dialectics as a guide in order to engage in theoretical thinking, but, in reality, their dialectics is only the eclectic combination of several

Mao　　　　　　*Ai Siqi*

propositions of formal logic. Superficially, it seems as though they are using dialectics to sublate formal logic, yet, in fact, they are eliminating dialectics in formal logic.

Dialectics' sublation of formal logic, obviously, is not only rejection, for at the same time it assimilates the positive elements of formal logic. But, this assimilation is just like Mr Zhang says: it is not only preservation. Yet eclecticism draws us entirely to this extreme. It says formal logic still has a domain within dialectics; its scope is merely reduced somewhat. Looking at this as a whole, formal logic is still led and "controlled" by dialectics, but looking at it from a partial perspective, eclecticism still governs formal logic. The dialectics of Ye Qing, then, is an example of this eclectic distortion.

(a18) Ye Qing admits that the inductive and deductive methods are founded on form-al logic, and need to be sublated by dialectics. However, he also says: "In their application we can treat

(b18) For example, the inductive and deductive methods. Ye Qing admits thatthese two methods are founded on formal logic and need to be sublated by dialectics. He says, "dialect-

Mao

the inductive method and the deductive method categorically, using them at the appropriate occasion in the dialectical process of research". In this way it is acknowledged that the complete process of research is dialectical, but in this process there are times when one needs to use the inductive method and the deductive method. The combination of these methods, then, becomes the complete dialectical process of research.

(a19) The inductive method seeks out from amongst a great many complex, particular things their general, pure common points; the method it adopts is analysis. The deductive method uses general principles to explain particular things; the method it adopts is synthesis. The former proceeds from the particular to the general and from the concrete to the abs-

Ai Siqi

ics controls the inductive and deductive methods". However, how does this so-called control do this controlling? "In their application we can treat the inductive method and the deductive methods categorically, at the appropriate occasion in the dialectical process of research". The meaning of this is that although the complete process of research is dialectical, at various occasions in this process, there are times when one needs to use the inductive method, and there are times when one needs to use the deductive method. The combination of these methods becomes the complete dialectical process of research.

(b19) We know that the inductive method needs to seek out from amongst a great many complex, individual things, their general, pure common points; the method it adopts is analysis. The deductive method uses general principles to explain particular things; its method, contrary to the inductive method, is synthesis. The inductive method proceeds from the partic-

Mao	*Ai Siqi*
tract; the latter proceeds from the general to the particular and from the abstract to the concrete. According to Ye Qing's method, the whole of dialectics is merely the mechanical and eclectic combining of the inductive and deductive methods.	ular to the general and from the concrete to the abstract; the deductive method, on the contrary, proceeds from general to the particular and from the abstract to the concrete. According to Ye Qing: our "use of dialectics in research then includes the inductive and deductive methods" and, in the complete dialectical process of research the inductive and deductive methods each has its appropriate place; in that case, the whole of dialectics is merely a question of here the inductive method, there the deductive method - this mechanical, eclectic combination.
(a20) Ye Qing's formulation appears to be dialectical research, and proceeds from the particular to the general and from the general to the particular; it is the inductive and deductive method; in fact, this is wrong.	(b20) Perhaps Ye Qing may say he is using dialectics in studying things and that he proceeds from a great many concrete, individual things to the discovery of general laws, and that he again applies these general laws to individual concrete things. The former stage of the process being the appropriate place for induction and the latter stage of the process belonging to the deductive method. In fact, this is wrong.

Mao	Ai Siqi

Mao

(a 2 1) Although, in dialectics, at the stage of from the particular to the general, ordinary inductive methods such as observation, comparison, and analysis are used, they are only used as key elements. Because the inductive method only uses the method of analysis here, it only grasps determinations that are simple and one-sided. Dialectics is not like this, not only is it analysis, at the same time it is synthesis. It not only grasps determinations that are simple and one-sided, but it needs to seek out determinations that are all-sided and unities of contradiction.

In the process of the general to the particular, will it do to only use the deductive method, adopt the method of synthesis, apply general laws to, and synthesize, individual things? No! If dialectics is to be implemented, then, one does not only use laws and adopt synthesis, but in doing this, one still needs to analyze the concrete conditions of these individual things and discover the tendencies of new particular contradictions.

Ai Siqi

(b 2 1) Although, in dialectics, at the stage of the process from the individual to the general are used ordinary inductive methods such as observation, comparison, and analysis, they are only used as key elements. Not only must dialectics be employed at this stage of the ascent of the particular to the general, the dialectical method must be implemented and not here replaced with a totally unchanged inductive method. Here, the inductive method only uses the method of analysis. From complex, diverse things it only grasps determinations that are simple and one-sided. Here, however, dialectics not only analyzes, but at the same time, it uses synthesis. It not only grasps determinations that are simple and one-sided, but it seeks out determinations that are all-sided and unities of contradiction. According to Ye Qing, the research process of the general to the particular should be characterized as the appropriate place for the deductive method; if it only uses the method of synthesis, only applies general laws to individual things and

Mao

Ai Siqi

synthesizes individual things, then this will do. In fact, one must implement dialectics here; dialectics not only uses laws here, and not only needs to synthesize, but at the same time, it still needs to analyze the specific conditions of these individual things and discover the tendencies of new particular contradictions.

(a22) No matter whether it is from the general to the particular or from the particular to the general, our methods are both basically dialectical. The inductive and deductive methods have only an application as respective elements of the process of research. They cannot be separated from each other and stand alone. They are not simply rejected, nor are they simply preserved, but are assimilated, digested, and transformed. Dialectics is the whole of dialectics and is not the piecing together of the inductive and deductive methods.

(b22) In this way, no matter whether it is from the particular to the general or from the general to the particular, our methods are both basically dialectical. The inductive and deductive methods have only an application as respective elements of the process of research. They cannot be separated from each other and stand alone. Although they are not simply rejected, neither are they simply preserved. They are assimilated, digested, and transformed. Because dialectics is itself the whole of dialectics, it is not the piecing together of the inductive and deductive methods.

(a23) The quality of things does not change in the process of quantitative change; at this

(b23) This distortion of dialectics by Ye Qing can also be seen in his interpretat-

Mao

time, in terms of quality, it is at relative rest, however, in terms of quantity, it is in motion throughout. Because relative rest is still a particular form of absolute motion one still needs to use dialectics in studying relative rest; only then will one be able to see things in a profound way. Formal logic can only see the aspect of rest, moreover, it can overstate this aspect and forget basic states of motion. Since dialectics can grasp the all-sidedness of things, and even the aspect of formal logic is contained in it, why does one still want to use formal logic in studying relative rest?

Ai Siqi

ion of the relation between states of motion and states of rest. Although, verbally, he acknowledges the absolute nature of motion and the relative nature of rest, in reality, he has already put motion and rest on an equal footing: "they engender each other and are mutually supportive as well as mutually determining". He completely misunderstands what the significance of absolute as well as relative is. As Mr Zhang says, rest is only a particular form of motion; things at rest are essentially still in motion. For example, the quality of things does not change in the process of quantitative change. At this time we can say, with regard to the aspect of quality, that it is at relative rest. However, with regard to the aspect of quantity, it is in motion throughout. On the surface, a stone does not move or change; internally, however, it continuously undergoes a process of quantitative change (although, this is very slow). The change of feudal society is often very sluggish, but you cannot say it has not

Mao

Ai Siqi

changed. Because relative rest is basically a manifestation of the state of motion, we still need to use dialectics in our study of relative rest. Only then will one be able to see things in a very profound way. We are not saying that research using formal logic is completely without merit, but that formal logic can only see the aspect of rest, moreover, it can overstate this aspect and forget basic states of motion. Since, for us, dialectics can grasp the all-sided (the formal logic aspect is embodied in this) we do not still need to use formal logic to grasp it. Is not the way of Ye Qing, which considers that by relying only on formal logic relative rest can be completely grasped and which considers that the domain of formal logic will be permanently preserved, an extremely vulgar distortion?

(a24) Ye Qing says: "Understanding the basic character of the Chinese economy is obviously a study of a state of rest and consequently is a question undoubtedly established on the basis of formal logic".

(b24) When he discusses the study of the economic character of China this eclectic distortion is even more evident. He considers that understanding the basic character of the Chinese economy is obviously a study

Mao

This is wrong; this is eclecticism. According to his opinion, it is only the study of the development of China's society that is the study of a state of motion and a dialectical question. Form, quality, and relation, etc., are only the study of states of rest and ought to belong to formal logic. Is not this obvious eclecticism?

Quality and relation and such questions are the starting point of development; although it cannot be regarded as development itself, if we are faithful to dialectics, we should at least see in them the motive force of development, see in them specific contradictions; can formal logic do this? Formal logic only sees one side; it can only become formalism. For example, feudal society needs a capitalist revolution; this is a formula. Because China's economy is feudal it is then said that China needs a capitalist revolution and the establishment of capitalist society. In formal logic, this kind of deduction is very coherent, and we can only say this, but China's specific conditions are denied. The

Ai Siqi

of a state of rest, and consequently is a question undoubtedly raised on the basis of formal logic. In Ye Qing's opinion it is only the study of the development of China's society that is the study of a state of motion and a dialectical question. The study of "form, quality, and relation, etc.", however, are studies of states of rest. This is such obvious eclecticism! In fact, quality and relation are the starting point of development. Without this starting point there is no development. Ye Qing himself says, "Economics needs to be understood before it is known at what stage of evolution Chinese society is, and what revolution is needed". As to this starting point: although we cannot regard it as development itself, if we are faithful to dialectics, we at least need to see within it the original motive force of development, as well as a variety of specific contradictions. This, then, is not something formal logic can grasp. Naturally, if you definitely base yourself on formal logic and advance this question, of course, that suits

Mao	*Ai Siqi*

specific conditions of China do not permit that it will be restricted historically to a capitalist revolution, nor do they permit the establishment of capitalist society. All questions like this are questions that formal logic cannot solve, only dialectics can. The formalism of Plekhanov to Ye Qing cannot solve any question.

you, but this way you only see one side or it becomes formalism. This is to say: you want to use the deductive method, so first you adopt a general formula, then, you look to see what the nature of the Chinese economy is, then, relying on this formula, you determine China's needs. For example, feudal society needs a capitalist revolution, this is a general formula. The answer to your research tells you that China's economy is a feudal one, thereupon, you say China needs a capitalist revolution and the establishment of a capitalist society. In formal logic this, naturally, is very coherent. But, do the specific conditions of Chinese society comply with this formula? Your deduction cannot manage this. However, Chinese society cannot comply with your deductive formula. Although Chinese society is feudal, its special conditions do not permit that it will undergo a Western European style capitalist revolution, nor do they permit the establishment of capitalist society. This can only be done through dialectical study, for none of

Mao	*Ai Siqi*
	this can be seen by the deductive method of formal logic. In understanding Chinese economics, people who are faithful to dialectics must implement it. They cannot assign a domain to it here, thus giving empty formalism room to establish itself. (Plekhanov, esteemed by Ye Qing, made the mistake of formalism precisely because of this kind of thing.)
(a25) Two thousand years ago Greek sophists regarded motion as innumerable points of rest in space, and therefore concluded that there are only innumerable points of rest and no motion. Ye Qing says rest is the cessation of motion and motion is the accumulation of rest; this is the return to life of sophism.	(b25) First, he says motion is the accumulation of rest, and rest is the cessation of motion. This is just like Mr Zhang says, not only does it eclectically combine rest and motion, but it does it to the extent that as a result it eliminates motion in rest. Two thousand years ago Greek sophists had already developed this theory. They regarded motion as the sum total of innumerable points of rest in space and consequently concluded that there are only innumerable points of rest and no motion. Who would have thought that sophism would return to life in the mouth of "twentieth century" Ye Qing. This truly makes people want to "acclaim it as the height of perfection".

Mao

Ai Siqi

(a26) Lenin says, "a simple judgement is also a unity of contradiction. For instance, the proposition 'Ivan is a man' has the meaning of 'the particular is equal to the general'". Formal logic often makes this kind of proposition, "a youth is a shop-assistant", but not, "a youth is a youth", and this is because formal logic itself cannot strictly abide by the law of identity without making itself untenable. When formal logic uses this kind of proposition it naturally has not considered that it contains a contradiction, and therefore it cannot be said that this is an application of the law of the unity of contradiction. However, we cannot deny that this kind of proposition in essence contains a unity of contradictions.

(b26) Secondly, in formal logic the proposition "the youth is a shop-assistant" is common, and this must be so for formal logic becomes untenable if strictly according to the law of identity one is only able to say "the youth is a youth". When we say "the youth is a youth" contains a contradiction, it is to indicate that formal logic itself cannot strictly abide by the law of identity. When formal logicians use this proposition they naturally have not thought that it contains a contradiction, and therefore this proposition is certainly not an *application* of the law of the unity of contradiction. But we still cannot deny that this kind of proposition in essence *contains a unity of contradictions*. Ilyich, in his *Philosophical Notebooks*, says, "a simple judgement is also a unity of contradiction. For instance, the proposition 'Ivan is a man' has the meaning of 'the particular is equal to the general'". It is not known whether Ye Qing understands this point or not.

(a27) Ai Siqi says: "Things that are different are not con-

(b27) Thirdly, things that are different are certainly not

Mao

Ai Siqi

tradictions, for instance, a pen, ink, and chair are not contradictions. But if the principles of development and change are understood then it is known, that under certain conditions, things that are different are able to transform themselves into contradictions. If at the same time and place two definite things begin to act on each other in a mutually exclusive fashion, then they become contradictions. For instance, a shop-assistant and a writer are basically without contradiction, but if a certain shop-assistant has an interest in writing and thinks of becoming a writer, the two then become mutually exclusive within an entity and form a contradiction. If it is thought only such things as good and bad, male and female are contradictions and other things cannot transform themselves into contradictions, then, it is a formalistic differentiation. Is this distinguishable from Zhang Dongsun's formalistic division of "contrary, contradiction, and opposition"? The basic principle is correct but

contradictions, and so such things as a pen, ink, and a chair are not contradictions. However, if dialectics is truly "understood" and the principles of development and change are understood, then it must be known that under certain conditions things that are different can also transform themselves into contradictions if at the same time and place these two different things begin to act on each other in a mutually exclusive fashion. For example, a shop assistant and writer are two different, totally unrelated things. However, if someone who is a shop-assistant is very interested in writing as well as dissatisfied with his or her existing state of affairs and thinks hard about becoming a writer, at that time two different things - a shop-assistant and writer, within an entity, become mutually exclusive. Can you say this is not a contradiction? Can you say this shop-assistant has not experienced a contradiction in his or her life? If you insist that only good and bad, male and female, etc. can be con-

Mao

Ai Siqi

the formulation "difference is not contradiction" is not. One should say that, under certain conditions, all things that are different are contradictions. A person sits at a chair, dips a pen into ink to write an essay. Because a person and writing, these two definite conditions, temporarily unites the things that are in contradiction, one cannot say these differences are not contradictions. When a cook prepares food, he takes firewood, rice, oil, salt, sauce, vinegar, and vegetables and, under certain conditions, unites them. Under certain conditions, a shop-assistant and a writer are also able to unite. Part work-part study can unite work and study. Difference is each and every thing, all being under certain conditions, conntradictions; therefore, difference itself is contradiction; this is what is called a concrete contradiction. Ai's formulation is unsatisfactory (Mao Zedong's opinion).

(a28) The formula "A is B or not B" of the law of the excluded middle, in fact, con-

sidered contradictions and other things cannot transform themselves into contradictions, then what is the difference between this formalistic method of differentiation and Zhang Dongsun's division of "contrary, contradiction, and opposition", etc. Can this be the thinking of a person who "understands" dialectics?

(b28) Fourthly, in formal logic, "a youth is a shop assistant" suits only the form-

Mao

Ai Siqi

tains a contradiction: that is, "A is not A but is B", or "B can be B or not B"; Hegel has already criticised this.

ula A is A of the law of the excluded middle; everybody understands this. But the focus of our attention is to indicate: can a proposition of formal logic fundamentally find a role in dialectics and be "under the jurisdiction of moving logic"? We do not want to classify the law of the excluded middle with the law of the unity of contradiction. The formula "A is B or not B", in fact, already contains a contradiction: that is, "A is not A but is B" or "B can be B or not B"; Hegel has already criticised this. But, perhaps for Ye Qing it is not easy to understand because from start to finish he only knows how to use a formal mind to carry out rigid classification, and he is unaware of development and change.

(a29) Although external cause may not be overlooked, it cannot determine necessity in things. What determines necessity is internal change. Ye Qing says, "one must acknowledge the interaction of internal and external cause". This is mechanical interaction where the two sides are with-

(b29) Although external cause may not be overlooked, it cannot determine necessity in things. What determines necessity in things is internal cause. At this point the two must be distinguished in terms of superiority and inferiority. Ye Qing says dialectics must acknowledge interaction.

Mao

Ai Siqi

out a relative superiority or inferiority. This, then, forms Ye Qing's eclectism. Dialectical interaction is not like this. In it, the two sides are distinguished by a primary and secondary significance.

Ye Qing's question is admitted, "Mechanics need an external motive force: water encounters external heat and vaporizes; the evolution of organisms is due to the environment; are these not facts?" This is not a question of simple denial. However, at the same time the activity of the thing itself in [this process of] change must be acknowledged; this is the determining factor in [the process of] change in things. Mechanics has movability; water has the property of vaporization; it is the nature of organisms to evolve. Because of this, external causes such as motive force, heat, and the environment have a function. Internal cause determines the necessity of change in things, not external cause.

Therefore, there must be an interaction between internal and external cause. However, one knows that when speaking of interaction there is the difference between mechanical and dialectical interaction. Mechanical interaction is reciprocal. The two sides are without a relative superiority and inferiority. This kind of interaction can only form Ye Qing's eclecticism. In dialectical interaction, however, the two sides are distinguished by a primary and secondary significance. In the interaction between internal and external cause dialectics stresses the primary determining function of internal cause. This is what is meant by saying "what is called the occurrence of internal action, then, is considered to be the reason for necessity in things". Ye Qing has put several questions to me, "Mechanics needs an external motive force, is this not a fact; water encounters external heat and vaporizes, is this not a fact; the evolution of organisms is due to the environment, is this not a fact?"

Mao

Ai Siqi

I naturally reply "yes". I cannot simply deny it. However, acknowledging these facts is not the same as acknowledging that external cause determines necessity. If you ask, "Motive force causes mechanical movement, is this necessity? Heat causes water to vaporize, is this necessity?" I naturally will answer in the affirmative. However, if you again ask, "Well then, is not the determination of this 'necessity' precisely motive force, heat, etc.?" To this I will reply in one word "no". Why is the answer "no"? Because Ye Qing himself must acknowledge that, "External cause must depend on internal cause to become external cause. If mechanics lacks dynamism, motive force cannot become the motive force of mechanics. If water lacks the property of vaporization, heat then becomes the heat of water and it cannot vaporize".

Internal and External Cause

(a30) General things will always manifest themselves through particular forms. No

(b30) This is to say general things often will be manifested through particular

Mao

Ai Siqi

thing in the world exists in a purely general sense. What is called "the particular is contained in the general" indicates a general thing manifesting itself in a particular form. It does not say that there is some particular thing independent of the general (like Ye Qing saying the theory of internal causes is a general principle, yet China's development does not conform to a law). The general and particular are a unity of contradictions; there is no purely general and there is no purely particular independent of the general.

(a31) The distinguishing feature of dialectical materialism consists in its grasp of the kernel of facts, the essence of facts, and the regularity of the internal development of facts. It does not consist in esteeming the appearance of facts. Mechanical materialists, empiricists, and pragmatists also respect facts, but they only respect superficial facts. Respecting superficial facts is the preliminary stage of knowledge and the preliminary stage of science. Seventeenth and eighteenth

forms. Absolutely no thing in the world exists in a purely general sense. Therefore, what is called "the particular is contained in the general" indicates a general thing manifesting itself in a particular form. It does not indicate the particular independent of the general. The general and particular are also a dialectical unity. There is no purely general, at the same time, there is no purely particular thing apart from the general.

(b31) The distinguishing feature of dialectical materialism does not consist of its respect for facts, but in its ability to grasp the kernel of facts and its ability to grasp the internal regularities of development. What dialectics needs to respect is the essence of facts and not their appearance. Esteeming superficial facts is the preliminary stage of knowledge and the preliminary stage of science. Seventeenth and eighteenth century mechanical materialism and the science of mech-

Mao

century materialism and the theory of the science of mechanics are like this. It is not denied that superficial facts can also give people some knowledge. Seventeenth and eighteenth century mechanics has already furnished a great many truths. Pragmatism, compared to the empty talkers who present a false picture of peace and prosperity, is able to see more of a few things. To a great extent, it was able to expose the crimes of the enemy invasion and the mistake of absolute non-resistance. However, this esteem of immediate facts, that only see the invasion of the enemy and not the nature of the invasion, that only see the mistake of non-resistance and not the prospect of the resistance of the masses, is completely different to materialist dialectics. It is only a superficial fact that mechanical motion is due to external force; the essence of fact is that mechanics itself has the potential for movement. The science of the age of the outlook of mechanics only paid attention to the study of external force. This was be-

Ai Siqi

anics is like this. We do not deny that esteeming superficial facts can give us some knowledge. Seventeenth and eighteenth century mechanics has already furnished a great many truths. The pragmatism of Hu Shi (provided he is able to put into practice his doctrine) compared to empty talkers who always present a picture of peace and prosperity, is more capable of seeing more of a few things. Also, it was still able, to a great extent, to expose the invasion of the enemy and the mistake of absolute non-resistance. However, this alone is not enough. This crawling esteem for only seeing immediate facts that simply see the invasion of the enemy and not the nature of the invasion, that simply see the mistake of non-resistance and not the prospects of the resistance of the people, is completely different to materialist dialectics. Yes, mechanical motion is due only to external force, this is a fact; however, this is only a superficial fact; essentially, the capacity of external force to cause this mechanical mov-

Mao

Ai Siqi

cause science at that time was still at a preliminary stage; it was not able to penetrate through to the essence of movement. Arriving at the high level stage of the theory of relativity made people aware of the use of internal cause in explaining mechanical movement. In Newton's time they only knew how to use gravitation (external force) to explain the movement of heavenly bodies; the theory of relativity, however, uses the property of movement itself to explain this.

ement is due to the potential of mechanics itself for movement. The reason one's hand pushes a small stone is because the small stone can move. If one pushes a wall it will not work. This is what our paper has said several times, so much so that even Ye Qing himself cannot deny it. Ye Qing's so-called science of the age of the outlook of mechanics only concentrated on the study of external force. This was because science at that time was still at a preliminary stage. It was not a time when it was able to penetrate through to the essence of things. The arrival of science at a higher stage, like the present emergence of the theory of relativity, makes us insist on the use of internal cause to explain mechanical movement. For example, in Newton's time the movement of heavenly bodies was explained by external force (gravitation), but the theory of relativity uses the property of movement itself to explain this.

6 Philosophical Annotations and Marginalia

Annotations on M. Shirokov and A. Aizenberg et al., A Course on Dialectical Materialism, translated by Li Da and Lei Zhongjian (third edition).

[pp. 14-15]

(p. 6) The essence of dialectics, namely the law (*faze*) of the unity of opposites.

[pp. 193-196]

(p. 14) Materialist dialectics is the determining element of Marxism.

The objective world develops, and so too does subjective knowledge.

(pp. 15-16) Reflection is not a passive absorption of the object, but an active process. In production and class struggle, knowledge is an active element which leads to the transformation of the world.

Source: *Mao Zedong zhexue pizhuji* [The philosophical annotations of Mao Zedong] (Beijing: Zhongyang wenxian chubanshe, 1988), pp. 1-189. The translation is of a selection only of the most significant and coherent of Mao's annotations on two Soviet texts on philosophy. The annotations date from November 1936 to July 1937. Page numbers in round brackets refer to *Mao Zedong zhexue pizhuji*; those in square brackets refer to the Chinese translations of the Soviet texts which Mao was annotating. Translated by Nick Knight.

(p. 17)   To change the world is at the same time to change oneself.
(p. 20)   Plekhanov ... did not understand the essence of dialectics (the law of the unity of opposites)...
(p. 21)   The mechanistic outlook - this perceives only mutual interconnections, and not mutual interpermeation (*shentou*).
[pp. 203-213]
(p. 22)   No question regarding knowledge of the world can be solved except through practice.
        The subject of cognition is social class.
(pp. 23-24) The first stage: very shallow, [the proletariat] does not understand the essence of capitalism, adopts incorrect methods of struggle, and is still in the stage of a "class-in-itself".
        The second stage: the practice of everyday struggle and the development of the reality of capitalism, leads the proletariat to an understanding of the essence of capitalism (exploitative relationships and the relations of class struggle), Marxism appeared, and the proletariat achieved the stage of a "class-for-itself".
(pp. 24-25) From the perceptual stage move to the rational stage, and from the rational stage move to revolutionary practice.
(p. 25)   The purpose of knowledge is to achieve logical understanding from perceptual data, the two stages are different, but cannot be separated.
(p. 26)   Perceptual knowledge: one-sided, superficial, external connections.
        Rational knowledge: totality, essence, internal connections.
(pp. 28-29) Perceptual knowledge cannot be separated from rational knowledge, perceptual knowledge already contains within it the sprouts of rational knowledge. The general is already contained in that which is concrete, but what is contained is only the external and not the internal connection. From the shallow to the deep, from the outside to the inside, from the particular to the general, it is only thought with practice as its basis which succeeds. This is the movement of the deepening of knowledge, it is sudden change of knowledge. It

is only with this deepening and sudden change that nature can be reflected relatively correctly and completely.

(p. 29-30) Practice proves: things that are perceived cannot immediately be comprehended, it is only things that are comprehended that can be more deeply and correctly perceived. Perception solves the problem of phenomenon, comprehension solves the problem of essence and it is only in the process of practice that the essence of a thing can be revealed and understood.

(p. 33)   Practice is the proof of truth.

[pp. 213-216]

(pp. 33-34) Theory is produced from practice; if the process of development of the objective external world is correctly reflected, and if subsequently this theory is applied in practice, then this theory can be made manifest in practice, and thus completes the process of knowledge.

[pp. 253-257]

(p. 44)   It is necessary to indicate all of the particular characteristics of a process, especially the fundamental particularity; only then is it possible to know the laws of development of a process, because the laws (*faze*) are contained in the development of the contradictions of the basic particularity.

(p. 46)   It is necessary not only to know the basic characteristics of an entire process, it is also necessary to know the different characteristics of the various stages of the process.

[pp. 258-260]

(pp. 48-49) The process of development has its origin in the change of intrinsic essence to non-essence, has its origin in the change of non-essence to essence. This distinction is essential, otherwise there will be errors.

[pp. 265-267]

(p. 50)   A process has both qualitative and quantitative aspects.

(p. 52)   Quantitative change promotes qualitative change.

[pp. 272-276]

(p. 59)   The acknowledgement of development through leaps is one of the central characteristics of dialectical materialism.

(p. 60)   Nature, society, thought, all undergo leaps (*feiyue*). At the moment of the leap, the old quality is eliminated and a new quality is produced (with the old quality as the basis).

The quality and quantity of the old object are terminated, and the new quality and quantity begin to emerge.

The old process is the preparation for the new process, the old stage is the preparation for the new stage.

The new process or stage retains remnants of the old quality, and while there is furthermore a lengthy period in which the old and new intermesh in a complex manner, there is dominance of one over the other.

(p. 62)   Dialectics must pay attention to the specific character of leaps.

[pp. 277-280]

(pp. 64-66) Two viewpoints.

The first viewpoint, the mechanistic view of development, sees development resulting from an increase or decrease in quantity. It sees problems only one-sidedly and externally rather than completely and internally, and cannot explain the reasons for the development of a thing.

The second viewpoint, the dialectical materialist view of development, reveals the source of movement within a process. So-called knowledge of a process is the revelation of the various aspects of the contradictions replete within a process, the determination of the mutual relations between these aspects, and the search for the movement of the contradictions of a process.

If we take cognisance of a process during its dissociation (*fenlie*), observe the parts of the contradictions replete within the process and the mutual relations of these parts, we can then know the development of a process from emergence to elimination. As Lenin has therefore stated: The essence of dialectics is knowledge of the dissociation of a unified entity and the parts of the contradictions replete within it.

It is necessary but not sufficient to have knowledge of the mutual distinctions of a process, of the many aspects and attributes of the mutual opposites of a process, including a knowledge of the mutual connections of these aspects and attributes;   it is necessary also to know the fundamental

contradiction which allows development of the process, for that is the source of movement of the process.
[pp. 281-286]
(p. 67)   In the contradiction between the social character of production and the private character of ownership can be seen the contradiction between the forces and relations of production, and this is the fundamental contradiction.   From this fundamental contradiction emerges all other contradictions, because this fundamental contradiction determines the development of capitalism.
(p. 69)   The principal contradiction in the transitional stage in the Soviet Union is the contradiction between socialism and capitalism, and the basis for the continual emergence of this contradiction is the existence of a rich peasantry. All other contradictions are determined by this principal contradiction. It will only be with industrialisation and the socialisation of agriculture that this principal contradiction will be resolved; but there is the possibility that this contradiction can be resolved through the use of internal force.
(p. 71)   The unity of contradictions and their dissociation is also a law (*faze*) of thought.
Knowledge is determined by practice and the history of society.
(p. 72)   The so-called unity of opposites is the dissociation of a unified entity to become mutually exclusive opposites, and includes the mutual connections between these opposites. This is the source of the so-called principal contradiction, of so-called self-movement.
The particularity of contradictions is different as the contradictions of each different process are different.
(p. 73)   Qualitatively different contradictions require different methods for their resolution.
[pp. 287-292]
(pp. 73-74) The national contradiction between China and Japan requires for its resolution a united front with the bourgeoisie. The internal (*guonei*) contradiction after 1927, however, was resolved through a united front with the peasantry and petty bourgeoisie. During normal times, the contradiction between labour and capital will be resolved through a united front of the

workers. In the contradiction between the correct line and incorrect tendencies within the Party and revolutionary ranks, use the method of ideological struggle for its resolution. Internationally, revolution is to be employed to resolve the contradiction between the proletariat and the bourgeoisie. Industrialisation and the collectivisation of agriculture are to be used in resolving the contradiction between the proletariat and the peasantry in the Soviet Union. Develop the productive forces to resolve the contradiction between society and nature. As the contradictions of processes are different, so too are the methods for their resolution.

(p. 74)   In looking at a problem from a dialectical materialist perspective, it is necessary to expose the particularity of contradictions within any process, and at the same time it is necessary to know the particularity of contradictions of the various aspects of a process.

(p. 75)   Opposed aspects are a condition for the existence of each other, only if one aspect exists can the other exist.

(p. 79)   The central task of dialectics is to study the mutual permeation (*shentou*) of opposites, namely the identity of opposites.

(p. 81)   If there is no concrete study of a process, there is no way that the identity of opposites, that is their mutual permeation, can be understood.

[pp. 293-299]

(pp. 83-85) Although contradiction exists universally, antagonism only emerges when the contradictions of certain processes have developed to a definite stage. The contradictions between oppressing and oppressed classes, between oppressing and oppressed nations, between state and state, between party and party, etc., all have circumstances in which antagonism is developed. Antagonisms within the social process adopt the form of oppression and war; those within the process of nature adopt the form of clash and conflict; and scuffles and plotting between individuals are of the same order. Many contradictions do not develop to an antagonistic form: within the Communist Party, the contradiction between correct and incorrect; in the realm of culture, the contradiction between advanced and backward; in the realm of the economy, contradictions between town and countryside, between value and use value, between mental and manual labour, between production and consumption; in class relations, the contradiction between workers and peasants; under socialism, the contradiction between the forces and relations of production; in the natural world, between life and death, positive and negative, inheritance and variation, attraction and repulsion, cold and warm, and between ocean and continent. None of these has yet achieved a condition under which it bursts asunder, none of these contradictions contains antagonism. The method for the resolution of contradictions and that for the resolution of antagonism are different. This is the particularity of contradiction and the particularity of the method for the resolution of contradiction, a question which requires distinctions to be made.

(pp. 87-90) A complex process has many contradictions, and amongst these one is the principal contradiction and the others are secondary contradictions. Because the development of the principal contradiction determines the development of the various secondary contradictions, if one cannot distinguish between the principal and secondary contradictions, between the determining contradiction and those that are determined, one cannot seek out the most essential thing of a process (provide examples). However, within a contradiction, regardless of whether it is principal or secondary, the two aspects of the opposites are not only in opposition and struggle, but are moreover in mutual reliance on the opposing aspect with which it carries on opposition and struggle. The result of the struggle of the two aspects is the emergence of the change of mutual interpermeation, namely a transformation to achieve identity, a transformation to its opposing aspect, and this is the indivisible interconnection of the two opposed aspects. However, it is a big mistake to look at the two aspects of any contradiction as though they are equal. Of the two aspects, one is inevitably the principal and the other the secondary aspect, and the former is the aspect which plays the contradiction's so-called guiding role. This book has already provided the four examples of value and use value in which value is the principal aspect, of forces and relations of production in which the forces of production are the principal aspect, of theory and practice in which practice is the determining aspect, and of socialism and capitalism in the Soviet Union of which socialism is the principal aspect; all prove the determining function of the principal aspect in relation to the other aspect. It is not, as Plekhanov's mistaken explanation has it, simple mutual combination; neither is it, as Luppol's explanation has it, a case of alternating mutual determination; it is rather one aspect performing the principal and determining function. In actuality which aspect is principal? It is necessary to observe the situation of the development of a process, and it will be determined under definite conditions. For a long period in capitalist society, the bourgeoisie were the principal aspect, but on the eve of the revolution and during its aftermath, the proletariat changes to become the principal aspect. In a capitalist state, capitalism is the principal aspect while feudal forces are the secondary aspect. Feudal forces were the principal aspect in pre-revolutionary Russia, as they are in present-day Japan, with capitalism playing a secondary role. In Chinese society, dominance belongs to imperialism and the feudal forces, such that they exercise a determining effect on all else. The invasion by Japanese imperialism determines all manner of changes. Thus, during the vigorous development of the great revolution between 1925 and 1927, in the confrontation between the Southern revolutionary forces and the Northern warlords, the Southern forces changed from secondary status to being dominant, while the power of the Northern warlords changed in the opposite direction. In the example of the contradiction between the proletariat and the bourgeoisie, because the bourgeoisie still has a firm grasp on the economic arteries, to this day it still occupies a dominant position; however, in terms of revolutionary leadership, because of the level of consciousness and the thoroughness of the proletariat and the vacillation of the bourgeoisie, the proletariat occupies the dominant position. This particular point has an influence on the future of the Chinese Revolution. If the proletariat is politically and materially to occupy the dominant position, it must unite with the peasantry and petty bourgeoisie. If the majority of the workers, peasants, and petty bourgeoisie can become conscious and get organized, then the proletariat will assume the

determining and dominant role of the revolution. In the situation of hostility between China and Japan, the Chinese elements are currently changing from a secondary to a principal position, and that is because if the national united front is established broadly and is consolidated, and with the addition of international factors (the Soviet Union, the Japanese masses, and other peaceful states), there will be created a superiority over the Japanese aspect. In the contradiction between the peasantry and the proletariat, the proletariat is dominant. In the contradiction between industrial workers and handicraft workers, industrial workers are dominant. In the contradiction between skilled and unskilled workers, skilled workers are dominant. In the contradiction between town and countryside, the town is dominant. In the contradiction between economic base and superstructure, the economic base is dominant. In the contradiction between perceptual knowledge and rational knowledge, perceptions are dominant. In the contradiction between the main force of the Red Army and the guerilla units, the main force of the Red Army is dominant. In the contradiction between the military tactics of offence and defence, offence is dominant. In the contradiction between strategy and tactics, strategy is dominant. In the contradiction between mobile and positional warfare, mobile warfare is dominant. Of the various arms of the services, the infantry is dominant. In the contradiction between mental and manual labour, manual labour is dominant. And who is to decide? When the development of a process reaches a definite stage, the strength of the two sides in the struggle will determine it. The dominant and the non-dominant change from one to the other.
[pp. 303-308]
(pp. 92-93) In the motion of contradiction in all processes, identity is relative while struggle is absolute; all processes are thus. However, because the nature of the contradiction is different in each process, and the internal structure of each process is different, it is very apparent that the method by which absoluteness and unity are made manifest will also be different.
(pp. 93-94) It is correct but insufficient to recognise that contradiction gives rise to motion; it is also necessary to understand under what kind of conditions contradiction gives

rise to motion. In a condition of unity, although contradiction is in motion it is a particular state of motion, namely a relative state; this is commonly called rest, invariability, immobility, death, static, standstill, deadlock, stalemate, peace, gentleness, and is relative, temporary, and conditional. It is necessary to recognise the general condition of motion, namely the dissociation of a unified entity, its struggle, conflict, movement inconstancy, life, action, dynamism, warfare, mutual disputation, and this is absolute. Identity, unity, rest, death, peace, and so on, which are the relative condition of contradiction, are contained within the absolute condition of contradiction. It is metaphysical and mechanistic not to understand this truth, and in fact is a rejection of dialectics.

(p. 99)   It is not the unity of opposites which is the essence, it is the struggle of opposites.

[pp. 316-324]

(pp. 105-106) The contradiction between the forces and relations of production, namely society's internal contradiction, has a determining influence on the contradiction between society and nature; in other words, humanity can triumph over nature. It has been thus ever since the production of instruments of labour.

(pp. 112-113) The Left and the Right are linked, and this is because they both are divorced from a correct understanding of a process; they arrive at a vacuous understanding which is abstract and general, which pays no heed to the content of a process, and which does not analyse concrete stages, conditions, possibilities, and so on.

(p. 113)   The so-called dialectical process of the development of reality and knowledge is a process of mutual transformation of quality and quantity, of the unity of contradictions, and the negation of the negation.

[pp. 324-327]

(p. 115)   Engels' words on the three laws are correct.

[pp. 329-334]

(pp. 119-121) The error of formal logic is in its perception of negation as an external negation between one process and another, which is moreover regarded as an absolute negation; this approach completely misunderstands reality. The opposite of this approach is dialectical materialism, that is, scientific observation and study. Material reality is self-motion, and moreover this self-motion is interconnected. Any process itself moves forward because of the struggle of contradictions, and through a sudden transformation it changes to move in an opposite direction. The entire history of development of any process is constructed of a thesis, an antithesis which negates the thesis, and a synthesis which is a negation of the negation of the antithesis. The thesis already contains contradiction or antithesis within it, the antithesis also contains the thesis within it, and the synthesis incorporates both the thesis and antithesis. So-called negation, as Lenin has stated, "is neither random nor complete negation, is neither sceptical nor vacillating negation; it is rather negation as an element which preserves connection, an element of affirmation, i.e., without any vacillations, without scepticism".[1] Negation does not destroy everything and make a clean break with the past, it is not absolute; things that are in front contain things that come later, and things that come later contain things that are in front. Without the motion of negation, there can be no motion of affirmation. All processes are like this.

(pp. 124-125) Negation is the ever-higher development of a process.

A dialectical negation does not constitute a complete break with the past or its complete elimination.

The first negation creates the possibility of the second negation.

A dialectical negation is the cause of movement of a process of development, and this negation manifests itself as two aspects: one aspect manifests itself as sublation, namely the overcoming of the principal things of the old entity which are incompatible with preservation; the other aspect manifests itself as affirmation, namely the provision of status to and the preservation of the various things of the old entity which are still temporarily compatible with existence.

Annotations on M.B. Mitin et al., Dialectical Materialism and Historical Materialism, translated by Shen Zhiyuan (Volume I).

[pp. 179-180]
(p. 142)   Practice is the criterion of truth.
[pp. 181-185]
(p. 143)   Correct theory actively guides practice.
(p. 144)   Practice develops, theory too should develop.
(pp. 145-146) Perceptions and thought are a product of social life. As social life changes, so too do perceptions and thought.

Material production is the foundation of the variegated life of humanity.

All knowledge is the result of the struggle of production and the class struggle.

Before Marx, all materialism examined the problem of knowledge apart from the social nature of humankind and apart from its historical development, and was therefore incapable of understanding the dependence of knowledge on social practice.
[pp. 187-188]
(p. 152)   The purpose of the study of philosophy is not to satisfy one's curiosity, but to transform the world.

Know the laws of the world, find correct theory in order to guide practice effectively, and transform the world.
[pp. 194-201]
(p. 161)   The fundamental theme of the view of development of materialist dialectics is that it is the contradictory nature of any phenomenon which leads to the development of that thing.
(p. 165)   Different processes have different contradictions.
(p. 166)   It is because there are different characteristics and different contradictions that there are all sorts of different forms of motion.

Knowledge of matter is knowledge of the form of motion of matter.
(p. 169)   [The law of the unity of opposites] is the universal law (*faze*) of the objective world and knowledge, and all

processes fall within its ambit.
[p. 207]
(p. 175)   Every difference contains contradiction.
Mutual dependence is a manifestation of the struggle of opposites, the absolute exists in the relative.
[pp. 216-222]
(p. 178)   With regard to the Chinese Revolution, we should emulate Lenin's analysis of the Russian Revolution.
(p. 181)   Scientific research must commence from a knowledge of the distinguishing characteristics of quality.
The various and different forms of the motion of matter. Each entity has a definite form of motion, and there are a wide variety of forms of motion; however, there is of necessity one form of motion which manifests any one particular quality of matter. Different forms of motion manifest the different qualities of matter or composition of substances.
(p. 185)   Quantity too is objective, and the concept of quantity is a reflection in human consciousness of those quantitative relations within phenomena themselves. Scientific research should come to know [objective reality] not only on the basis of qualitative difference, but also on the basis of quantitative complexity.
(pp. 185-186) Within an entity, quality and quantity constitute an indivisible identity, an identity of different substances, namely an identity of opposites.
However, the quantitative change of an entity can only emerge on the basis of a certain quality compatible with it, and within a definite period, quality restricts the development of quantity. Feudalism, imperialism, and socialism are three examples.
(pp. 186-187) Quantitative change is restricted by the nature of quality, but at the same time quantitative change also has an influence on quality. That is to say, an entity which is determined by a definite quality will remain thus up to the moment at which quantitative change reaches a definite qualitative limit; quantity will then demand a change of quality. At the same time, this change is a change from quality to

quantity. Once the old quality has passed away, a new quantity can then develop in a forward direction.

Only through quantitative change can qualitative change emerge.

Note

1.   The quote is from Lenin's "Conspectus of Hegel's *Science of Logic*", in *Collected Works* (London: Lawrence and Wishart, 1963), Vol. XXXVIII, p. 226.   The Chinese translation used by Mao does not, however, reflect very faithfully the original.   See also *Mao Zedong zhexue pizhuji*, pp. 516-517, note 84.

COMPILED BY NICK KNIGHT
AND JEFF RUSSELL

7 | On Mao, Philosophy and Ideology: A Select Bibliography of English Language Sources

Philosophy

Arndt, Andreas, "The synthesis of Chinese and Western philosophy in Mao Tse-tung's theory of dialectic", *Studies in Soviet Thought*, 22:3 (1981), pp. 196-205.

Borsa, Georgio, "On Mao's contribution to a theory of dialectics", *Politico*, 42:3 (September 1977), pp. 503-514.

Bulkeley, Rip, "On 'On Practice'", *Radical Philosophy*, 18 (Autumn 1977), pp. 3-9, 15.

Chin, Steve S.K., *The Thought of Mao Tse-tung: Form and Content*, translated by Alfred H.Y. Lin (Hong Kong: Centre for Asian Studies Papers and Monographs, 1979).

Chu, Theresa, "Some reflections on Mao Zedong's thought", in Adelmann, F.J. (ed.), *Contemporary Chinese Philosophy* (The Hague, Boston, and London: Martinus Nijhoff Publishers, 1982), pp. 97-116.

Creel, H.G., *Chinese Thought from Confucius to Mao Tse-tung* (Chicago: Chicago University Press, 1953).

Creel, H.G., "Comments on harmony and conflict", *Journal of Chinese Philosophy*, 4 (October 1977), pp. 271-277.

Doolin, D. and Golas, P., "On Contradiction in the light of Mao Tse-tung's essay on 'Dialectical Materialism'", *China Quarterly*, 19 (July-September 1964), pp. 38-46.

Dunayevskaya, Raya, *Philosophy and Revolution: From Hegel to Sartre, and From Marx to Mao* (New York: De Lagorte Press, 1973).

Duncanson, Dennis, "Mao Tse-Tung and the Spencerian Dual Code", *Contemporary Review*, 234:1356 (1979), pp. 33-38.

Fann, K.T., "Mao and the Chinese Revolution in philosophy", *Studies in Soviet Thought*, 12 (June 1972), pp. 111-123.

Fann, K.T., "Mao's revolutionary humanism", *Studies in Soviet Thought*, 19:2 (March 1979), pp. 143-154.

Fitzgerald, C.P., "Mao and the Chinese cultural tradition", *Politico*, 42:3 (1977), pp. 483-493.

Friedman, Edward, "Einstein and Mao: metaphors of revolution", *China Quarterly*, 93 (1983), pp. 51-75.

Fu, Charles Wei-Hsun, "Confucianism, Marxism-Leninism and Mao: a critical study", *Journal of Chinese Philosophy*, 1 (1974), pp. 339-371.

Fu, Charles Wei-Hsun, "Rejoinder to Professor Howard Parsons' critical remarks on 'Confucianism, Marxism-Leninism and Mao'", *Journal of Chinese Philosophy*, 2 (Summer 1975), pp. 447-454.

Fu, Charles Wei-Hsun, "Marxism-Leninism-Maoism as an ethical theory", *Journal of Chinese Philosophy*, 5 (1978), pp. 343-362.

Gandhi, Madan G., "Mao's theory of contradiction", *Indian Journal of Politics*, 11:1 (April 1977), pp. 43-54.

Glaberman, Martin, "Mao as a dialectician", *International Philosophical Quarterly*, 8 (1968), pp. 94-112.

Hill, Jerome Dalton, *Epistemology and Politics: The Unity of Theory and Practice in Dewey and Mao* (Michigan: University of Michigan Press, 1981).

Ho, David Y.F., "The conception of man in Mao Tse-Tung Thought", *Psychiatry*, 41:4 (1978), pp. 391-402.

Holubnychy, Vsevolod, "Mao Tse-tung's materialist dialectics", *China Quarterly*, 19 (1964), pp. 3-37.

Hsiung, James Chieh, "Confucian 'harmony', Maoist 'struggle', and their Western counterparts: a dialectical comparison", *Journal of Chinese Philosophy*, 4 (1977), pp. 261-269.

Jung, Hwa Yol and Jung, Petee, "Revolutionary dialectics: Mao Tse-tung and Maurice Merleau-Ponty", *Dialectical Anthropology*, 2:1 (February 1977), pp. 33-56.

Kim Hyung-chan, "Some thoughts on Mao Tse-tung's views of man, society and human knowledge", *Journal of Thought*, 7 (April 1972), pp. 77-84.

Koller, John M., "Philosophical aspects of Maoist thought", *Studies in Soviet Thought*, 14 (1974), pp. 47-59.

Liu, J., "Mao's 'On Contradiction'", *Studies in Soviet Thought*, 11:2 (June 1971), pp. 71-89.

Madsen, Richard P., "The Maoist ethic and the moral basis of political activism in rural China", in Wilson, Richard W., Greenblatt, Sydney L., and Wilson, Amy Averbacher (eds.), *Moral Behaviour in Chinese Society* (New York: Praeger, 1981).

Mohanty, M., "Mao Tse-tung's law of unity of knowing and doing", *Indian Journal of Political Science*, 37:3 (July-September 1976), pp. 64-71.

Mohanty, M., *The Political Philosophy of Mao Tse-tung* (Columbia, Mo.: South Asia Books, 1979).

Nivison, David S., "Communist ethics and Chinese tradition", *Journal of Asian Studies*, 16:1 (1956), pp. 51-74.

Noumoff, S.J., "Mao as philosopher", in Gibson, J.M. and Johnston, D.M. (eds.), *Canadian Essays on Revolutionary China* (Toronto: Canadian Institute of International Affairs, 1971), pp. 55-64.

Parsons, Howard L., "Remarks on Charles Wei-Hsun Fu, 'Confucianism, Marxism-Leninism and Mao: A Critical Study'", *Journal of Chinese Philosophy*, 2 (Summer 1975), pp. 429-445.

Ram, Asha, "Mao Tse-tung: theoretical framework of his thoughts", *Indian Philosophical Quarterly*, 4 (January 1977), pp. 215-231.

Ram, Asha, "Practical aspects of the thoughts of Mao Tse-tung", *Indian Philosophical Quarterly*, 7 (January 1980), pp. 289-300.

Riepe, Dale (ed.), "Maoism: a twentieth-century Chinese philosophy", in *Asian Philosophy Today* (New York: Gordon and Breach, 1981).

Schram, Stuart R., "Mao Tse-tung as Marxist dialectician", *China Quarterly*, 29 (January-March 1967), pp. 155-165.

Schwartz, B.I., "The philosopher", in Wilson, Dick (ed.), *Mao Tse-tung in the Scales of History* (Cambridge: Cambridge University Press, 1977), pp. 9-34.

Singh, Bhola Prasad, "The philosophical foundations of Mao's peasant communism", *Indian Journal of Political Studies*, 1:1 (January 1977), pp. 59-70.

Soo, Francis, *Mao Tse-tung's Theory of Dialectic* (Dordrecht: D. Reidel, 1981).

Wakeman, Jr., Frederic, *History and Will: Philosophical Perspectives of Mao Tse-tung's Thought* (Berkeley: University of California Press, 1973).

Whitehead, Raymond L., *Love and Struggle in Mao's Thought* (New York: Orbis Books, 1977).

Wittfogel, Karl and Chao, C.R., "Some remarks on Mao's handling of concepts and problems of dialectics", *Studies in Soviet Thought*, 3:4 (1963), pp. 125-160.

Wu, J.S., "Understanding Maoism: a Chinese philosopher's critique", *Studies in Soviet Thought*, 15:2 (June 1975), pp. 1-118.

Ideology

Amin, Samir, *The Future of Maoism*, translated by Norman Finkelstein (New York: Monthly Review Press, 1983).

Andors, Stephen, "Mao and Marx: a comment", *Modern China*, 3:4 (October 1977), pp. 427-433.

Blumier, Jay,"On the correct handling of contradictions within Mao Tse-tung", *Socialist Commentary* (July 1957), pp. 5-7.

Chang Chi-yun, "Antitheses between San-Min-Chu-Yi and Maoist communism", *Chinese Culture*, 20:3 (September 1979), pp. 1-25.

Chang, Maria Hsia and Gregor, James A., "Maoism and Marxism in comparative perspective", *Review of Politics*, 40:3 (July 1978), pp. 307-327.

Chen Yung Ping, *Chinese Political Thought: Mao Tse Tung and Liu Shao-Chi* (The Hague: Martinus Nijhoff, 1966).

Ch'en, Jerome, *Mao* (New Jersey: Prentice-Hall, 1969).

Ch'en, Jerome (ed.), *Mao Papers: Anthology and Bibliography* (London: Oxford University Press, 1970).

Ch'en, Jerome, "The development and logic of Mao Tse-tung's thought, 1928-49", in Johnson, Chalmers (ed.), *Ideology and Politics in Contemporary China* (Seattle and London: University of Washington Press, 1973), pp. 78-114.

Chiao Chien, "New wine in old bottles: Some characteristics of the study of Mao Tse-tung's thought movement in the sixties", *Journal of the Chinese University of Hong Kong*, 3:1 (1975), pp. 207-216.

Chin, Steve S.K., "Identity and contradiction: An explanation of the Mao-Liu struggle from an ideological point of view", *Studies in Soviet Thought,* 10:3 (September 1970), pp. 227-254.

Chin Ssu-Kai, "The essence of the development of Marxism-Leninism by Mao Tse-tung", *Asian Thought and Society,* 2:1 (1977), pp. 124-134.

Chou Tzu-ch'iang, "Elements of Chinese culture in Mao Tse-tung's works", *Issues and Studies*, 9:6 (1973), pp. 35-56.

Christensen, Peter Moller and Delman, Jorgen, "A theory of transitional society: Mao Zedong and the Shanghai School", *Bulletin of Concerned Asian Scholars*, 13:2 (April-June 1981), pp. 2-15.

Cohen, Arthur A., "How original is 'Maoism'?", *Problems of Communism*, X:6 (November-December 1961), pp. 34-42.

Cohen, Arthur A., *The Communism of Mao Tse-tung* (Chicago and London: University of Chicago Press, 1964).

Cohen, Arthur A., "Maoism", in Drachkovitch, M.M. (ed.), *Marxism in the Modern World* (Stanford: Stanford University Press, 1965).

Corrigan, P., Ramsay, H., and Sayer, D., *For Mao: Essays in Historical Materialism* (London: Macmillan, 1979).

D'Encausse, Helen Carrère and Schram, Stuart R., *Marxism and Asia: An Introduction With Readings* (London: Allen Lane, The Penguin Press, 1969).

Deshingkar, G.D., "Mao against Confucius?", *China Report*, 10:1-2 (1974), pp. 4-7.

Deutscher, Isaac, "Maoism - Its origins and outlook", *Socialist Register* (1964). Reprinted in Isaac Deutscher, *Ironies of History* (London: Oxford University Press, 1966).

Devillers, Philippe, *Mao* (London: Macdonald, 1967).

Dirlik, Arif, "The predicament of Marxist revolutionary consciousness: Mao Zedong, Antonio Gramsci, and the reformulation of Marxist revolutionary theory", *Modern China*, 9:2 (April 1983), pp. 182-211.

Dorrill, William F., "Transfer of legitimacy in the Chinese Communist Party: Origins of the Maoist myth", in Lewis, John Wilson (ed.), *Party leadership and Revolutionary Power in China* (Cambridge: Cambridge University Press, 1970), pp. 69-113.

Dow, Tsung-I, "Mao Tse-tung and Marxism", *Asian Profile*, 7:2 (April 1979), pp. 97-117.

Eastman, Lloyd, "Mao, Marx and the future society", *Problems of Communism*, 18:3 (May-June 1969), pp. 21-26.

Esherick, Joseph W., "On the 'restoration of capitalism': Mao and Marxist theory", *Modern China*, 5:1 (January 1979), pp. 41-78.

Forster, Keith, "Mao Tse-tung on the transition period from capitalism to communism", *Journal of Contemporary Asia*, 6:1 (1976), pp. 101-106.

Frame, William V., "Mao, Stalin, and Khrushchev: the role of materialism in the Sino-Soviet dispute", *Asian Thought and Society*, 2:3 (1977), pp. 290-317.

Franke, Wolfgang, "The revolutionary theory and practice of Mao Tse-tung: a contribution to the discussion of the history of communism", *Modern World* (1960-1961), pp. 48-53.

Friedman, E., "Neither Mao, nor Che: the practical evolution of revolutionary theory", *Comparative Studies in Society and History*, 12 (April 1970), pp. 134-139.

Friedman, E., "Marx and Mao and ...", *Modern China* 3:4 (October 1977), pp. 419-426.

Friedman, E., "The future of Maoism", *Telos*, 59 (Spring 1984).

Geltman, E., "Khrushchev vs Mao", *Dissent*, 10 (1963).

Goldman, R., "Mao, Maoism and Mao-ology", *Pacific Affairs*, 41 (1968), pp. 560-574.

Gouldner, A.W., "Marxism and Mao", *Partisan Review*, 40:2 (February 1973), pp. 137-144.

Gurley, John G., "The symposium papers: discussion and comments", *Modern China*, 3:4 (October 1977), pp. 443-463.

Hak, Han and Van Ree, Erik, "Was the older Mao still a maoist?", *Journal of Contemporary Asia*, 14:1 (1984), pp. 82-93.

Harris, Nigel, *The Mandate of Heaven: Marx and Mao in Modern China* (London: Quartet Books, 1978).

Hsiung, James Chieh (ed.), *The Logic of "Maoism": Critiques and Explication* (New York: Praeger, 1974).

Hsiung, James Chieh, *Ideology and Practice: The Evolution of Chinese Communism* (New York: Praeger Publishers, 1970).

Hwang Shao-tzu, "Anatomy of Mao Tse-tung's thought", *Asian Outlook*, 3 (December 1968), pp. 9-12.

Jung, Hwa Yol and Jung Petee, "The hermeneutics of political ideology and cultural change: Maoism as the Sinicization of Marxism", *Cultural Hermeneutics*, 3:2 (August 1975), pp. 165-198.

King, A.Y.C., "Voluntarist model of organization: the Maoist version and its critique", *British Journal of Sociology*, 28 (September 1977), pp. 363-374.

King, Sarah S. and Sanderson, Richard A., "Mao and Mac: a cultural perspective", *Journal of American Culture*, 1:2 (Summer 1978), pp. 454-461.

Knight, Nick, "The form of Mao Zedong's 'Sinification of Marxism'", *The Australian Journal of Chinese Affairs*, 9 (January 1983), pp. 17-33.

Knight, Nick, "Mao Zedong and the 'Sinification of Marxism'", in Mackerras, Colin and Knight, Nick (eds.), *Marxism in Asia* (London and Sydney: Croom Helm, 1985), pp. 62-93.

Knight, Nick, "Mao Zedong and the Chinese road to socialism", in Mackerras, Colin and Knight, Nick (eds.), *Marxism in Asia* (London and Sydney: Croom Helm, 1985), pp. 94-123.

Koichi, N., "Mao's thought and the Chinese revolution", *The Japan Interpreter*, 5 (1967).

K'ung Te-liang, "First appearance of 'Mao Tse-tung's Thought'", *Issues and Studies*, 9:5 (February 1973), pp. 34-41.

Lee Chen-chung, "Trotsky's theory of the 'permanent revolution' and Mao Tse-tung's theory of the 'continuous revolution'", *Issues and Studies*, 8:7 (April 1972), pp. 29-39 (Part 1); 8:8 (May 1972), pp. 60-76 (Part 2); 8:11 (August 1972) pp. 61-72 (Part 3); 9:2 (November 1972), pp. 68-85 (Part 4); 9:5 (February 1973), pp. 73-87 (Part 5); 9:6 (March 1973), pp. 73-80 (Part 6).

Lew, Roland, "Maoism and the Chinese revolution", *The Socialist Register* (1975), pp. 115-159.

Li, K., "The dilemma of Mao's political thought", *Issues and Studies*, 9:8 (May 1973), pp. 29-37.

Lowe, Donald M., *The Function of "China" in Marx, Lenin and Mao* (Berkeley and Los Angeles: University of California Press, 1966).

MacInnis, Donald, "Maoism: The religious analogy", *Christian Century* (January 10, 1968), pp. 39-42.

Marchant, Leslie Ronald, *To Phoenix Seat: An Introductory Study of Maoism and the Chinese Communist Quest for a Paradise on Earth* (Sydney: Angus and Robertson, 1973).

Masamichi, Inoki, "Leninism and Mao Tse-tung's ideology", in London, K. (ed.), *Unity and Contradiction: Major*

Aspects of Sino-Soviet Relations (New York: Praeger, 1962).

Masi, Edoarda, "Mao's thought and the European Left", *Socialist Revolution*, 1:4 (July-August 1970), pp. 15-38.

Meisner, Maurice, "Harmony and conflict in the Maoist utopian vision", *Journal of Chinese Philosophy*, 4 (October 1977), pp. 247-259.

Meisner, Maurice, *Marxism, Maoism and Utopianism: Eight Essays* (Madison: University of Wisconsin Press, 1982).

Meisner, Maurice, "Utopian goals and ascetic values in Chinese communist ideology", *Journal of Asian Studies*, 28:1 (November 1968), pp. 101-110.

Meisner, Maurice, "The Maoist legacy and Chinese socialism", *Asian Survey*, 17:11 (November 1977), pp. 1016-1028.

Meisner, Maurice, "Leninism and Maoism: Some Populist perspectives on Marxism-Leninism in China", *China Quarterly*, 45 (January-March 1971), pp. 2-36.

Meisner, Maurice, "Utopian socialist themes in Maoism", in Lewis, John W. (ed.), *Peasant Rebellion and Communist Revolution in Asia* (Stanford: Stanford University Press, 1974).

Meisner, Maurice, "Mao and Marx in the scholastic tradition", *Modern China*, 3:4 (October 1977), pp. 401-405.

Michael, Franz H., *Mao and the Perpetual Revolution* (New York: Barron's, 1977).

Mohanty, M., "Mao's portrait of Stalin", *China Report*, 11:4 (1975), pp. 19-29.

Mohanty, M., "Mao, Deng and beyond: dialectics of the early stage of socialism", *China Report*, 20:4-5 (1984), pp. 123-132.

Moore, S., "Utopian themes in Marx and Mao", *Dissent*, 17:2 (April 1970).

"More on Maoism", *Problems of Communism*, 16:2 (March-April 1967), pp. 9-99.

Munro, Donald J., "Comments", in Ping-ti Ho and Tang Tsou (eds.), *China in Crisis* (Chicago: University of Chicago Press, 1968), Vol. 1, Book 1, pp. 389-396.

Nakanishi, T., "The Chinese revolution and Mao Tse-tung thought", *Chinese Law and Government*, 4:12 (1971), pp. 5-37.

Naryanswamy, Ramnath, "Mao on Stalin", *China Report*, 16:4 (July-August 1980), pp. 27-38.

Natoli, Aldo, "Mao Tse-tung and Marxism", *Politico*, 42:3 (September 1977), pp. 465-482.

Nomura, Koichi, "Mao Tse-tung's thought and the Chinese revolution", *Developing Economies*, 5 (March 1967), pp. 86-104.

Pachter, H., "Mao vs Marx", *Dissent*, 14 (1967).

Perelomov, L.S., "Mao, The Legalists, and the Confucianists", *Chinese Studies in History*, 11:1 (1977), pp. 64-95.

Pfeffer, Richard M., "Mao and Marx in the Marxist-Leninist tradition: a critique of 'the China field' and a contribution to a preliminary reappraisal", *Modern China*, 2:4 (October 1976), pp. 421-460.

Pfeffer, Richard M., "Mao and Marx: understanding, scholarship, and ideology - a response", *Modern China*, 3:4 (October 1977), pp. 379-386.

Pischel, Enrica Collotti, "What is dead and what is still alive in Mao", *Politico*, 42:3 (September 1977), pp. 423-444.

Powell, D. "Mao and Stalin's mantle", *Problems of Communism*, 17:2 (1968), pp. 21-30.

Ray, D.M., "Mao and the classless society", *Survey*, 77 (Autumn 1970), pp. 30-50.

Reeitsu, Kojima, "A reconsideration of Mao Zedong's theories of socialism", *The Developing Economies*, 18:2 (June 1980), pp. 147-159.

Rejai, M., "Redefinition of 'Maoism'", *Journal of Asian and African Studies*, 2:3-4 (July-October 1967), pp. 186-191.

Rius, *Mao For Beginners* (New York: Pantheon, 1980).

Rossanda, Rossana, "Mao's Marxism", *Socialist Register* (1971), pp. 53-80.

Schram, Stuart R., "Chinese and Leninist components in the personality of Mao Tse-tung", *Asian Survey*, 3:6 (1963), pp. 259-273.

Schram, Stuart R., "Comments", in Ping-ti Ho and Tang Tsou (eds.), *China in Crisis* (Chicago: University of Chicago Press, 1968), Vol. 1, Book 1, pp. 380-389.

Schram, Stuart R., *The Political Thought of Mao Tse-tung* (Harmondsworth: Penguin, 1969, revised ed.).

Schram, Stuart R., "What makes Mao a Maoist", *New York Times Magazine* (March 8, 1970), pp. 36-37.

Schram, Stuart R., "Mao Tse-tung and the theory of the permanent revolution, 1958-69", *China Quarterly*, 46 (1971), pp. 221-244.

Schram, Stuart R., "Mao and Maoism", in Gibson, J.M. and Johnson, D.M. (eds.), *A Century of Struggle: Canadian Essays on Revolutionary China* (Toronto: Canadian Institute of International Affairs, 1971), pp. 118-132.

Schram, Stuart R., "Some reflections on the Pfeffer-Walder 'revolution' in China studies", *Modern China*, 3:2 (April 1977), pp. 169-184.

Schram, Stuart R., "Comment", *Modern China*, 3:4 (October 1977), pp. 395-400.

Schram, Stuart R., "The Marxist", in Wilson, Dick (ed.), *Mao Tse-tung in the Scales of History* (Cambridge: Cambridge University Press, 1977), pp. 35-69.

Schram, Stuart R., "Modernization and the Maoist vision", *Bulletin* (International House of Japan), 36 (1979), pp. 1-22.

Schram, Stuart R., "Mao: the Man and his Doctrines", *Problems of Communism*, 5 (1966), pp. 1-7.

Schram, Stuart R., "Mao Tse-tung", in Bottomore, Tom (ed.), *A Dictionary of Marxist Thought* (Oxford: Basil Blackwell; and Cambridge, Mass.: Harvard University Press, 1983), pp. 298-301.

Schram, Stuart R., "Mao studies: retrospect and prospect", *China Quarterly*, 97 (March 1984), pp. 95-125.

Schurmann, Franz, *Ideology and Organization in Communist China* (Berkeley: University of California Press, 1971, revised ed.).

Schwartz, Benjamin I., "On the 'originality' of Mao Tse-tung", *Foreign Affairs*, 34:1 (October 1955), pp. 67-76.

Schwartz, Benjamin I., "The legend of the 'legend of 'Maoism'", *China Quarterly*, 2 (April-June 1960), pp. 35-42.

Schwartz, Benjamin I., "China and the West in the 'Thought of Mao Tse-tung'", in Ping-ti Ho and Tang Tsou (eds.), *China in Crisis* (Chicago: University of Chicago Press, 1968), Vol. 1, Book 1, pp. 365-379.

Schwartz, Benjamin I., *Communism and China: Ideology in Flux* (New York: Atheneum, 1970).

Schwartz, Benjamin I., "A personal view of some thoughts of Mao Tse-tung", in Johnson, Chalmers (ed.), *Ideology and Politics in Contemporary China* (Seattle and London: University of Washington Press, 1973), pp. 352-372.

Schwartz, Benjamin I., "Mao Tse-tung and communist theory", *New Leader*, 43 (April 1960), pp. 18-21.

Schwartz, Benjamin I., "New trends in Maoism", *Problems of Communism* (July-August 1957), pp. 1-8.

Schwartz, Benjamin I., "Modernization and the Maoist vision: some reflections on Chinese communist goals", *China Quarterly*, 21 (January-March 1965), pp. 3-19. (Also published in *Dissent*, 21 (Spring 1974), pp. 237-248.)

Schwartz, Benjamin I., "The essence of Marxism revisited: a response", *Modern China*, 2:4 (1976), pp. 461-472.

Seiji, Imabori, "Ups and downs of Mao Tse-tung thought and its evaluation in history", *Communism and International Politics* (The Japan Institute of International Affairs, Tokyo) (January-March 1977).

Selden, Mark, "Karl Marx, Mao Zedong, and the dialectics of socialist development", *Modern China*, 3:4 (October 1977), pp. 407-417.

Sharma, T.R., "From Marx to Lenin and Mao: The process of inversion", *Indian Political Science Review*, 12:2 (1978), pp. 179-193.

Soo, Francis, "Mao's vision for China", in Adelmann, F.J. (ed.), *Contemporary Chinese Philosophy* (The Hague, Boston, London: Martinus Nijhoff Publishers, 1982), pp. 63-80.

Spitz, A., "Mao's permanent revolution", *Review of Politics*, 30 (October 1969), pp. 440-454.

Starr, John Bryan, "Maoism and Marxist utopianism", *Problems of Communism* (July-August 1977), pp. 56-62.

Starr, John Bryan, "Conceptual foundations of Mao Tse-tung's theory of continuous revolution", *Asian Survey*, 11:6 (June 1971), pp. 610-628.

Starr, John Bryan, "Mao Tse-tung and the Sinification of Marxism: theory, ideology, and phylactery", *Studies in Comparative Communism*, 3:2 (April 1970), pp. 149-157.

Starr, John Bryan, "On Mao's self-image as a Marxist thinker", *Modern China*, 3:4 (October 1977), pp. 435-442.

Starr, John Bryan, *Continuing the Revolution: The Political Thought of Mao* (Princeton: Princeton University Press, 1979).

Strong, Anna L., "The thought of Mao Tse-tung", *Amerasia*, 11:6 (June 1947).

Strong, Anna L., *The Thought of Mao Tse-tung* (n.p.: Chefoo News Co., 1947).

Sweezy, P., "Theory and practice in the Mao period", *Monthly Review*, 28:9 (February 1977).

Tan, Chung, "Maoism to remember", *IDSA Journal*, 9:3 (January-March 1977), pp. 267-298.

Tang, Peter S.H., "Mao Tse-tung thought since the Cultural Revolution", *Studies in Soviet Thought*, 13:3-4 (September-December 1973), pp. 265-278.

Taraki, Bariman, "Rationality, Motivation and Productivity: The Maoist Critique", *Western Sociological Review*, 8:2 (July 1977), pp. 187-209.

Taylor, Charles, "The death of Maoism", *Progressive*, 31 (March 1967), pp. 12-16.

Thomas, Paul, "The Mao-Marx debate: a view from outside China", *Politics and Society*, 7:3 (1977), pp. 331-341.

Todd, N., "Ideological superstructure in Gramsci and Mao Tse-tung", *Journal of the History of Ideas*, 35 (January-March 1974), pp. 148-156.

Tsou, Tang and Halperin, Morton H., "Maoism at home and abroad", *Problems of Communism*, 14 (July-August 1965), pp. 1-13.

Wakeman, Jr., Frederic, "A Response", *Modern China*, 3:2 (April 1977), pp. 161-168.

Walder, Andrew G., "Marxism, Maoism and social change", *Modern China*, 3:1 (January 1977), pp. 101-118; and 3:2 (April 1977), pp. 125-159.

Walder, Andrew G., "A Response", *Modern China*, 3:4 (October 1977), pp. 387-393.

Walker, R.L., "Mao as superman", *Journal of International Affairs*, 26:2 (1972), pp. 160-166.

Wang Shao-lan, "Mao Tse-tung's thought", *Chinese Communist Affairs*, 4:2 (April 1967), pp. 19-25.

"What is Maoism? a symposium", *Problems of Communism*, 15:5 (September-October 1966), pp. 1-30.

Wittfogel, Karl A., "The influence of Leninism-Stalinism on China", *Annals of the American Academy of Political and Social Science* (September 1951).

Wittfogel, Karl A., "The Legend of 'Maoism'", *China Quarterly*, 1 (January-March 1960), pp. 72-86; and 2 (April-June 1960), pp. 16-34.

Womack, Brantly, "Theory and practice in the thought of Mao Tse-tung", in Hsiung, James Chieh (ed.), *The Logic of "Maoism": Critiques and Explication* (New York: Praeger, 1974), pp. 1-36.

Womack, Brantly, "The historical shaping of Mao Zedong's political thought", in Adelmann, F.J. (ed.), *Contemporary Chinese Philosophy* (The Hague, Boston, London: Martinus Nijhoff Publishers, 1982), pp. 27-62.

Womack, Brantly, *The Foundations of Mao Zedong's Political Thought, 1917-1935* (Honolulu: University Press of Hawaii, 1982).

Wylie, Raymond F., "The emergence of 'Mao Tse-tung's Thought' in 1943: The domestic and international context", *International Studies Notes*, 2:2 (1975), pp. 1-11.

Wylie, Raymond F., *The Emergence of Maoism: Mao Tse-tung, Ch'en Po-ta and the Search for Chinese Theory 1935-1945* (Stanford: Stanford University Press, 1980).

Wylie, Raymond F., "Mao Tse-tung, Ch'en Po-Ta and the 'Sinification of Marxism', 1936-38", *China Quarterly*, 79 (September 1979), pp. 447-480.

Yin Ch'ing-yao, "The ideological origin of Mao Tse-tung's theory of 'permanent revolution'", *Issues and Studies*, 6:3 (1969), pp. 39-51.

Yin, Ch'ing-yao, "On Mao Tse-tung's 'continuous revolution'", *Issues and Studies*, 10:7 (April 1974), pp. 87-96.

Yin, Ch'ing-yao, "Mao Tse-tung's theory of two stages and two alliances", *Issues and Studies*, 9:3 (December 1972), pp. 63-71.

Young, Graham, "Ideology, authority and Mao's legacy", *The Australian Journal of Chinese Affairs*, 9 (1983), pp. 153-170.

Young, Graham and Woodward, Dennis, "From contradictions among the people to class struggle: The theories of uninterrupted revolution and continuous revolution", *Asian Survey*, XVIII:9 (September 1978), pp. 912-933.

Young, Graham and Woodward, Dennis, "Chinese conceptions of the nature of class struggle within the socialist transition", in Sawer, Marion (ed.), *Socialism and the New Class: Towards the Analysis of Structural Inequality within Socialist Societies* (Bedford Park, S.A.: APSA Monograph No. 19, 1978), pp. 28-45.